DESIGNING WITH
PALMS

DESIGNING WITH
PALMS

JASON DEWEES

PHOTOGRAPHS BY CAITLIN ATKINSON

TIMBER PRESS

PORTLAND, OREGON

In memory of
E. John "Slim" Harbett and
Nancy Harbett Dewees

Frontispiece: Fronds of Canary Island date palm grow over trapezoidal stairs, while *Rhapalostylis* spp. and *Howea forsteriana* offer support.

Published in 2018 by Timber Press, Inc.

The Haseltine Building
133 S.W. Second Avenue, Suite 450
Portland, Oregon 97204-3527
timberpress.com

Printed in China

Text design by Stacy Wakefield Forte
Cover design by Anna Eshelman and Michelle Leigh

Library of Congress Cataloging-in-Publication Data

Names: Dewees, Jason, author. | Atkinson, Caitlin, photographer.
Title: Designing with palms / Jason Dewees; photographs by Caitlin
   Atkinson.
Description: Portland, Oregon: Timber Press, 2018. | Includes
   bibliographical references and index.
Identifiers: LCCN 2017046009 | ISBN 9781604695434 (hardcover)
Subjects: LCSH: Palms. | Landscape design.
Classification: LCC SB413.P17 D48 2018 | DDC 635.9/77484—dc23 LC
   record available at https://lccn.loc.gov/2017046009

A catalog record for this book is also available from the British Library.

According to the Greeks, trees are alphabets.

Of all the tree letters, the palm is loveliest.

—Roland Barthes, *Roland Barthes by Roland Barthes*

(translated by Richard Howard)

CONTENTS

FOREWORD

n 2003 I had just transitioned from owning a small landscaping business to owning a ramshackle urban palm nursery. The nursery was an empty double lot on a block of Victorians in San Francisco's Mission District. My business partner and I, who together had almost zero qualifications for running a nursery, were spending the day, along with my brother and some friends, literally wielding machetes against the bramble that owned a third of the nursery we'd just taken possession of. We were taking what would turn out to be one of very few breaks that our new business would allow in the coming years, sitting in the shade, covered in sweat and minor injuries from fighting the bramble, eating popsicles.

In walks Jason Dewees, who makes a beeline for a row of rare palms and asks, "Is this a *Rhopalostylis sapida*?" My partner and I, who had been cramming to get up to speed on the names of the plants our new role demanded we be authorities on, had memorized the name of that particular palm the week before, and knew, as well, that it was the rarest in the nursery. We offered Jason a popsicle, and he pulled up a lawn chair.

Jason's love for and knowledge of palm trees shaped our new nursery and my point of view as a designer. When we purchased The Palm Broker, we intended to transform it into the design-focused nursery we imagined. We didn't understand the palms or recognize right away what a palm can do.

Now, years later, we are so delighted that this book will give you the chance to learn from Jason, as we did, about what a palm can do.

Jason's passion for palms is infectious, and everyone at Flora Grubb Gardens caught the bug. With Jason's leadership, Flora Grubb Gardens now raises a long list of palms once nearly impossible to find in Northern California. We love each of them for what it offers the garden, for what it can do, for its ability to transform a space, to set a mood, and to solve a long list of design problems that few other plants can address.

I've always said that although I own a rare plant nursery, I am not really a plant person. I am a garden person. The difference? I won't really tolerate the rarest, most interesting plant if it doesn't perform its purpose well in the garden. That is why I adore palm trees. When used correctly, when designed into a garden with skill, palms do their jobs so well.

This book will teach you to employ these noble plants to their best use, and you'll find that every garden you add them to will be transformed by their presence. Palm trees are so lucky to have Jason Dewees as their champion, and you are lucky to have him as your teacher.

—*Flora Grubb, owner, Flora Grubb Gardens*

PREFACE

For most people, the palm hides in plain view. So charismatic, instantly recognizable, palms get lost in the glare of their own beauty.

Most of us first fall for palms when the shush of waves on the sand mixes with the overhead rustle of their fronds. Relaxed, half-naked, our skin warmed by the sun, our toes cooled by the sea, we are, for that moment of bliss, in paradise

Next we notice the amazingly tall row of palms not far from our house. Our palm love swells and deepens in an encounter with wild California fan palms in a desert canyon echoing with birdsong. Or maybe we fall in love in that moment on screen when palms wave shadows over Kathleen Turner's sexy villain character at the end of *Body Heat*, conferring an ineffable mood to the scene. Even the simple grace of a potted palm in the corner of the room can charm us into affection for this distinct plant family.

My mother adopted a neanthe bella palm (*Chamaedorea elegans*) around the time I went to kindergarten. Friends from my nursery school left the houseplant with her when the family moved away from San Francisco to New York. It had the classic palm-tree shape, but in miniature: a rosette of feather-shaped leaves on top of a green ringed stem no more than an inch thick, with stilt roots emerging from the base into the soil in a fertilizer-stained clay pot. I remember nubby root tips dotting the length of the stem. Every week or two, my mother hand-washed the plant with soap to treat a case of scale, the music of Stevie Wonder or Carole King filling the house. That plant must have lasted a long time in her care, for it was later on in childhood I wondered why the periodically appearing flower stalks never made fruits—or were those little kernels that dried and dropped off actually fruits? Sometimes I would peel the husky leafbases from the trunk, exposing a pale internode that would slowly green up in response to the light. Even now, I find grooming a chamaedorea palm one of the most satisfying of garden tasks. My crush for neanthe bella lives on.

I believe it was the archetype of the palm tree that drew me to that miniature at home. Palms were regular but infrequent elements of the landscape where I grew up in California, and holiday visits to my mother's side of the family in Miami exposed me to a place where palms were abundant. Their image preceded in my mind the arrival of that houseplant. Recognizing a miniature version of the icon gave me the child's thrill of connecting a cat to a tiger.

This first crush grew into a love of the palm family, plants, and gardens—and has since become my passion and vocation. I work as a palm specialist and horticulturist and have been able to focus on this exceptional plant family's attributes and contributions. I share my love of palms with many in the design, planning, architectural, and gardening fields and help create landscapes that challenge conventional planting design. It is a joy and a mission. The satisfaction of working with a client to choose the right species for her garden design and her subtle, modern house on a spectacular, blustery site overlooking Point Reyes National Seashore comes from puzzle-solving, sweaty exertion, and elation at both the results and the relationship we've developed in working together. Along the way, I have found that the palm's icon status is both portal and obstacle to working with palms in design.

Palms are among the earliest trees depicted by the human hand. They are stamped on Roman and Israeli coins from two millennia ago, portrayed at Egypt's Tomb of Sennedjem from the late 1300s BC, carved in 5800-year-old petroglyphs in Saudi Arabia, and seen in rock art at Tassili n'Ajjer, Algeria, from 6000 BC. The date palm of the Fertile Crescent was likely one of the earliest cultivated fruit trees, bound to the origins of Western agrarian civilization. These ancient portraits are potent, distilled images signifying the satisfaction of hunger and thirst. However enrobed in our jet-age perspective such elemental satisfactions may now be, images of palms remain ubiquitous today, still signifying respite and bounty. If any plant is an icon, it is the palm.

Pictured at the Dick Douglas garden in Walnut Creek, California, the silver Mediterranean fan palm from the Atlas Mountains of Morocco and Algeria, *Chamaerops humilis* var. *argentea*, rewards scrutiny with a revelation of color.

INTRODUCTION

It's time to look clearly at palms—observe their qualities, habits, and needs—and to bring their many beautiful and useful forms into gardens beyond the tropics. This book aims to release the palm from the prison of iconography so that it can take a natural place in the garden and enrich landscapes alongside the other plants in the plant kingdom.

Palms are the Cate Blanchetts and Denzel Washingtons of the plant world, distracting stars who are still powerful when stripped of their celebrity.

I will explain uses, characteristics, and cultural requirements of palms. I'll introduce the most commonly available and hardy species, plus an array of tempting rarities. And I will celebrate their allure—all to give readers confidence in and excitement for using palms in gardens.

We all know a palm when we see it. A crown of feathery leaves atop a leaning trunk casts swaying shadows on the sand. A cluster of yellow coconuts—or are those golden dates?—hangs below the crown, feeding the desert islanders—or oasis-dwellers—who live amidst these whispering trees.

What child in school cannot draw a palm tree? Few renderings of palms hanging in museums, meanwhile—even paintings by artists seemingly intent on achieving landscape realism—capture the actual character of palm species, let alone individual plants. Artists, dedicated to observation, are gobsmacked by the singularity of the palm form.

We must forgive those artists: most people are blinded by an icon. And we gardeners and designers are just like most people in that way. Behind the glare, palms' amazing variety and usefulness demand closer attention in garden design. The icons live up to the hype. You believe the hype. But the hype might be muting your own fresh experience of the view. This book will help focus your attention.

Not everyone feels their pull. Many people register the palm's form so quickly and indifferently that they neglect to see the details that compose it. Even for the interested gardener, young containerized palms in a garden center hardly distinguish themselves as varied species and barely hint at their mature forms. And if we're glancing up at palm trees, they may just be too tall or wind-tossed to reveal themselves. I hope to enable readers to choose the right kinds for designing gardens.

Meanwhile, their mistreatment, misuse, and myths repel many other people from palms. Palms sometimes even sustain hatred, scorn, and moralism. Opponents of planting palms see unpruned skirts of dead leaves hanging beneath a sickly spot of green up in the glare of a smoggy sky; or they see a youngster of a huge species misplaced, smothering a bungalow. Or they hear stories of rats' nests and profligate price tags. Misplacing conspicuous plants is tacky. Charisma spoiled spawns strong feelings. Symbols out of context bewilder, seem absurd. To the objection that palms don't belong, the first response is this: If it contributes to the beauty of the landscape, why not? I hope even the bewildered, repelled, and skeptical reader will stick with me, catch a bit of my enthusiasm, look more closely at these plants and their thoughtful use, and understand them better.

Terremoto Landscape designed a Mid-City, Los Angeles, garden with a reordered demotic LA plant palette mixed with new varieties, adding an unusual-for-California triangle palm (*Dypsis decaryi*). Its keeled leaves fall in three ranks, creating a compelling presence and perfect scale as well as an echo of older palms out on the urban horizon.

IS IT A PALM?

In making, or remaking, a garden, gardeners and designers apply a critical eye to plants, as well as to space, climate, animals, light, soil, and architecture. The Enlightenment's founder of Western plant taxonomy, Carl Linnaeus, called palms the princes of the plant kingdom. If this noble group is to be of use to gardeners, we must inspect it, too, and identify it as a member. Leaves are the best way to start.

WATCH OUT FOR IMPOSTORS

Lots of plants get called palms but aren't. Tree ferns, for instance, such as those in the genera *Dicksonia*, *Cibotium*, and *Cyathea*, cut silhouettes similar to those of palms, but ferns' uncurling fiddleheads, often yielding double- and triple-pinnate fronds once mature, give them away as palm imposters. The conspicuous spore-bearing organs spotting the fern fronds seal the distinction from palms. These palm imposters often make complementary garden plants, however.

Yuccas, dracaenas, pandanus (screw pines), cordylines, and beaucarneas—these plants' leaves are strap-shaped, not fan- or feather-shaped, and unfurl like a flag in the center of the crown instead of unfolding. These non-palms also often produce branching and swelling aboveground trunks.

Cycads are convincing palm imposters, with palmy, feather-shaped leaves; their new leaves, however, resemble a fern in the way they uncurl on their way to maturity. Many cycad species, especially when mature, produce clutches of leaves in flushes—picture a sea anemone recoiling in reverse. Palms, by contrast, push up new leaf spears one at a time, and they do not uncurl or unfurl but unfold like an accordion, to realize their mature form. Also, many cycads branch above ground, and older plants will produce conspicuous cones in the center, reminiscent of giant pine or spruce cones. Branchy palm inflorescences rarely look like cones. And only in a few cultivated palms (such as *Corypha* spp. and *Tahina spectabilis*) are inflorescences seen at the top of the stem.

The hardness of the stem at maturity distinguishes palms from the very few other groups of plants possessing pleated leaves that seem to unfold as they emerge, such as Panama hat palm (*Carludovica palmata*) in the cyclanth family and palm grass (*Curculigo capitulata*) in the hypoxis family. Palm stems at maturity (of flowering age) are hard as bone.

Banana plants (in the genera *Musa* and *Ensete*) are commonly and mistakenly called banana palms, but their stems (technically pseudostems) are fleshy, as is the thick, buried rhizome from which they emerge. Bananas share with giant birds of paradise (*Strelitzia nicolai*) and traveler's palms (*Ravenala madagascariensis*, also called traveler's trees) other characteristics that set them apart from palms: new leaves that unfurl like flags and big, showy flowers. Look for the unfurling habit of the newest emerging leaf, because the leaves of bananas, birds of paradise, and traveler's trees can be deceptively feather-shaped, especially when torn into segments by the wind. And the hard stems of the latter two look and feel like palm trunks.

A palm imposter, *Cycas taitungensis* uncurls a simultaneous flush of a dozen feather-shaped leaves in Joe Le Vert's garden in Augusta, Georgia. This habit of leaf emergence distinguishes it from palms and points to its membership among the cycads, an ancient group of gymnosperms related to pines and ginkgos.

far right: In Roger Raiche's garden near California's Russian River, *Yucca rostrata*, a non-palm with a crown of simple, spear-shaped leaves, stands next to the stiff and folded fan leaves of *Trachycarpus fortunei* 'Wagnerianus' palms.

LEAVES: FEATHER OR FAN

How do you know if you're looking at a palm? If the leaf is feather-shaped or fan-shaped, it's strongly in the running to be a palm. Held up to the light, the candidate's foliage will show veins running in parallel. Palms' large and complex leaves are sometimes mistaken for branches, which most palm species lack; aerial branching of the trunk, or stem, is rare among palms. Each palm leaf begins in a single shoot near the top of the trunk, pushing upward as a spearlike body that unfolds into its mature feather or fan shape. Even if the leaf is undivided, resembling a banana leaf, it will be in one of these two shapes, its pleats attesting to having been folded in the spear. Thus a plant with a fan or feather leaf produced in a process of unfolding is most likely a palm.

The rolling hills of Santa Monica's Tongva Park, designed by James Corner Field Operations in collaboration with meadow guru John Greenlee, employ a grassland base coat for an orchestration of plantings, including trees, succulents, perennials, and palms. This view includes silver Mediterranean fan palms (*Chamaerops humilis* var. *argentea*) and Australian fan palms (*Livistona australis*, known in Australia as cabbage palms).

STEM AND BUD

On most palms, the leaves gather in a group toward the top (the apex) of the trunk; we call it a crown. All the leaves you see in the crown of a palm originated in that single bud, and they all attach to the developing trunk (technically called the stem) at a node, a ring around the stem. Other stems may grow from the base of the stem you're examining, but the stems of the vast majority of ornamental palms don't branch above ground. (Exceptions are found among the climbing rattan palms such as species of *Calamus*; the doum palms, *Hyphaene*; and in certain species of *Dypsis*.)

FLOWERS

Apart from a few species (whose sole flowering event is their death knell, as in many agaves), palms' flowers develop from buds at the nodes where the leaves attach to the stem. The small, profuse individual flowers perch on a branched structure called an inflorescence. Some palms have unbranched, wandlike inflorescences. All palm inflorescences start out enclosed in sheathing structures called bracts, or spathes. These can range from fleshy, to papery, to woody.

TO THE SENSES

Now that you've determined that this is a palm you're admiring, soak in its aesthetic qualities. Look at the color and texture of the leaves in all their parts. Look at the way they move in the wind. Listen to the accompanying sound. Does the foliage shine? Color and reflectivity often differ between the upper and lower sides of the leaf, and diverse colors and waxy or fuzzy textures can flow onto the leaf stem. Admire the architecture. No other plant group boasts such powerful geometry—radial symmetry, tensile arcs, leaflets like parallel blinds, spiraling crowns of leaves. Lower leaves on most species naturally turn yellow before dying to straw, but some fall just as chlorophyll fades. Many palms bear thorns on their leaf stems or trunks, sometimes in contrasting colors and fascinating shapes. Peek into the crown for flowers and fruit. Many species' fruits take on showy red, yellow, or black pigments, or subtle ivory or jade colors. The scent of some palm flowers carries on the breeze. Do the fruits glisten? Some are warty, scaly, or spiny. They almost all change in ripening—they might make a mess or the fruits could be insignificant, so plan accordingly.

What is the texture of the trunk? Trunks can range from smooth to furry, colorful, green, gray, or brown. In certain species, the bases of dead leaves can attach to trunks for a long time. Entire leaves may remain hanging indefinitely if unpruned, accumulating into a skirt or beard of strawlike material merging into the green crown. Pruned leafbases can rise in a pleasing spiral up the trunk, reflecting the geometry of how new leaves are laid into the crown. Look at the proportions of the plant. How thick is the trunk in relation to the diameter of the crown? It's possible in some palms to prune dead leafbases from the trunk to change those proportions while transforming the trunk's texture and color. How do the roots emerge at the base? They may not be visible at all, root tips may appear high on the trunk, or only a few new roots show at the soil line.

Do you see many young crowns or older trunks emerging from the same area at the base? Are they connected underground to the central or largest stem, or might they just be seedlings, independent of the main trunk?

Absorbing these details will equip you to use and manage palms fluently in landscapes.

THE ROLES PALMS PLAY

In our princely plant icon we uncover particular qualities and the work it can perform with them. Preeminent among trees in regularity of form, palms such as the royal palm (*Roystonea regia*) make perfect avenue trees, as they do on Royal Palm Way in Palm Beach, Florida, where the evenly spaced columns make any driver's arrival on that wealthy island a waltzing procession. Perhaps no landscape use is so common for palms, especially away from the tropics, because the architecture of each species is so dependable, particularly among the solitary tree palms.

Many of the roles palms can play are unknown or unexpected in regions outside the tropics, despite the increasing availability of gorgeous and diverse hardy species. Some species are naturally shrubby, with many stems emerging from a single rootstock. These shrubs can be swaths of foliage, mounds, or hedges. With age, some of the suckering species graduate to form copselike clusters, dynamic and muscular or stately and aloof. Other species grow as vines, climbing high into surrounding trees, or as delicate ground-dwelling shade plants. The classic tree form ranges from giant-trunked behemoths dominating their surroundings, to reedy stemmed treelets defying gravity and wind. Ecological habits differ tremendously, too: savannas, where palms pepper—and even help form—the grassy ground plane; scrublands, where palms join the shrub assemblage; forests, in which palms scatter themselves widely among woody trees, vines, and bamboos;

Indigenous California fan palms (*Washingtonia filifera*), their Baja California cousin the Mexican fan palm (*W. robusta*), and a hybrid between them (*Washingtonia ×filibusta*) form the dominant planted structure of this natives-rich, desert-embracing garden designed by Steve Martino in Palm Springs, California.

oases in arid zones; or palm-dominated stands, in which they reign to the near exclusion of other arborescent plants.

A plant from the Atlas Mountains of Morocco and Algeria, the sun-loving silver Mediterranean fan palm (*Chamaerops humilis* var. *argentea*) grows as a shrub—suited in this case to its dry, chaparral-like scrub habitat—its leaves a waxy bluish or silvery green. It is adaptable to climates from Hawai'i to England, useful in containers or in the ground, in sun or light shade, by the sea or in the mountains. This palm has become available in nurseries in recent decades and hardly resembles the iconic coconut or date palms of our internalized media feed. Its leaves resemble fans, not the feathers of coconut and date palms; it produces numerous growing points at its base, the source of its shrubbiness; and it burgeons where coconuts fail, in frosty zones and in Mediterranean climates.

TAKE ON THE MYTHS

There's no sense ceding palms to the stereotypes that dominate society's view of them. They offer too much beauty and too many uses to hand them over only to exotic, tropical-themed, and desert-oasis gardens. Give them a place in plantings for their inherent aesthetic and functional qualities, not just for the familiar stories they inspire.

Still, it is undeniable: No plant better symbolizes the tropics than the palm. Palms are essential to tropical style in the garden. The palm family, Arecaceae, finds its greatest diversity of species in wet, tropical lowlands such as those of the Amazon basin, Indonesia, and Madagascar. Coconut palms (*Cocos nucifera*) on tropical shores won't survive long where frosty or gloomy winters prevail. Even more than the orchid or the hibiscus, the palm deserves its symbolic, iconic role. And thanks to the date palm (*Phoenix dactylifera*)—a keystone fruit tree and source of building and craft materials in warm-desert regions from Morocco, to India, to Palm Springs—no plant better advertises water and fecundity in the desert than the palm.

But as observant travelers to London, Tokyo, and Vancouver will attest, hardy palm species add beauty even to winter-afflicted regions. Let's not typecast palms.

Wherever they originate, palms are quite valuable to people who live among them and use them. A friend who recently returned to San Francisco from a vacation in Hawai'i told me about a conversation she had with a tree-trimmer who was cutting young coconuts and lower leaves off a tall coconut palm for the safety of visitors soaking up the rays on the beach below. A chef, journalist, and food writer—and always curious about ingredients—she learned from the climber that the immature nuts he'd brought down were good for the water inside but still too young to use for the nutmeat. For most of us raised in the temperate zones, palms' aura of vacation

Coconut palms (*Cocos nucifera*) planted at Punta Roquena, a private botanical garden maintained by D'Asign Source in the Florida Keys, mark the scene as a place of warmth, relaxation, and seclusion from workaday cares. As a source of water, nourishment, construction, and craft materials, the species is an economic mainstay for people living on tropical shores around the globe.

time clouds their importance to human life. The third-most economically important plant family, palms are used wherever they are native for food, drink, craft, construction, even medicine. Posh destinations such as the atolls of the Maldives might be uninhabitable without the coconut palm and the drink, food, and shelter materials it provides. The palmyra palm (*Borassus flabellifer*) alone has 800 uses in its range from India to Indonesia—for food, medicine, sugar, alcohol, cordage, building, furnishings, clothing, writing material, and boat-building. It is likely that the first gardens we might recognize in the Western tradition, in Mesopotamia, Egypt, or Iran, offered inhabitants the fruit and the beauty of the date palm. It may be that the richness of palms' contribution to human life summons our feelings and interest at an unconscious, ancestral level, while their air of relaxation follows from the past two centuries of leisure travel. Common between these realms is a feeling of plenitude.

A painting by Edith Bergstrom of fan palm (*Washingtonia filifera*) leaves in the Southern California desert embodies the spirit of the place by rendering the palm with thrilling accuracy.

A rigorous reading of palms would also unearth stories of colonialism, empire, environmental disruption, and global economic relations that are beyond the scope of this book.

As trees, palms act as intermediaries between us humans in our modest size bodies and the vastness of sea, sky, mountain, and forest. Our picture of coconut trees by the sea conjures this phenomenon. Tree palms' crown-and-trunk form evokes a standing person, our attention concentrated at the head. In a group they seem social, their phototropic growth causing them to lean apart, mutually accommodating the others' need for sun. Their motile crowns clap, swing, and rotate; fronds yield and rebound to the wind, while their swaying trunks recall the balancing movements we make to stay standing. Palm trees can look like Martha Graham's troupe in a slow spell of a dance or children swinging their arms as they await the return of their parents' attention. They stand next to us, conversant with our perspective. We look up to them; we look over to them. Their fronds bend to us as we explore the garden but their spines remind us to be cautious in our plots of cultivated nature.

SOUTH FLORIDA IMPRESSIONS

The foot of the Bailey Palm Glade at Fairchild Tropical Botanic Garden in Florida conveys a vista with hints of André Le Nôtre's gardens at Versailles, an axis here flanked by Chinese fan palms (*Livistona chinensis*) and royal palms (*Roystonea regia*).

The verdant landscape of South Florida is where, as a child visiting my grandparents in the southern suburbs of Miami, my fascination with palms expanded from my mother's potted plant into the garden. Bitten severely by the palm bug on my third-grade winter break in Florida, I brought home back to San Francisco a habit of doodling coconut palms, and then staring with new interest at a quartet of Mexican fan palms framed in our classroom's windows. By the end of that school year I had learned their botanical name, *Washingtonia*. My interest became an obsession in high school, after I spent a spring break with my grandparents in Miami, a city whose seal (rendered in pink) features a palm silhouette. My grandmother gave me her copy of *Palms of the World* by James McCurrach to take back to California with me, and from then on I was able to revel in palm images and knowledge at will, and to interpret what I was observing so intensely in the landscapes around me.

Every visit to Florida thereafter included a stop at Fairchild Tropical Botanic Garden, home to hundreds of palm species beautifully planted and interpreted for the public. Named for Dr. David Fairchild (1869–1954), a global plant explorer for the United States Department of Agriculture and author of the classic book, *The World Was My Garden*, the garden opened in 1938 with a collection of tropical plants. A repository of the fruits of American global expansiveness dedicated to tropical botany, the garden was designed by landscape architect William Lyman Phillips, a member of the Frederick Law Olmsted partnership, who was retained by the garden until 1954. Phillips invented a new garden form—a palm glade, cut and nested partly below grade with a small pond at its tucked head—just for palms. It's just one example of the founders' magisterial vision for this premier tropical garden.

Cycling between reading plant books and visiting gardens has, since then, been my primary way of experiencing my love of plants—especially palms—and has fueled my aspirations for seeing them used well in the design of landscapes.

My grandparents, with whom I'd spent that winter break, appreciated the native habitats of their home, regularly visiting the Everglades, taking weekend excursions to Sanibel Island over on the Gulf of Mexico, and cultivating native plants amid the declining remnants of the pine rockland habitat where they'd bought their house in the early 1970s. Their garden absorbed a great deal of their interest as they explored horticultural

societies—including the Palm Society—nurseries, and Fairchild Tropical Botanic Garden sales for native plants, palms, fruit trees, and exotic plants with which to landscape the suburban lot. My grandmother held that if you've got the restricted climate for extraordinary tropical plants, why not grow them instead of the more common hardy plants that people settle for farther north? Carting me and my little brother around the yard in his wheelbarrow, my child-of-Kentucky grandfather showed off his banana patch, mango tree, Valencia orange, winter vegetable plot, and his favorite palm, the royal palm, *Roystonea regia*, a Florida native. He had been a pro tennis coach who trained players such as Doris Hart and Bobby Riggs as well as swells vacationing on Miami Beach such as Walter Winchell, and was later a tennis teacher for the City of Miami. My grandfather took pride in his acre garden; it connected him in retirement to the agricultural milieu of his birth, while resorty ornamental plants—like palms—exemplified his boom-time escape from the burden of real farming into Miami's opportunities and good life—sustained in part thanks to his city pension.

Planted largely with Florida native plants, especially palms, landscape architect Raymond Jungles's former office garden perches on the limestone banks of the Miami River and affords views of the Miami-Dade County Courthouse beyond a row of golden coconut palms and passing boats.

The title of the Marx Brothers' 1929 comedy about the Florida land boom, *The Cocoanuts*, captures the palm's role as advertisement for the life his family bought into back then.

The ancient reef stone beneath my grandparents' old garden underlies the peninsula, raising it barely above sea level. At the edge of the Gulf Stream lives a (quite threatened) coral reef, a contemporary hint of the ancient origins of the bedrock. Sandy barrier islands such as Miami Beach and the limestone spine of the Keys are the first dry land encountered as you proceed inland from the Atlantic, followed by the mangrove-fringed Biscayne Bay and Intracoastal Waterway. Everything is amazingly flat. Look upward for the drama of thunderheads, rain columns, and cumulus clouds against deep skies. Ocean and bay reveal their shallows in blue-green tints.

A ridge of porous limestone reaching a dozen or so feet above sea level is the foundation of the Miami metropolis; where it reaches north under Fort Lauderdale and West Palm Beach, it's buried under sandier, less alkaline soils. I recall my grandfather showing me how to find cavities in the stony ground where, using a digging bar to crack the sharp, convoluted, pale rock, he would excavate planting holes large enough for the new palms and trees I was so excited to put in the ground. This band of higher land indiscernibly declines on its western margin to the vast, mucky heart of South Florida—the seasonally wet grassland, sloughs, hardwood hammock woods of the Everglades, and the Big Cypress Swamp. These function as a broad river draining south from Lake Okeechobee, rising in the summer and fall wet season, drying back to bird-squawked waterholes in the winter and spring, and emptying west and south through mangroves—tree baskets approximating a shoreline in tidal shallows—into the Gulf of Mexico and Florida Bay.

A Seminole and Miccosukee structure thatched with palmetto, a chickee stands between copernicia and beccariophoenix palms in Mike Harris's Broward County, Florida, garden.

In November of 2015, my photographer colleague, Caitlin Atkinson, and I drove west from Miami across the tip of Florida toward the Naples Botanical Garden. We witnessed the bleached autumnal aspect of South Florida in the leafless bald cypress woods hanging with gray Spanish moss along the road. It was my first foray into the Everglades since seeing them three decades before with my grandparents. When the cypresses petered out and we reached a stretch with thousands of palmettos studding the vast river of grass, I was seeing something new, one of nature's most beautiful designs with palms, and I knew we were on the right track for this book.

A feather (pinnate) palm, *Marojejya darianii* (back), and a fan (palmate) palm, *Licuala grandis* (front), demonstrate the palm family's two basic leaf forms and show off the folded architecture of palm leaf blades at Hale Mohalu, Big Island, Hawai'i.

THE
FASCINATING
PALM FAMILY

Palms are a much more varied and important plant family than most people imagine. A bit of attention to their details combined with an overview will, I hope, expand the ways of using and dealing with palms in designing landscapes.

Palms are a family (Arecaceae) of flowering plants (phylum Anthophyta) in the monocot clade (Liliopsida). As monocots, their closest relatives are plant families such as grasses, lilies, and bromeliads. Coconut palms (*Cocos nucifera*) and date palms (*Phoenix dactylifera*) may be the most famous and deliciously useful of palm types, but they are only two out of a botanical family of around 2400 diverse species. Taking the form in habitat of jungle vines, shrubland components, understory dwellers, savanna constituents, mangroves, clusters, and tall trees, palm species contribute a special verve to gardens and landscapes. They play powerful, central roles, but they also succeed in filling supporting, background positions.

Getting the best out of palms in the landscape also comes from learning more about how they grow with other plants in habitat, what garden conditions—soils, moisture levels, fertility—they prefer, and which climates and ecosystems they come from. A peek into palm origins around the world naturally enriches designs using palms.

WHERE PALMS COME FROM

A family of plants most profuse and diverse in moist, lowland equatorial environments such as the Amazon basin, palms are also found in nature from latitudes of 44°N (in Italy) to 44°S (in New Zealand). In North America, palms are indigenous in a swath from North Carolina through Florida, to Texas, Oklahoma, and Mexico, and in Arizona and California. Hawai'i is home to about twenty-five native species of palms.

The family's biogeographic range is surprising: Palms grow in habitats at the upper reaches of cloud forest in the Andes, more than 11,000 feet (3350 m) above sea level, where dawn reveals frost-whitened pastures and afternoon high temperatures barely reach 65°F (18°C). Palms preside over the fog-shrouded semiarid slopes of the Canary Islands off the coast of northwestern Africa and Mexico's Guadalupe Island off the west coast of the Baja California peninsula. Palms push up through forests of birch, fir, and oak in sight of glacier-burdened Himalayan peaks. Palms commingle with camellias and maples. Palms dwell in forests rich in deciduous tree species high on slopes of Mexico's Sierra Madre Oriental—and in low-lying pine woods of the American Carolinas. Palms line the scorching watercourses of deserts in California and Egypt, and they stand athwart the Roaring Forties winds in coastal forests of New Zealand's South Island.

Some palms prefer the cooler mountain areas of the tropical and subtropical world and grow well in nontropical regions. The genus *Trachycarpus*, including the widely cultivated Chinese windmill palm, *T. fortunei*, occupies the Himalayan

ABOUT CLIMATE

A good starting point for understanding climate for plant cultivation is the Köppen classification system. It provides general categories for the climates in which palms can be grown: A, for tropical and moist; B, for dry and desert; C, for temperate; D, for continental or cold temperate (where very few palm species can be grown, on the margins and with extra care); and E, for polar (no outdoor palms).

Within these general climates, letter codes designate more specific climate types.

Within tropical group A, climate type Af indicates a rainforest climate with year-round rainfall and warmth: windward Hawai'i, for instance, and regions of year-round rain nearer the equator in Central and South America, Central Africa, windward Madagascar, the Malay Archipelago and New Guinea, and northeast Australia. Type Am indicates a tropical monsoon climate with plentiful rainfall, alternating with a drier season around the winter solstice: regions scattered in southern India to Myanmar, Southeast Asia, Central and West Africa, the Amazon, Atlantic Brazil, Central America, Mexico, and the Caribbean. Type Aw indicates a tropical savanna climate. This type is also characterized by alternating wet and dry seasons, but with more drought stress, either because the annual dry season is more severe than in the tropical monsoon climate (Am), or because the overall rainfall is lower. The dry season often occurs near the winter solstice, but in some locations, such as leeward Hawai'i, it occurs near the summer solstice, in which case the type As

is used, the "s" indicating dry summer, the "w" indicating dry winter. Find extensive areas of tropical savanna climate in South America, Central America, Mexico, and the Caribbean, Sub-Saharan Africa, northern Australia, leeward Madagascar, inland Southeast Asia, and India. Am, Aw, and As climates tend to have more temperature variation than Af climates both across seasons and from day to night.

Within the dry and desert climate group, B, temperature and irrigation determine which palm species can grow. Climate type BSh, the hot, semiarid climate, and BWh, the hot, desert climate, allow ample use of palms. Few or no palms tolerate the colder BSk and BWk climate types.

I use a vernacular of climate terms throughout the book.

» Tropical climates experience year-round warm to hot conditions with seasonal variation marked largely by rainfall and humidity patterns, such as Bangkok.

» Cool tropical climates have milder temperatures and include higher elevation and some higher latitude sites, such as Hawai'i or San José, Costa Rica.

» Subtropical climates are warm and hot for the preponderance of the year, with a significantly cooler winter season but rare frost, such as South Florida or Brisbane, Australia.

» Warm temperate climates have seasonal temperature variation, from warm to hot in summer, to extended cool winter weather, with frost a possibility in some locales, such as Sydney, Australia.

uplift between India, Southeast Asia, and China. It has even naturalized in Switzerland. Another exclusively montane genus, *Ceroxylon*, achieves the family's highest habitat elevation and adapts to cool, mild temperate zones. Its most famous member, *C. quindiuense*, Colombia's national tree, grows to the greatest height of all palms—200 feet (61 m).

But those are the exceptions that contribute their noble beauty to landscapes beyond the tropics. Palms are most prolific in moist tropical forests, where many species—some seen as interior plants—live their entire lives in shade, and others prefer sun in canopy breaks or as canopy components. Many palms also occur in exposed seaside locations, where vacationers expect them. The most famous of these is the coconut palm (*Cocos nucifera*), but other well-known species such as the palmetto of the Southeast United States (*Sabal palmetto*) are found in sunny coastal dunes, scrub, marsh, and shaded woodland alike. In Florida, as in many subtropical and tropical areas, a lot of palm diversity can be found in coastal locations. In the Florida Keys, a half-dozen species flourish on the scrubby limestone islands subject to salty winds and seawater inundation during tropical storms.

The fan-shaped blades of cold-hardy Chinese windmill palm (*Trachycarpus fortunei*) leaves catch a light snowfall in Doreen Wynja's garden in Oregon. Native to China, this species is the most cold-tolerant tree palm and is cultivated throughout temperate parts of East Asia as well as in Scotland and Canadian British Columbia. Photographer, DoreenWynja.com.

above: An Andean wax palm, *Ceroxylon ventricosum*, grows at the Sullivan garden in Ventura, California. This genus of palms with wax-coated trunks occupies the highest altitude of all palms—up to 11,480 feet (3500 m) in the Andes of South America—and includes the tallest palm species, *C. quindiuense*.

right: Florida and Bahamas native silver thatch palm, *Coccothrinax argentata*, ornaments the low coastal vegetation of Bahia Honda State Park in the Florida Keys.

PALMS FOR THE COAST—OUTSIDE THE TROPICS

Images of the languid coconut palm (*Cocos nucifera*) fringing tropical beaches make palms seem like the right plants for a coastal garden, even in non-tropical environments such as in California or Vancouver, British Columbia, where bracing fog and wind and storms, as well as drought, can pose a challenge for the hardiest of plants. And, indeed, certain palms hold up pretty well to the onslaught of weather by the ocean: they can be among the toughest plants for coastal gardens. But it's important to choose the right species and give these plants regular fertilizer and watering, especially in gritty, salty soils found at the beach.

Natural coastal elements so dominate our experience of a landscape that "the coast" often becomes the garden's style by default. Each region has its particular assemblage of plants, geology, topography, fisheries, shipping, architecture, and folkways that characterize its meeting of land and water. In many places, palms are part of that assemblage of native plants; in others, palms can join the palette easily. Their penchant for movement in the wind and susurration complement the ocean's perpetual wave action.

In the southeast United States, native tree palms such as *Sabal palmetto* thrive in coastal habitats amidst dune grasses, brackish marshes, and seacoast live oak woodlands. The palmetto's gregarious, vertical, cabbage-top, sometimes drunk-leaning presence characterizes the coast of the Carolinas (it is the state tree of South Carolina, after all), Georgia, and Florida, while its usefulness in cultivation extends westward along the Gulf Coast and the Texas coast—where it is often joined by the heftier native Texas palmetto, *S. mexicana*. (With irrigation, both species can grow successfully, if more slowly, in Southern and Central California coastal gardens as well.) The palmetto inhabits oak and pine woods alongside waterways and ornaments barrier-island neighborhoods, fitting its house-height staff of vital greenery into the tight spaces of dense vacation communities and grand strands.

These two palmettos are tree palms, but other, largely trunkless, native North American fan palms add luxuriant texture to the understory and low ground in these coastal landscapes: *Serenoa repens*, the saw palmetto, and *Sabal minor*, the dwarf palmetto. Short of stem and branching at the base, saw palmetto is the most common native palm in the United States, with natural populations occurring in a range from Louisiana eastward through Florida to South Carolina, often as the understory of pinewoods. The dwarf palmetto—singular, trunkless, with a larger leaf and dramatic vertical flower stalks—naturally ranges from east Texas to northeast North Carolina, where it often grows in very moist locations in bald cypress (*Taxodium distichum*) swamps and along rivers, belying its ability to grow as well in drier, beachy gardens and colder zones.

The ubiquitous Mexican fan palm (*Washingtonia robusta*), native to Baja California, rules the beaches and bluffs of Southern California, reaching skyline heights over time in Santa Barbara, growing in pure sand at Venice Beach, and framing the sparkling Pacific from the heights of La Jolla. On the Central California coast it's useful as well, but by the time you get north along Highway 1 toward San Francisco, its appearance remains appealing mostly on protected, south-facing exposures like Santa Cruz. North of San Francisco, foggy summer conditions and intense winter storms make it scrappy, although it can survive at least as far north as Brookings, Oregon.

The shrubby, multiple-stem Mediterranean fan palm (*Chamaerops humilis*) takes the low ground in California, at least while young. Over time its stems can build up and out to heights up to 20 feet (6.1 m), and picturesque leaning clumps complement red-blooming mounds of *Aloe arborescens* and violet-flowering pride of Madeira shrubs, *Echium candicans*, both Old World exotics settled into the West Coast's seaside shrublands. The "Med fan" is useful in bright spots on the wooded

above: Desert oasis and grassy savanna habitats show off palm forms to great advantage. Here California's native palm, *Washingtonia filifera*, dominates spring-fed areas along the San Andreas Fault near Palm Springs (Thousand Palms Oasis, Coachella Valley Preserve).

right: Fall color on streamside cottonwood, alder, willow, and sycamore mixes with the evergreen crowns and gray thatch of California fan palms (*Washingtonia filifera*) in their Colorado Desert habitat.

Pacific Northwest coast, too, where specimens can be seen in the beautiful gardens of Shore Acres State Park on the Oregon Coast and in Seattle, at the Carl S. English Jr. Botanical Gardens near the Ballard Locks. Both the Mexican fan palm and the Mediterranean fan palm also thrive on Atlantic and Gulf coastlines, although the Mexican fan palm's leaves are burned at around 23°F (–5°C), putting it at a disadvantage to the hardier *Sabal palmetto* in outbreaks of extreme cold that can reach such places as Corpus Christi, New Orleans, Pensacola, and Charleston from November to March.

As for less common exotic species, the feather-leafed pindo palm, *Butia odorata*, from Brazil and Uruguay, makes a strong contrast to the fan palms of the US coasts, where it also proves tolerant of salty winds. Its flounce of recurved, grayish or olive-green leaves atop a stout, usually short trunk, and its tasty, golden fruit can bring a cheery presence and strong form at human height to coastal gardens from the Pacific Northwest to Baja and from Virginia Beach (Virginia) to Mobile (Alabama), Miami, and South Padre Island (Texas). Its pinnate leaves have the advantage of offering a discernible reference to the feathers of coconuts, that holy grail of coastal palms.

DESERT AND SAVANNA PALMS

Desert oases—areas of permanent fresh water—are home to several ornamental palm species, including *Washingtonia filifera*, the sole species native to the states of California and Arizona, and the date palm, *Phoenix dactylifera*. Along with tolerances to heat, wind, fire, and sun, many desert palms are also cold-tolerant, and despite being limited in habitat to areas of permanent water, they can often endure drought conditions. Savanna palms, such as *Trithrinax campestris* from northern Argentina, often share these traits, although many palms from more tropical savanna habitats lack tolerance to cold.

The idea that palms are only tropical is belied by their appearance in natural plant assemblages that seem anything but tropical to North American eyes—such as the deciduous riparian desert tree corridors and Southeast pine and oak forests in which native palms mingle.

Picturing palms in the full range of their natural distribution dispels myths and widens the possibilities for designing with them.

THE PARTS OF PALMS

Just as oaks have their acorns and pines have their needles, the palm family has a vocabulary for describing its forms. Often, these words set them apart from other plants. To use palms assuredly in garden design, you'll find it helpful to recognize and understand their constituent parts and anatomy. You should be able to recognize a palm and distinguish it from other, similar, plants, and you'll also need to observe and learn more about identifying and using them.

As a designer, your knowledge of palm anatomy enables you to understand how palms grow, bloom, and fruit, so that you can place them and care for them in the long term. And deeper knowledge brings greater appreciation and joy in working with them.

The significance of palms in economics, botany, and ecology is fascinating and adds to their beauty and interest in the landscape.

A woodland on Kiawah Island, South Carolina, is home to palmetto (*Sabal palmetto*), loblolly pine (*Pinus taeda*), and live oak (*Quercus virginiana*).

WHAT MAKES A PALM

A palm is a flowering plant with leaves that look like feathers or fans and that unfold like accordions as they emerge into mature form. (The bud that produces the new leaf is the source of the edible palm heart; because it's the sole vegetative bud on the stem, harvesting it kills the entire stem.) The leaf can be modest in size (as small as a human hand) to very large (up to 82 feet, or 25 m, long). Picture a seagull feather as a symbol for one group and a hand fan for the other: the entire feather or fan is part of a single leaf, or frond. (This more figurative word

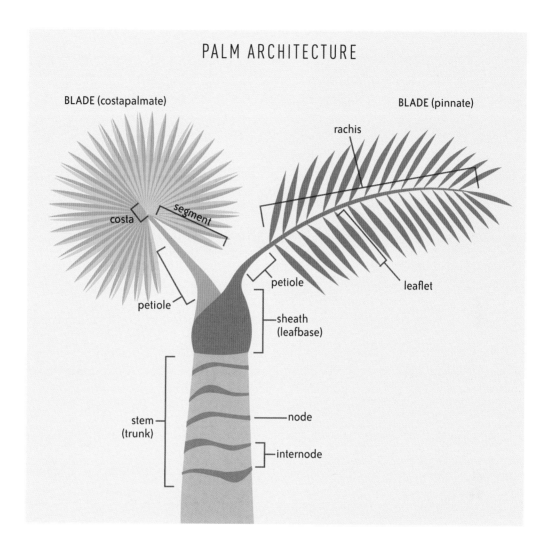

PALM ARCHITECTURE

BLADE (costapalmate)

BLADE (pinnate)

rachis

segment

costa

leaflet

petiole

petiole

petiole

sheath
(leafbase)

stem
(trunk)

node

internode

for palm leaves is also frequently associated with the leaves of ferns, and ferns are not palms or even flowering plants.) It will also be useful to know that pinnate means feather-shaped and palmate means fan-shaped. The difference between pinnate and palmate leaves is important: it's the first detail you will examine as you start identifying types of palms, and it is the fundamental distinction in palm horticulture.

Palm leaves comprise three parts: leafbase or leaf sheath, petiole, and blade. The leafbase encircles and connects to the trunk. The petiole is the stalk that connects the leafbase to the blade; it is sometimes so short as to be absent, but where present, it accounts for the mistaken impression that the leaf is a branch. The leaf blade is most conspicuous and familiar—it's the part of the leaf that looks like a feather (pinnate) or a fan (palmate) with pleated segments.

PINNATE, OR FEATHER, PALMS

The classic palm form is the flat pinnate leaf blade of the coconut palm or the kentia palm (*Howea forsteriana*) that is grown indoors nearly everywhere. The petiole ends on pinnate leaves where the first segments, or leaflets, begin. The rachis comprises the continuation of the petiole, a midrib that bears the folded segments or leaflets. Picture a quill pen, its stylus and shaft analogous to the petiole, the midrib of the feather an analog to the rachis. Several variations on the pinnate leaf blade occur: flat, keeled, entire (undivided), plumose, and bipinnate.

The pinnate leaf resembles a seagull feather's form, with leaflets arranged in an even row in a single plane along the rachis. On many flat pinnate palms, the leaflets may be clustered or bunched along the rachis, but this phenomenon occurs more often in plumose palms—those with pinnate leaves that resemble an ostrich feather, with leaflets emerging at different angles from the rachis to produce a full, fluffy, three-dimensional plume. Royal palms (*Roystonea* spp.) and queen palms (*Syagrus romanzoffiana*) are common plumose-leaf pinnate palms. Keeled leaf blades have leaflets attached at an upward angle along the rachis, creating a V-shape trough in cross section, as seen, for example, in the genus *Butia* and in *Dypsis decaryi*. Entire, or undivided, pinnate leaves can resemble banana leaves and are more frequently seen in tropical lands. Undivided leaves often grow in the seedling phase of pinnate palms, most famously in the coconut. The metallic palm, *Chamaedorea metallica*, a pinnate palm with undivided leaves, is often used as an interior plant. (A less popular divided leaf form also exists.)

The genus *Caryota*, whose species are known as fishtail palms, includes the only bipinnate palms in the family. It's a more complex feather leaf. Bipinnate means that secondary rachises are attached to the leaf's primary rachis—the stalk of the feather carries a series of subsidiary stalks. Leaflets resembling the fins of a fish are attached to the secondary rachises. The bipinnate structure can lend these palms the semblance of a fern frond. Well-placed caryota palms cast a herringbone-mosaic canopy against the sky.

PALMATE, OR FAN, PALMS

The palmate leaf resembles a handheld fan, with the petiole an analog to the handle of the fan, and the blade the folding semicircle that makes a personal breeze. The pleated segments of the palmate leaf radiate out from a hub where the petiole meets the blade. A common variant on the palmate leaf is the costapalmate leaf, characterized by an extension of the petiole (the costa) into the blade. Some of

A planting with three variations on pinnate leaves: In front, the light green leaves with V-split tips are entire, feather-shaped, with leaflets connected; at center are flat pinnate leaves, with separate leaflets regularly arranged in one plane; and in back are plumose pinnate leaves, with leaflets attached to the rachis in several planes and in clusters. A palm imposter pictured is the banana-like plant with dark green leaves and reddish undersides.

the segments of the blade radiate from the hub of the fan, while other segments begin on the costa.

LEAFBASES

The leafbase on all palms begins as a cylindrical sheath inside the crown of leaves attached to the developing trunk. By the time leafbases show on the outside of the crown at the end of the functional life of the leaf, they vary tremendously among species. Many pinnate palms have crownshafts. A neat and attractive leafbase variant, the crownshaft is a continuous, fleshy, usually green, cap on the trunk—like the tall brim of a chef's hat beneath a pouf of fronds—consisting of the leafbases, with the leafbase of the oldest leaf exposed as the intact, cylindrical sheath, alive with chlorophyll until it peels off along the node encircling the trunk.

Contrast the leafbases of the crownshaft with the many kinds of split leafbases (fibers, latticework, basket-weave, even armature) on other palms, particularly fan palms.

The skirt, or beard, that accumulates beneath the crowns of the two species of *Washingtonia*—*W. filifera* and *W. robusta*—results from marcescence, the retention

far left: This clustering fishtail palm (*Caryota mitis*) has bipinnate leaves. Secondary rachises branch off from the primary rachis and bear the leaflets. The twice-pinnate structure of the leaf blade is limited to this popular genus and is the most conspicuous variation on the architecture of feather-leaf palms.

left: Linear variegation on the palmate leaf of this lady palm (*Rhapis excelsa*) in Paul Humann's Broward County, Florida, garden highlights the radial structure of the blade.

center: A Sonoran palmetto, *Sabal uresana*, at the Bergstrom Gardens in Atherton, California, demonstrates the costapalmate variant of palmate leaves. The

riblike costa in the center of the leaf blade appears as a backlit line on the upper leaves; it contributes to the outward recurvature of the leaf.

right: Leafbases in the crownshaft of *Satakentia liukiuensis* contribute a rosy brown warmth along with their green to the palette of a patio at the Naples Botanical Garden, Florida.

far right: Typical of many fan palms, leafbases on *Corypha umbraculifera*, the talipot palm, at Villa Paradiso, Franco D'Ascanio's garden in the Florida Keys, are split beneath the toothed petioles into an inverted V-shape and remain attached to the trunk in youth, collectively creating a gecko-green, latticed pattern.

of dead leaves attached to the stem after withering. Many palms exhibit marcescence, especially in youth. The very popular Mexican fan palm, *W. robusta*, begins spontaneously releasing its dead leaves beneath the crown at a great, mature height. Sometimes newly released leaves in the stack will push off others that have been retained for decades.

The natural marcescent habit presents several design choices: Leave the palm untrimmed to preserve the skirt, trim the leaves at the point where petiole meets leafbase to reveal a more-or-less regular latticework pattern on the trunk (called "natural" in the California palm trade, despite being a form of grooming), or remove the leaves along the node where the leafbase attaches to the stem to reveal a mostly smooth trunk surface (called "skinned" in California palm-growers' parlance). Freshly uncovered surfaces—of trunk or leafbase—on washingtonias will often seem reddish before fading to gray with sun exposure. It's also possible to treat the trunk with all three methods, skinning the base, leaving the leafbases midway up, and allowing a beard to remain below the crown. For arborists and tree-trimmers, managing the skirt is a high-risk endeavor. The dry leaves can be a fire hazard, and the process of removing the leaves from below can unleash a lethal avalanche of heavy, thorny fronds.

Leafbases of the Florida silver thatch palm (*Coccothrinax argentata*) remain attached just beneath the crown, but unlike those of washingtonias, dead leaves break off at the petiole close to the leafbase. Apart from the petiole stub portion, the sheath resembles a fine linen fabric. Indeed, on many palms, the sheath splits into a weave that one might see as inspiration for the invention of cloth, especially when it peels neatly off the trunk like a swatch of fabric. It's appealing for use in floral design and plant craft. Other sheaths can be rough like burlap, fine like muslin, frayed and hairy, and, of course, smooth and green in those species forming crownshafts.

Trunks of palmettos (*Sabal palmetto*) with their leafbases (boots) attached make an unmistakable pattern in the landscape. Key to achieving the look is to cut all the petioles at the same distance from the leafbase. Epiphytes such as ferns thrive in these boots, adding a jungly look or softening the geometry, depending on one's taste and design intent.

above: Leafbases of the California fan palm (*Washingtonia filifera*) remain attached indefinitely to the trunk along with the rest of the leaf (petiole and blade). The accumulated dead leaves form a skirt, or beard, of straw-colored foliage, neatly cropped here at California's Thousand Palms Oasis to accommodate visitors walking on the boardwalk.

right: The two contrasting textures on this *Sabal* species arise from the two integral parts of each leafbase: fibrous sheath and smooth petiole stub. Before these leaves withered and

their petioles were neatly cut (by Joe Le Vert and students at Aquinas High School in Augusta, Georgia), the petiole stub and its inverted-V-split base (called boots in the US Southeast and Texas) provided the leaf's vascular connection to the stem. The remainder of the sheath encircling the trunk is made up of the hairy-looking fiber.

far right: Leafbase stubs give a reptilian air to the trunk of a *Butia odorata*, pindo palm, at the late Richard Douglas's garden in Walnut Creek, California.

Instead of remaining as fibers or staying intact as green tubes, the leaf sheaths on many palm species disintegrate to the point of nearly disappearing. The lowermost leaves of Chilean wine palms (*Jubaea chilensis*), for example, are affixed to the trunk only at the enlarged base of the petiole, with little remaining of the rest of the sheath besides the line that encircles the trunk and marks the leaf node. When the leaf falls off the trunk (abscises), a rounded-diamond shape remains as a leafbase scar on the clean trunk, often weathering away over time.

THE STEM, OR TRUNK

Stems that emerge above ground are usually called trunks, especially in tree-size palms. However, palm stems can also be subterranean rhizomes, viny, or so thin or short that the word "trunk" does not fit. But "stem" always correctly describes the section of the plant below the leaves, however miniscule, immature, or obscured by

the soil or leafbases it may be. Immature palms may not have a stem that you can touch without digging in the soil (or around the leaves and roots at the base), and in a very young plant it may be too small or soft to recognize as a stem.

A key feature of palm stems is that they don't thicken much once they emerge below the crown of foliage. They don't make secondary growth or form true wood. Once the stem achieves mature girth, its only significant growth is in length or height; when marginal increases in diameter at this point occur it is due to expansion of the cells in the stem, not from the proliferation of cells that occurs in the trunks of woody trees such as oaks or pines. A cross section of a palm stem reveals a pattern of vessels throughout rather than the rings laid down in woody trees by cycles of cells proliferating.

Although not wood-producing, most palm stems have a substantial, woody texture and are solid, lacking the air-filled center chambers that characterize most bamboos, for example. Scratch the stem with your fingernail to encounter a density of bone or wood. They can be tall, straight, and columnar; bulging and cigar-shaped; spindle-shaped or bellied like a pregnant stick figure; leaning; spiraling; curling and vinelike; subterranean and prostrate; or like a squat cone.

left: Palms are either single, solitary-stem species such as the *Brahea calcarea* in the foreground, or clustering, multistem species such as the *Phoenix reclinata* in the background.

above: The clustering stems, or trunks, of this Everglades palm (*Acoelorrhaphe wrightii*) at Fairchild Tropical Botanic Garden, Florida, arise from the same rootstock and are parts of a single plant.

above: The subterranean stems of the Brazilian seashore palm, *Allagoptera arenaria*, grow horizontally in the dunes at the Naples Botanical Garden, Florida, branching and making multiple crowns of plumose leaves that appear to rise directly from the ground. On occasion, plants have short aboveground stems.

right: The genus *Hyphaene* from Africa, the Arabian Peninsula, and the Indian subcontinent includes several species whose trunks naturally branch dichotomously—their buds splitting in two and continuing to grow—including this *H. compressa* at Fairchild Tropical Botanic Garden.

The iconic palm is solitary and monopodial (one-footed): it produces one stem with a crown of leaves. A single bud at the top of the stem produces the leaves and continues the growth of the stem. Caespitose, or clustering, palms grow more than one stem from a single base of roots, like clumping bamboo. The individual stem has the same aerial form of a solitary palm, but it shares its rootstock with conjoined identical siblings. Another word for this clustering habit is sympodial (same foot) growth, indicating shared footing of the stems. The effect can range from the twin palm of Brazil, *Syagrus cearensis*, with its tendency to make a perfect pair of trunks, to the thicketlike growth of the bamboo palm (*Chamaedorea seifrizii*) or the Everglades palm (*Acoelorrhaphe wrightii*), with scores of stems.

The most prevalent form of palm branching takes place underground in the clustering palms. In a few groups—spectacularly in the doum palm, *Hyphaene* spp., inconspicuously in many of the vining rattan palms and in several *Dypsis* species, for example—aboveground branching is characteristic, but otherwise consider palm branching an underground phenomenon.

FLOWERS AND INFLORESCENCES, FRUITS AND INFRUCTESCENCES

My friend Roger Raiche, the pioneering California horticulturist and garden designer, once pointed out to me that palms are the superlative foliage plant. It's their dramatic leaves as well as overall form that attract people. But palm fruit and flowers make an impact, too, and it's important to consider their aesthetics, their ecological contributions, and the maintenance challenges they can present.

The complete flowering organ of the palm, the inflorescence, comprises a complex branching structure enclosed in a tubular sheath that bears numerous small flowers. (A few palms bear spikey, unbranched inflorescences.) It can emerge among or below the leaves, or above the crown. When flowers are pollinated and fruits begin to form, the same structure, now bearing the fruits, is known as an infructescence. Think of a spray of cherry tomato flowers: when the buds emerge and flowers open, it is an inflorescence; once flowers are pollinated and the tomatoes begin to form, it becomes an infructescence.

On palms closely related to coconuts, a conspicuous bract encloses the inflorescence, splitting to one side and becoming woody and canoe-shaped. These bracts

are prized for décor and floral design. Although individual flowers are not showy, the many forms of palm inflorescences and infructescences can be powerful elements in arrangements.

The profusion of flowers on palm inflorescences and their progressive flowering create an efficient site for pollinators that visit and return to gather their nectar and pollen, and for predators that find their insect quarry here. In addition, people eat young inflorescences of several species of *Chamaedorea* as a vegetable.

In light of palms' economic value to humans, it's no surprise that their nutrient-rich fruits are also important to wildlife, as are other parts of palms. According to Jennifer Purcell of The Living Desert Zoo and Gardens in California, among the many animals that take advantage of the desert fan palm, *Washingtonia filifera*, are hooded orioles that use the leaves to weave their suspended nests; coyotes that eat the fruits; great horned owls, western yellow bats, and greater

left: Palm fruits and infructescence branches, such as these of *Pinanga coronata*, change color from the flowering phase to seed set, to ripening and fruit drop.

above: The prolific sprouts of baby palms emerge from fallen seeds among palm roots on the ground. The smooth skin and juicy flesh of the fresh fruits have decayed, revealing fibrous coats around the hard seeds.

A NOTE ABOUT SMELL AND TASTE

left: Individual palm flowers are generally quite small, as on this hardy bamboo palm, *Chamaedorea microspadix*. Male and female flowers grow on separate plants in this genus. The flowers pictured are pistillate (female), containing an ovule with the potential if pollinated to develop into a fruit with fertile seed.

center: The flowers of two different palm species mingle on the ground in a Hawaiian garden. Like almost all palms' flowers, they have three petals. The monocot clade, to which palms belong along with grasses, agaves, bromeliads, and tulips, is characterized by flowers with parts in multiples of three.

right: Sweet, purple-black December fruits of the desert fan palm (*Washingtonia filifera*) at Thousand Palms Oasis, California, hang like a necklace across a skirt of dead leaves attached to the trunk. The local Cahuilla nation recounts eating the fruits fresh, grinding dried fruits for flour, and soaking them in water for a flavored drink.

The flowers of many palms are sweetly fragrant—an unexpected treat, as unshowy palm flowers don't often draw us in for a sniff. Other palm flowers can smell unpleasant. Some palm fruits are edible, of course (and, remember, many are not!). Fruit can also introduce fragrance into the garden—appealing, overripe, or objectionable.

roadrunners that make their homes in them; and the bees, wasps, hummingbirds, and butterflies that browse the flowers.

Aside from those palms chosen for their colorful foliage, potent palm color often comes as a pleasant bonus. The color attraction of fruits does vary by species—with plenty of small, dull, olive-green or black fruits among them—and by sex: pistillate (female) Canary Island date palms (*Phoenix canariensis*) bedecked with orange dates alternate with quieter, staminate (male) partners along California avenues, the latter's flowers but a subtle cream amid the voluminous green crowns. There's no predicting sex on immature plants, leaving erratic patterns of colorful (pistillate) and less-colorful (staminate) individuals in mass plantings. Among palms planted with fruit color in mind, Manila palms (*Adonidia merrillii*) and many *Veitchia* species, with their bright red fruits conspicuous below the crownshaft, are popular in tropical and warm subtropical areas.

When a palm is thriving and fruiting, it will produce ample fruit crops, leading to messes and even safety issues. Placement (over deep groundcover, for example) can take care of the mess, but the risks to people have to be managed. Pruning coconuts in urban and resort areas saves people from getting bonked on the head by the big nuts but also leaves the palms looking gelded with diminished, hemispherical, even tufted crowns; planting an alternative such as small-fruited *Beccariophoenix* species, *Parajubaea* species, or *Syagrus amara* provides a similar feeling without the risk of falling coconuts, the management cost, or the reduction of the plant's vigor and potential beauty.

No matter how prized the parent palm, its seedlings can be weeds. As with any weed, but especially large, arborescent weeds, it's important to root them out early to save effort later. Well-placed spontaneous seedlings, however, can be favored in a landscape as they develop, enhancing the coherence and site-settled ease of a planting.

Propagation by seed, a topic beyond the scope of this book, generally works best with fresh seed; viability of most palm seeds is limited, especially of species from moist climates. On all but the most cool-growing species, use bottom heat and a clean seedling mix (such as equal parts coir, perlite, and sand). Clean the seed down to the endocarp (the shell beneath the flesh or husk), place the seed shallowly in the mix in the tray, maintain a moist but not wet medium and moderate to high humidity, and wait. Many different requirements exist per species, however, with some types requiring deep pots for successful germination, some preferring sun exposure on the seed bed, and some performing better without removal of the flesh or husk, or needing a drying period before sowing and watering.

right: The stilt roots of a pair of walking palms, *Socratea exorrhiza*, have intertwined in a garden in Hilo, Hawai'i. Above ground or below, palms regularly produce new roots from the base of their stems. Roots are at their thickest as they emerge from the trunk, branching and becoming thinner as they spread outward in the earth to absorb nutrients and water and to anchor the plant.

far right: After the seed germinates, all subsequent palm roots are adventitious—meaning they emerge from the stem. Spiny, branching roots of *Cryosophila williamsii*, a highly endangered Honduran species at Fairchild Tropical Botanic Garden, form a protective armature along the trunk above ground while underground roots serve the usual functions of absorption and stabilization.

ROOTS

The roots of palms also set them apart from woody trees. The primary root of monocots (the larger group of plants to which palms belong) functions only in the earliest, seedling, stage of development. Secondary roots start to take over as the tiny primary root withers. These adventitious roots growing from the incipient stem will continue to push out, one after the other, for the life of the palm. The root pushes through soil, sand, rocks, and humus, absorbing water and nutrients and anchoring the plant with flexible, cable-like strength. You'll often see root tips at the base of palm trunks. A protective layer covers the tips, enabling them to navigate rocky abrasive elements and reduce nibbles from animals. Behind the tip is the root's absorbing surface.

It's this regular process of root development from the root initiation zone at the stem's base that enables full-size trees of many palm species to be transplanted easily compared to woody trees. It's important to pay attention upon planting to the root initiation zone. Especially in dry locales such as California, palms planted too high can suffer, because new roots wither in dry air before they reach moister soil, weakening the plant and slowing its growth. Planting too low, especially in wet regions, can deprive roots of the oxygen they need to function or can lead to rot.

The horizontal, decumbent stem of some species functions as rhizome, with roots emerging along its length. Some arborescent species produce roots high on the stem that function as armature. In some species, aerial roots, seeming to start uselessly well above the ground, await events such as a landslide, a blowdown of the palm, or just speedy accumulation of humus to grow out and add support in newly contacted medium.

ARMATURE

The palm family defends itself with more mechanical than chemical means. Strongly fibrous leaves, stems, and roots are difficult to browse and may not be worth large herbivores' energy to digest. However, palms are certainly not immune to herbivores: In California, for example, rabbits and gophers are adept at devouring palms, especially young, trunkless individuals. Insects and mites, with their ability to bypass tough fibers to sap a palm's vitality, are another matter, being common pests of palms in cultivation.

Armature, an additional mechanical means of defense, includes sharp spines, teeth, and thorns, and bladelike edges and points of leaves. These sharp parts derive from modified roots and leaves, or they are simply integral to the plant's organs—mostly leaves and stems. It's important to take precautions in pruning and grooming those species with spines; watch out for petioles with teeth.

above: This fiercely armed *Acrocomia* species at the Naples Botanical Garden sports needle-sharp spines along the rings of the trunk in an attractive pattern, as well as on the length of the leaves, where the spines are less conspicuous but no less effective in causing pain to hungry animals and unsuspecting tree-trimmers.

right: Fruits of an Alexandra palm, *Archontophoenix alexandrae*, shower into a Hawaiian garden. These eager sprouts require regular weeding, not least because the species is invasive in wet lowland areas of the islands.

PALM PLANTING, CARE, AND MAINTENANCE

Start with a seed. Yes, some palms, such as the commercial date palm, are commonly grown from clonal divisions, but the beginning of most palms is a seed. The general rule for sprouting palm seeds is to soak them for a few days, clean off the outer flesh or husk, and provide consistent moisture and warmth; bright, indirect light; and a well-draining medium. The variations expand from there—and beyond the scope of this book. Shift seedlings from their sprouting bed to small containers when they have developed two or three leaves and can still be disentangled from their bed-mates without breaking their young roots. Move them up in size before root-confinement slows their growth, but don't overpot—too much soil volume can retain excess moisture, at the expense of the roots' need for aeration.

PLANTING

It is time to plant out a seedling once it reaches a large enough size to survive in the ground with regular garden care. For private and protected gardens, that size may be a two-leaf seedling; in a public landscape, it should be larger so as to put up with more potential abuse. Stake if you must to mark and protect the plant. Staking young palms is usually unnecessary, unless the plant is in danger of rocking in very windy sites. Be mindful that leaves may get thrashed if they blow against tall stakes. Shade cloth can help while a young palm roots in, protecting older leaves while new leaves acclimate to higher light.

Sea Crest Nursery, in Santa Barbara, one of California's premier sources for large, choice palms and cycads, maintains palm specimens in boxes, making them portable and reducing transplant shock in California's dry, often cool climate.

THE RECORD-BREAKING PALM FAMILY

» The largest seed in the plant kingdom comes from *Lodoicea maldivica*, the double coconut or coco de mer (to 40 pounds, or 18 kg).

» The largest leaf in the plant kingdom grows on *Raphia regalis* (to 82 feet, or 25 m, long).

» The largest inflorescence in the plant kingdom (to 26 feet, or 8 m, tall) is produced by *Corypha umbraculifera*, the talipot palm, with millions of flowers.

» The tallest plant among monocots is *Ceroxylon quindiuense*, the Andean wax palm (to 200 feet, or 61 m).

» The record for longest aboveground plant stem is held by *Calamus manan*, a rattan palm (about 650 feet, or 198 m, long).

» The third-most economically important plant family (after grasses and legumes) is the palm family.

» The oldest tree seed to germinate and grow to maturity came from a date palm, *Phoenix dactylifera* (2000 years old).

For all the benefits of starting small—widest choice of species, stronger and speedier growth, growth form that responds to the site, cost savings—palms are attractive to designers as instant trees. They tend to be easier to transplant at large, mature sizes than similar size woody trees because their new roots continually develop from the trunk base—there's no tap root. It is common to dig palm species amenable to the practice from a field or garden, prune and tie up lower leaves, and transport them to new planting locations. (More varieties are amenable in warm, humid climates where transpiration is lower and growth rates are faster.) There, in a hole about twice the volume of the existing root ball, backfilled with a well-draining medium (preferably horticultural sand), and given a plentiful moisture supply and time, a palm will likely grow new roots and leaves and soon look like a veteran of the site. When hoisting the tree, installers use a soft—and sufficiently weight-bearing—woven strap (usually nylon), tying it to the best balancing point on the woody trunk (not on any soft tissues); they apply carpet remnants between the trunk and strap for extra protection—any scarring is permanent. Rigging to the box can also work well for some specimens, such as multistem palms. Adding a balanced fertilizer at planting time and then a palm formula quarterly thereafter for the first one to three years will support vigorous growth.

Many specimen palms are also grown in containers. The root volume in the box remains undisturbed (though the roots that grow from the box into the underlying ground at the nursery will be lost) when the palm goes to its new landscape. Planting from container bypasses the shock of field-digging and enables a newly planted garden to appear healthy and full from the start. The greater expense yields greater success.

Keep in mind two rules of thumb for planting palms:

» Don't cut roots or manipulate the root ball of container-grown palms if this is not necessary—it can set back even the most resilient species and kill sensitive ones. Place the root ball intact in the planting hole, taking care not to drop and shock it. (Resilient species—those commonly planted as field-dug specimens—will likely recover from such root ball disturbance.)

» Place the plant so that the base of the stem, where new roots emerge (the root-initiation zone), remains below soil grade. In wetter areas, it is important to match the grade to the top of the root-initiation zone—no higher. In drier climates such as those in California, adding 1–2 inches (3–5 cm) of mulch over the rooting zone can be helpful, even if the mulch is touching the stem. No stem should be left on its tip-toes after planting: the base should be snugly in the ground, generally a bit lower than recommended for planting woody trees, with no air or cavity between the base of the stem and the ground.

Fill in air pockets and compact the backfill around the root ball to stabilize the plant. Some species will have aerial roots breaking out of the stem surface well above grade—above the expected rooting zone. It is best not to bury these.

In areas with a cool or dry winter, plant palms in spring or summer to take advantage of warm weather and increase chances for success. In tropical areas, plant them at the beginning of the rainy season—which often coincides with spring there.

FERTILIZING

Palms tend to be heavy feeders. Local soil and climate conditions will determine needs for fertilizer; getting soil tested may be helpful. Cold weather and heavy rainfall can pose nutritional problems. Nurture the soil flora with organic fertilizing and mulching practices if possible—palms take advantage of mycorrhizal relationships in habitat for nutrition and water uptake and can do so in exotic soils

VIGOR AND WEAKNESS: PLUSES AND MINUSES

M any plants growing at the limits of their tolerances may serve their purposes better than if they were grown in their ideal climate. Chinese fan palms (*Livistona chinensis*) planted more than three decades ago in Oakland, California, grow so slowly in the cool climate that they have remained a useful understory foliage element; in Hawai'i, on the other hand, the species is speedy and invasive. Minimal fruit production can be another benefit of zone-pushing. Cheap, fast-growing species such as *Syagrus romanzoffiana* have become common in areas where thirty- or fifty-year freezes can kill them. Add the cost of removal to low-cost marginal palms.

Because palm stems undergo no secondary growth and cannot heal over, the scar from a 1990 freeze remains forever on the trunk of the rightmost king palm (*Archontophoenix cunninghamiana*) at the Lakeside Palmetum of the Gardens at Lake Merritt, Oakland, California. The species is at the limits of its climate tolerance in the Bay Area. Otherwise still thriving, it has sown a seedling visible at lower right. Unblemished king palms to the left were planted after the freeze. A thirty-two-year-old Chinese fan palm (*Livistona chinensis*) mingles below.

with compatible organisms. Four times a year at Flora Grubb Gardens we apply an organic 3-2-4 nitrogen-phosphorus-potassium (N-P-K) formula with crucial micronutrients such as magnesium, calcium, and iron. The most frequent deficiencies we see are of magnesium and potassium, which should be corrected in tandem, lest the plant's uptake of one element block uptake of the other. Nitrogen deficiency is also common; applying a palm-specific fertilizer is the simplest approach.

WIRY ROOTS AND CONFINED SPACES

A special talent of palm trees is their ability to nestle in close to buildings and other palms. They require surprisingly little room for their roots, affording tree effects in tight spaces. Such proximity may have little effect on their vigor. Beware, however, that future growth of close-planted specimens will often respond to shade cast by the neighbor palms: I've seen once-straight palmetto specimens of equal height planted too close together with an abruptly angled trunk the result. The cause? After planting, they had turned their new growth away from each other in search of more light. Using crown diameter as a rule of thumb for placement can prevent such awkwardness, but this limits the dynamic effects palms can achieve in their phototropic growth (another plus for planting young). Had the palmettos' crowns been staggered in height, the planting would have worked, because the palms' growth angles would have been curving and graceful. Many nurseries grow multiple seedlings of solitary palms in one pot for a more graceful effect over time.

Palms' thin, fibrous roots pose much less of a problem for the integrity of foundations and retaining walls than the ever-thickening roots of woody trees. A problem can arise, however, when a large palm grows taller and heavier over time and adds pressure to soil next to a wall, which can cause damage to the wall.

Similarly, these wiry roots are much less of a problem for sewer and water pipes, again because they do not go through secondary thickening. On occasion, however, a profusion of thin, fibrous palm roots can cause a problem in a pipe. Big species are more likely to pose problems than small ones. Most established palms can bear having a small portion of the root mat cut away and isolated from a pipe.

STAKING AND RIGGING

In Florida and the southeast United States, landscapers routinely place diagonal base props, stakes and ties, or guy wires on the trunks of newly transplanted palms to reduce wind throw. Squalls or storm gusts might topple a newly planted tree just starting to regrow roots. Never apply rigging to the crownshaft, leaves, or

HARDY HYBRID PALMS

Hybrid palms may produce minimal fruit litter and grow with hybrid vigor. Increasingly popular among enthusiasts in colder climates, palm hybrids are often the product of a laborious, years-long process of growing parent plants to flowering age and performing intricate flower surgery, pollination, protection from vermin, germination, and test growing. Most involve a group of genera related to the coconut palm, such as *Butia*, *Syagrus*, and *Parajubaea*, although many *Phoenix* species hybridize within the genus in cultivation, producing useful and beautiful intermediates.

Hybrids produced from at least one cold-hardy species add variety to the limited palette of freeze-tolerant palms.

other soft-tissue portions of the tree—this could damage or kill the sole growing point. It is important to avoid penetrating the trunk with nails or screws; connect rigging to a tight ring or cuff around the trunk and remove the whole apparatus once the palm has become established—that is, when it has grown a new full crown and plentiful roots. In some cases, it may be necessary to leave guying or bracing indefinitely, such as when the swaying of a palm tree might bump into a structure. In California, rigging of transplants is less common but useful in windier areas and on leaning or exceptionally tall specimens. On bottom-heavy container-grown plants, it's rarely necessary.

It is best to mount landscape lighting to the ground or the built surroundings; mounting on the trunks of palms is unsightly and often requires penetrating the trunk, although this is done frequently—and lamentably.

PRUNING

Palms produce a lot of biomass—big, fibrous dead leaves; large inflorescences; fecund infructescences; leafbases often persistent or thorny; or unwanted stems on clustering species. In a manicured landscape, many palms demand regular grooming and pruning to look their best. At the same time, excessive pruning of live leaves in the crown, especially, can harm the form and even the structural integrity of a tree by depriving the bud of the energy needed to develop the natural thickness of its stem, which can narrow and weaken or break. An exception is upon transplanting, when it can be prudent to cut the lower half or more of the crown to reduce wind drag on the newly planted tree. Lower leaves will die off anyway, because the tree loses most of its roots when dug.

Mind this aesthetic directive: cut leaves where the petiole meets the leafbase (or along the node where the leafbase encircles the trunk, skinning the trunk). If cutting any distance out from that point, make sure all the petiole stubs are the same length and as short as possible.

Cutting along the leaf blade disfigures the frond. Such partial cuts ruin the arching balance of feather palms, while they blunt the radial expression of fan palms.

The unpruned, natural look in established palms, with lower leaves revealing their process of yellowing to straw, can be appealing and wildlife-friendly, but it must harmonize with the landscape context. Burgeoning, untrimmed palms in a stark, modern space may be just the right foil, or they could seem like feral interlopers.

For the healthiest impact, remove only leaves that have turned to straw color; palm trees reabsorb nutrients that remain in their leaves before shedding them. It's common, if not ideal, to cut the lower half of a crown, including green leaves, to a "nine-o'clock and three-o'clock" position, leaving a hemisphere shape and reducing the frequency of pruning.

Use new, sterile tools to minimize the spread of lethal fungal and bacterial diseases. Second best is to cauterize blades or soak them in a solution of one part bleach to one part water after a thorough cleaning. Rinse bleached blades thoroughly with fresh water before cutting.

A happy palm will produce a lot of fruit. Groundcovers can conceal small fallen fruits. When designing plantings over paving or gravel, consider the size and consistency (mushy? dry?) of fruit produced by the varieties of palms under consideration. Consider, too, the maintenance they will require—will it be smarter to remove inflorescences or unripe infructescences, or can the fallen fruit be easily raked up? Pruning before ripening can be more efficient on larger fruiting or seasonally fruiting species; it can be a once-a-year job. Pulpy fruit such as dates take an extra step to remove from paving. Species with hard, rolling fruit might pose a risk to pedestrians. Coconut trees growing anywhere people hang out pose a lethal risk from their 3-pound (1.4-kg) falling fruits. A species growing at the limit of its climate adaptations—or a male plant, or a single female plant lacking a pollinator—might not make any fruit but will perform well otherwise.

PALM SPRINGS IMPRESSIONS

On my first trip to Palm Springs I took a client's car full of orchids from San Francisco to set up in her new house. Driving away from the setting sun through San Gorgonio Pass between flanks of 10,000-foot-tall mountains, I lost the malls-cape of Southern California's Inland Empire and entered the terrain of giant wind turbines, dunes, creosote scrub, and national park views. Sunlight caught on the massif of Mount San Jacinto, a shadow the size of a small county stretching across the desert cities at the mountain's base, their cozy electric twinkle evoking a hideout.

My client's winter retreat in Rancho Mirage was a white modernist take on a Marrakech villa, an ample 1960s house with rooms, courtyards, pool, and guest house all locked in pleasing proportion to a square grid. I loved the intimate square dining room partitioned by Moorish-inspired wooden lattice screens, but it was when my client led me through the small loggia courtyard, past the trickling font at its center, to my guest room, that I marveled at the design. The room's door opened into a short barrel vault that let me into a larger barrel-ceilinged bedroom on the perimeter garden. Twenty feet out, a white wall blocked the bottom eight feet of suburban dusk, allowing into view only stony slopes, shimmering green palms, and sky.

The clear spaces of California's Coachella Valley contain many of the state's largest natural groves of its sole native palm. Mostly limited to the Colorado Desert (the low desert of California), the California fan palm, *Washingtonia filifera*, throngs the Indian Canyons on the Agua Caliente Indian Reservation just above Palm Springs, where perennial streams drain the grand San Jacinto and Santa Rosa mountains. The palm's bulky, jade-green crowns, thick trunks, and straw beards also rise in staggered generations from seeps among the granite faces of Joshua Tree National Park, and they congregate in spring-fed marshes along the San Andreas Fault rift. The palm's range extends south of the valley through Anza-Borrego Desert State Park and along the eastern slope of northern Baja California's mountainous spine.

The Cahuilla people of the Coachella Valley have used the palm for food, fuel, construction, clothing, and instruments. The tree's preference for moist, resource-rich locales made its shaded groves an attractive place for people to live. In the post–European-contact era, people have aided washingtonia's dispersal far beyond

Palm Springs and the surrounding desert cities are a community of privacy, in which high hedges enclose properties while tall palms, visible over great distances, bind the place together. Here at the Parker Palm Springs resort, the Mexican fan palm (*Washingtonia robusta*) performs that paradoxical trick in Judy Kameon's design.

the Colorado Desert, to Death Valley for instance, and it's likely the Cahuilla dispersed this valuable species in the region.

Joshua Tree, at the northeastern edge of the Coachella Valley, is the washingtonia's sole outpost within the higher and colder Mojave Desert. This ecological boundary foretells the palm's tolerance of extreme heat but less extreme cold (low teens, Fahrenheit, in dry climates). The palm thrives where average annual rainfall measures near the lowest and high temperatures near the highest in the United States. Palm Springs' average high temperature, 89°F (32°C), is fourth highest in the United States, and on average 181 days a year breach 90°F (32°C). Record low temperatures in the low 20s F (−5°C) occurred every few decades in the twentieth century. In the average year, only 14 days experience rains of 0.01 inch (0.25 mm) or more. Its average annual rainfall is about 6 inches (15 cm), and nearby weather stations experience even less rainfall.

The 10,000-foot rock slope of Mount San Jacinto swings its shadow over Palm Springs early in the afternoon, a reprieve in the many months when typically cloudless afternoons persist in the 100s F (high 30s C), and a chilling curtain in winter. The landscapes it buffers contain a multitude of palm trees—mostly Mexican fan palms (*Washingtonia robusta*), California fan palms, and date palms (*Phoenix dactylifera*)—and the shrubby Mediterranean fan palm, *Chamaerops humilis*. They're much more densely planted here than in Los Angeles, Orange County, or San Diego, and they tell visitors that this is an oasis, a haven for weekend retreats and winter sojourns. Irrigation-dependent, the citywide landscape oasis is borrowed from just up the road, where those palms grow naturally.

The valley floor rises on alluvial fans as you drive toward the vertiginous mountains, whose treeless slopes defy your instinctive measurement of scale. The city is a carpet of cultivated landscape thrown over this terrain, many gardens surrounded by hedges and walls. A rhythm of tall palm trees raises your gaze and offers a station on your eye's journey toward the desert crags. The palms peek above your matrix of privacy, waving from behind the hedges, linking home to resort hotel to golf course and supermarket parking lot, an urbanizing tree reminding you that you're in shared space in this spread-out community.

The motif of palms rising above hedges occurs again and again in the Californian desert cities, not just in Palm Springs but also in Rancho Mirage, Palm Desert, and Indian Wells. They are ubiquitous around pools; in front-yard plantings; languishing unirrigated on rocky, abandoned sites; and burgeoning on golf courses. Few other trees—pines, palo verdes, ficuses, mostly—reach the same height as the washingtonias or are as conspicuous. They add a dotted veil of green to the view of the city from upslope, a verdant haze to the suburban plain.

California's wild desert palms inhabit places where the Coachella Desert's precious water trickles down from the mountains or wells up from ancient aquifers.

In the agricultural districts east of the resort towns, date-palm orchards run in large tracts across the valley floor. These ranches produce dates of several varieties and sell full-size trees to be dug and transplanted for landscape use, especially those that have grown too tall for easy harvest. Here and in Arizona are the only commercial plantings of palms for food in the continental United States that I am aware of.

As a San Franciscan, I view this landscape with eyes of a traveler from another world. Perhaps no other place within California contrasts so sharply with San Francisco.

BETWEEN PEOPLE AND SEA Soaring and tenacious, animated and slightly anthropomorphic in their crown-and-trunk figure, coconut palms on the Puna coast of the Big Island of Hawai'i act as intermediary between the daunting Pacific Ocean and our mortal human perspective. Even coastal palm trees of other species bridge human and ocean (and sky) better than other tree types — an effect that partly accounts for their frequent use. And they leave views open.

PALM
SENSATIONS
AND
SERVICES

Gardens envelop us with the smell of dirt on our hands, the sweetness of a Barhi date, the sound of wind in the trees, the smack of morning chill. Gardens alter us, too, providing memories of a place and the feelings and events that occurred there.

Focused on sensation over symbolism, here is a portfolio of the sensory effects and functional roles of palms in the landscape. It is offered as an idea kit, an inspiration, along with cautionary notes. Plants play a primary role in our enchantment with gardens, and palms spark the romance of the tropics in the accumulation of the sensory memories they leave with us. Although it is impossible, and maybe unfair, to disentangle palms from the tropical places they often conjure, my hope is that looking closely at their aesthetic and functional qualities while holding symbolic meaning aside will equip gardeners and designers wherever palms grow to use them thoughtfully in landscape design.

Using plants first for their aesthetic effects in planting design is a commitment I draw from my work at Flora Grubb Gardens, where my colleagues create sometimes unlikely assemblages of plants, compatible in garden culture but disparate in the stories they evoke, that continually delight visitors to our gardens.

Because of what they can do and how they affect us, palms deserve a place in more design palettes.

ALLÉE

Breathtaking colonnades of Canary Island date palms at Stanford University's Palm Drive produce an open, regimented effect with a visual rhythm that mesmerizes the viewer and draws attention to the destination.

MUSEUM WAY
→ Cantor Arts Center
Rodin Sculpture Garden
Anderson Collection

BRIDGE TO THE SKY

Billowing *Bismarckia nobilis* palms draw the eye from a richly
planted ground plane toward the monumental skies above
Miami's Fairchild Tropical Botanic Garden. Spectacular palms
are useful bridges between South Florida's flat ground and
glorious cloud formations. No matter the topography, tall
palms seem to levitate in the sky.

CONTAINER COMPOSITION

left: Designer Christopher Reynolds uses chamaedorea and pygmy date palms (*Phoenix roebelenii*) for their neatness, upright habit, and soft linearity in a container composition for a modernistic building in San Francisco. Thanks to their root anatomy, container culture suits many palms.

SOUND

right: Flora Grubb's clara palm (*Brahea clara*) from Sonora, Mexico, provides overhead shelter, color harmony, and a soothing rustle for her Berkeley, California, garden. Each palm species renders a different sound in the wind, even differing among closely related varieties. Unlike Flora's clara palm, plants from the sibling population of *B. armata* in Baja California produce little sound in the wind, so stiff are the leaves. Each palm is an instrument.

GROVES AND COPSES

above: A copse of kentia palms (*Howea forsteriana*) at the Virginia Robinson Gardens in Beverly Hills, California, functions as a legible and animated foil to the stolid magnolia tree and cactus clump cornering the house. In place of the palms, a timber bamboo or a grouping of small trees would be opaque and pose greater maintenance challenges.

PACE A WALK

right: Carved into a populous grove of king palms (*Archontophoenix cunninghamiana*) at the Virginia Robinson Gardens, a stepped path gains comforting definition, while the palms' weighty trunks frame glimpses of the gardens beyond.

HEDGES

left: Modest-size hedges of lady palm are common in tropical and subtropical regions, dark green in shade but viable in humid sun, too. Even in cooler climates patient gardeners can use them for hedges. Many *Chamaedorea* species can be good small hedges, too, but with feather leaves, fragrant flowers, and colorful fruit. Palms combine nicely with other plants for a composed hedge or hedgerow.

BOUNDARIES

right: In Charleston, South Carolina, an interplanting of podocarpus with palmettos (*Sabal palmetto*) at regular intervals balances the fine texture and rectilinear form of the hedge with the energetic crowns of the palms: neatness, separation, and charisma make the match formal but not boring.

GROUNDCOVER

left: Finely clumping *Chamaedorea stolonifera* spreads into a thick mass of foliage at Ganna Walska Lotusland in Montecito, California. Low, solitary palms closely planted can serve the same purpose.

A TRICK OF SCALE

right: Young Chinese fan palms (*Livistona chinensis*) maintained for their big leaves along a walkway in Charleston, South Carolina, perform the paradoxical trick of enhancing the space. Properly chosen and placed, large-leaf palms—as foliage, shrubs, or trees—can confer grandeur onto confined places.

SHRUBS

Shrubby saw palmettos, *Serenoa repens*, frame a cascade at The Huntington Botanical Gardens in San Marino, California, adding a silvery foreground to live oaks. In its Florida and Southeastern habitat, saw palmetto often covers the ground plane in pinewoods and nestles in coastal dunes.

MIXED BORDER

A border at Seibels House and Garden in Columbia, South Carolina, designed by Jenks Farmer, incorporates shrubby saw palmetto (*Serenoa repens*), mondo grass (*Ophiopogon japonicus*), and a tree-sized palmetto (*Sabal palmetto*), backed by the seasonal color and bold form of deciduous oakleaf hydrangea (*Hydrangea quercifolia*).

BARRIER

top left: The beautiful and intricate armature of *Trithrinax campestris* leafbases and its daggerlike leaf tips create a good barrier against deer and other intruders. Many spiny palms, single-trunk or clustering, can be used to discourage animal or human intruders.

ECOLOGICAL SERVICES

right: A bee forages on the buffet of fragrant, nectar-rich flowers in the inflorescence of a *Sabal pumos*. Fruit and flowers tend to appear in profusion and make palms an efficient stop for animals in search of sustenance. Crowns of tough, fibrous leaves, often protectively armed, serve as shelter for birds and other animals as well. Inhabitants pay rent in nutrient rich droppings. In California, hooded orioles favor palms even in urban areas for building their pendant nests.

COLOR

left: Many specimens of the celebrated flamethrower palm, *Chambeyronia macrocarpa*, produce translucent red new leaves that convert within days to dark green. The dying oldest leaves of a palm often pass through a golden phase before falling off or fading to straw.

right: Leafbases of many palms deliver a hit of color, none so famously as the reds of the sealing-wax palm, *Cyrtostachys renda*.

COLOR
CONTRAST

Many palm trunks create
columns of color, often green,
gray, or brown, in the landscape.
In the Sullivan family garden
in Ventura, California, an
Andean wax palm, *Ceroxylon
ventricosum*, looms like a
banded marble column behind
a dark red ti plant (*Cordyline
fruticosa*). The palm's smooth
and waxy surface rewards touch
as well.

SENTINELS

Framing a paved drive in
Montecito, California, Thai
mountain giant fishtail palms
(*Caryota gigas*) serve as a pair of
grand and welcoming sentinels.

FOCAL POINT

right: Focus converges on a group of baby queen palms, *Chamaedorea plumosa*, and thus to a door opening to the street in a San Francisco garden designed by Davis Dalbok. The tracery of these little palm trees moves against smooth stucco in the area's constant breezes, casting a hint of canopy over the narrow walkway and pointing to architectural detail beyond.

AERIAL VOLUME

left: An unsung role for palm trees is their ability to activate volumes in and over landscapes—as these Caribbean royal palms (*Roystonea oleracea*) do in Jeff Seyfried's garden on the Big Island of Hawai'i. Garlands of Spanish moss (*Tillandsia usneoides*) add to the effect. Just as the campanile in St. Mark's Square in Venice is essential to the piazza's grandeur, even a single palm tree, with its energetic yet legible crown, can draw the eye upward through a bounded volume and thus expand the viewer's experience of a landscape. This function is especially useful in landscapes framed by buildings.

CANOPY

right: Friendly giants, Thai mountain giant fishtail palms (*Caryota gigas*) shade a courtyard garden designed by Eric Nagelmann in Montecito, California. Rather than crowding the intimate space, the shingled silhouettes of regularly spaced leaflets atop mammoth trunks generate a thrilling vertical dimension and provide canopy.

PUNCTUATE
A PATH

left: Starting between cycads, a path dances through trunks of solitaire palms, *Ptychosperma elegans*, at Punta Roquena, a private botanical garden in the Florida Keys, curated by D'Asign Source.

PUNCTUATE
THE GROUND

top right: A simple tableau comprises trunks of livistona palms meeting mulched ground at Ganna Walska Lotusland.

TEXTURE
AND TREES

Interplay between these wax
palms' (*Ceroxylon vogelianum*)
smooth trunks and the fine,
twiggy canopy and rough bark
of woody trees can be lovely
or awkward, depending on
planning and care. Skillful
placement of palms in relation
to woody trees can emphasize
the structural drama of each.
Thoughtful pruning of branches
to accommodate palms' vertical
thrust need not compromise the
tree's integrity.

ROLES ON SEPARATE STAGES

left: From the ground-level patio, Mexican fan palms (*Washingtonia robusta*) in a San Francisco garden designed by Christopher Reynolds are fully visible, their limited crowns adding a note of overhead protection while they annex the garden's airspace. The trunks intersect with and bolster the fence grid. Regular leafbase scars on the skinned trunks subtly parallel the lines of light through the fence, while wood and trunks share a reddish brown hue; together they will fade to gray. Views from the higher floors capture the green crowns of the palms.

SCALE TO AN EDIFICE

top right: Monumental Chilean wine palms (*Jubaea chilensis*) maintain their grandeur against the towering de Young Museum in San Francisco. Landscape architect Walter Hood chose to reuse a historic grouping of palms from around the museum's previous building, taking advantage of a correspondence between the palms' fronds, permeable to light, and the museum's perforated cladding. In Hood's nod to tradition, the specimen trees provide a natural antithesis to the structure designed by Herzog & de Meuron.

BALANCE

Palms ranging in size from moderate to grand fringe the Santa Barbara Courthouse in California, ornamenting without concealing its Spanish Colonial Revival grandeur and offering visitors and workers sound, movement, and green relief from the weight of the edifice.

THE BIG ISLAND: PALM HEAVEN?

My colleague Caitlin and I went to the Big Island of Hawai'I to see some of the most astonishing tropical gardens in the world to research and photograph for this book. With all its palm-studded landscapes, the Big Island sure looks like a tropical paradise, especially on its lush windward side. (The dry leeward side of this Connecticut-size island seems—and in some spots is—a desert by comparison.)

For all the palmy vistas, though, there are a few drawbacks for the ambitious gardener there: nightly rains and inconvenient daytime showers; persistent, sometimes devastating, volcanic activity; invasive pests and weeds; and the rare tsunami, earthquake, or tropical storm.

Most of us visitors who love gardening, however, envy people on the Big Island. The wet side is a place of wish-fulfillment, where garden plants grow as fast as Jack's beanstalk and fairy-tale rainbows appear every few hours. Hilo, the island's picturesque small city and seat of government, gets more than 100 inches (250 cm) of rain per year. The rains come year-round. They diminish concerns about drought that people in other parts of the world—including Florida, Texas, California, Australia, and the Mediterranean—must live with in designing and cultivating gardens. The Big Island's young lava substrates, while yielding few nutrients, allow for perfect drainage and easy modification for fertility and moisture retention. The frequent activity of the island's active volcanoes, Kīlauea and Mauna Loa, leaves dramatic topography, views, and colors for the garden designer to play with. Erosion and weathering have created picturesque landforms and vistas, including the slopes of the island's three inactive volcanoes, where the greatest growth in vacation resorts and population has occurred.

This island is a place of opportunity for people who want to create gardens for other reasons, too. Sugarcane fields left fallow after the withdrawal of the industry have been subdivided into multiacre plots. In the Puna District, south of Hilo, the chronic and imminent threat of volcanic activity from Kīlauea and associated inconveniences keep property values lower than elsewhere in Hawai'i. Land is affordable, rainfall is abundant, and local nurseries rival South Florida's in producing the widest array of palms and other tropical plants in the United States—many for export.

In this remarkable climate, not only do exotic palms from a wide range of habitats—from deepest tropical rainforests to cloud forest, mild temperate zones, and savannas—thrive, but gardeners also live in breezy comfort compared to those in other tropical and subtropical regions. Afternoon temperatures rarely rise above 85°F (29°C), and thanks to the enormous mass of the island's 13,000-foot (4000-m) volcanoes, cool air percolates down to sea level each night, making dawn feel fresh. Hilo's average low temperatures are in the 60°F to 70°F range (16°C to 21°C) nearly year-round. Nighttime's seaward movement of cool air meets and clashes with persistent onshore tradewinds and is responsible for the nighttime rains.

The Big Island may seem naturally palmy, but almost all of the species that grow there people brought from other tropical regions of the world, including the essential and ubiquitous coconut palm (*Cocos nucifera*). Some of the imports, such as the Alexandra palm, *Archontophoenix alexandrae*, from Queensland, Australia, have become invasive pests.

On the Hawaiian archipelago, about twenty-five beautiful species of palms in the genus *Pritchardia* occur naturally, mostly in moist forest habitats, with a few in drier zones of these ecologically diverse islands. They are endemic to Hawai'i, and most inhabit a single island. On the Big Island, at least five species grow in habitats ranging from brackish seaside environments to cool, mossy forests at three-quarters of a mile above sea level. Only three other members of the genus, two of them staples of tropical landscaping in the Hawaiian Islands, occur naturally elsewhere: the widely grown Fiji (*P. pacifica*) and Lau (*P. thurstonii*) fan palms, and the rare *P. mitiaroana*, native to the islands of Mitiaro in the Cook Islands and Makatea and Niau in French Polynesia.

Like so many of the state's native plants, most of Hawai'i's pritchardias are threatened or endangered by habitat loss and invasive species. Studies of ancient pollen records reveal that the islands' lowlands harbored extensive forests of *loulu* (the name for pritchardias in Hawaiian culture) before the first Hawaiians arrived in the islands in their sea-voyaging canoes—with stowaway Polynesian rats that, along with their cousins the brown and black rats arriving with European contact in the late eighteenth century, would come to feast on *loulu* seeds, thwarting future generations.

A few species of these charismatic and surprisingly adaptable fan palms are cultivated in Hawai'i, California, Australia, and elsewhere, but most are quite rare in gardens.

Both the windward and leeward sides of the Big Island are a magnet for palm collectors. The abundance of species and landforms enables designers there to teach lessons about designing with palms that we in harsher, more seasonal climates can apply with our more limited palm palettes.

THE
STORIES
PALMS
TELL

A garden designer once told me that we
were all catering to clients' clichés.
She was interviewing me for a job,
and, as interesting and respected and nice
as she was, I wasn't interested.

97

The stories that plants implicitly spawn do influence our experiences of landscapes. Entering dreamed-of realms (California's Sea Ranch, Bolivia's Tiwanaku, Cape Town's Kirstenbosch), finding the apotheosis of a notion (secure suburbia, wilderness, agrarian bounty), fulfilling a wish (preserving rare species, making walkable cities, gathering friends)—these are good reasons for spending time in a garden and for creating one. Clichés aren't tiresome (maybe just embarrassing) when we feel enlivened by them. But then they lose their allure and we recognize we're attached to a husk and it's time for a change.

That palms tell a few stories so loudly that we can't hear their other tales is another way to describe the conceit at the heart of this book. There are lots of possible garden experiences for palms to reveal.

Here I provide a portfolio about the moods and styles that palms can create, or enhance—the stories they can quicken and launch. My hope is that these photographs will help palms prompt new ideas, expand the feelings they inspire, and contribute new tales to the places where we dwell.

PERSIAN PARADISE

A rill trickling through a patio at the Virginia Robinson Gardens in Beverly Hills, California, hints at a Persian walled garden of paradise, evoking bounty in an arid place. Mediterranean fan palms (*Chamaerops humilis*) and king palms (*Archontophoenix cunninghamiana*) stand in for fruitful date palms while underscoring an early twentieth-century California version of paradise.

MODERN

above: A modernist approach to space and plant selection underpins this San Francisco landscape designed by Daniel Nolan for Flora Grubb Gardens. Building upon a tradition of city gardens begun by Thomas Church, Nolan delineates useable space with plain materials while creating a tableau to view from the house above—its most important function in the location's cool climate. Daring to combine three kinds of subtly varying fan palms— *Trachycarpus martianus* (tall, at center), *T. fortunei* 'Wagnerianus' (near left), and *Livistona chinensis* (far left and right)—Nolan embeds their radial energy into a gathering of calm, compatible greens—boxwood, pittosporum, ivy, and Japanese maple— allowing them to be just building blocks, and thereby freeing them of their symbolic freight.

SPANISH COLONIAL REVIVAL

right: Hollywood set design made permanent, the mandated rebuilding of Santa Barbara in a Spanish Colonial Revival style after the 1925 earthquake would have been incomplete without palms—innumerable kentias here at the Santa Barbara Biltmore. Renovations in the early 2000s brought more palm varieties grown by Sea Crest Nursery just up the coast. The kentias' romantic luxuriance helps create a California coastal idyll for holidaymakers.

bottom left: A picture of precipitous mountains behind exotic plantings in a Mediterranean climate inspires comparisons between the French and Italian Riviera and the Santa Barbara coast of California. Palms—kentias, Canary Island date palms (*Phoenix canariensis*), and nīkau palms (*Rhopalostylis sapida*)— imported both to Europe and California in the nineteenth century, please travelers, lure investment, and signal the global reach of horticulture and its patrons.

SURREAL

above: Like elfin spirits materializing from an opaque unconscious, Mediterranean fan palms pop out of a ficus hedge in front of Kelly Wearstler's Viceroy Santa Monica hotel in California.

SOUTHEAST ASIAN

right: Shaded by a bo tree (*Ficus religiosa*), a Thai-style pavilion accented with a *Licuala peltata* var. *sumawongii* anchors the Lea Asian Garden at the Naples Botanical Garden, Florida. The celebrated tropical landscape designer Made Wijaya designed the palm-rich space in homage to varied garden designs, old and new, of Southeast Asia, where plants of the genus *Licuala* pepper the natural flora and cultivated lands of the region.

POST-WILD

A master plan by Ellin Goetz, Ted Flato, Raymond Jungles, Herb Schaal, Bob Truskowski, and Made Wijaya integrates the exotic-plant collection at the core of the Naples Botanical Garden into a restored native landscape. Passing through the entrance structure of the visitor center—reminiscent of a lath house—visitors encounter exotic and native plantings designed by Jungles through its frames, followed by a progression of landscapes appearing ever more lightly constructed and open. Palms in lawn, such as these coconuts—not native to Florida—carry architectural parallels in their fronds, while gesturing toward a swath of native palmettos (*Sabal palmetto*) and royal palms (*Roystonea regia*) amid a river of native grasses (including Fakahatchee grass, *Tripsacum dactyloides*).

above right: Outward into the Preserve at the Naples Botanical Garden, royal palms frame a view of restored native landscape of slash pine (*Pinus elliottii*) and palmettos. Royal palms are charismatic natives but rare in the wild, creating an attractive guidepost to the quieter preserve. Fading rings on the trunks carry a hint of the architecture and exotic palms (such as *Dypsis cabadae*) that visitors see upon entering the garden.

CONTEMPORARY MODERNIST

A sheltered walkway floats through a garden designed by Raymond Jungles. Rising from a welter of plant textures, cabada palms (*Dypsis cabadae*) add their vital regularity to a contemporary modernist design by Lake|Flato Architects for the Chabraja Visitor Center at the Naples Botanical Garden.

BRAZILIAN MODERNIST

Miami landscape architect Raymond Jungles was mentored by Roberto Burle Marx (1909–94), the Brazilian artist celebrated for his modernist landscape designs rich with native plants—not least, palms. For the Kapnick Brazilian Garden at the Naples Botanical Garden, Jungles created an homage to Burle Marx, a dose of the artist's humane Brazilian modernism culminating in an elevated plaza, featuring a ceramic mural by the Brazilian master—the only one on public display in the United States. Integrating palms from varied Brazilian habitats, such as a huge *Attalea* (center) and a *Butia eriospatha* (right) reflected in the pool, Jungles's design concentrates an acre within the botanical garden where people gather, interact with plants, and participate in performances and classes.

URBAN WILD

above: Lincoln Road Mall is the pedestrian promenade at the heart of Miami Beach. Its final, westernmost block lacked the liveliness of the rest of the street until the opening of Herzog & de Meuron's mold-breaking building, 1111 Lincoln Road, and Raymond Jungles's brilliant redesign for the plaza and surrounding gardens. The banded paving evokes Roberto Burle Marx's sinuous two-tone Copacabana Beach sidewalk designs in Rio de Janeiro. Mature specimen plants of the Florida wild—live oak (*Quercus virginiana*), palmettos, air plants (*Tillandsia* spp.), bald cypress (*Taxodium distichum*, in autumn color), and red mangroves (*Rhizophora mangle*)—inject a sense of unruly nature into a city space that Jungles sculpted into layered platforms for seating and performances interlocked with water gardens. Walls impound the pools in biomorphic outlines that recall forms from Copacabana and bend the predominantly linear logic of the paving design. Water cascades between levels through molded spillways, ringing its element into the city corridor. Uniquely suited to the task, tall palmettos guide the eye from the bustle and through canopy trees to the landmark building and the changing skies eight stories up.

right: A clump of Everglades palm (*Acoelorrhaphe wrightii*) lines a public walkway between the landmark 1111 Lincoln Road building and a neighbor, a tracery of native flora in Raymond Jungles's design to fortify the circulation of the urban ecosystem. Heavier trunks of palmettos bracket the scene.

JAZZ AGE URBANE

Designer-hotelier Avi Brosch's discreet and luxurious beach lodge, Palihouse Santa Monica, is a quick stroll or bike ride to the beach and Third Street Promenade. Brosch and Surfacedesign landscape architects transformed the 1927 hotel into an urbane retreat. Palms serve the space with their unique effects—rustling canopy, vertical streaks of green trunks—while requiring minimal maintenance and holding the torch of Jazz Age chic that illuminates the Moorish-inspired Mediterranean Revival architecture.

DESERT

The Huntington Desert Garden in San Marino, California, is home to clara palms (*Brahea clara*) rising over a bed of cactus and succulents befitting their shared desert origins.

SYBARITIC OASIS

Judy Kameon, founder of Elysian Landscapes in Los Angeles and author of *Gardens Are for Living*, created a garden for playing—a dreamscape of pleasure and surprise—for the Parker Palm Springs, the resort hotel designed by Jonathan Adler that was pivotal in the city's remake as California's style-driven desert getaway. Given the opportunity to revamp the entire landscape with a fictional great-aunt's spirit of joie de vivre as her inspiration, Kameon reused the existing (and essential) palms, olives, citrus, and bougainvillea and replanted thickly with a palette ranging from shade trees and lavender to succulents, jasmine, Mexican sage, and pampas grass in a sequence of themed garden rooms connected by cozy passageways and leading to croquet, tennis, a lemonade stand, restaurants, spa, and swimming pools. The palm court invites napping in the shade of date palms (*Phoenix dactylifera*)—the quintessential oasis tree, signifying respite and fruitfulness.

VICTORIAN

left: A nineteenth-century California ranch style was to plant a pair of palms—often Canary Island date palms—at the entrance, or an allée along the drive (as at Stanford University). A San Francisco landmark, the Casebolt House, built in 1865 when its Cow Hollow neighborhood warranted the pastoral epithet, draws on this tradition.

GILDED AGE

above: The North Vista at The Huntington Botanical Gardens comprises an allée lined with Australian fan palms (*Livistona australis*) and eighteenth-century Italian sculptures. It defines a view from Arabella and Henry Huntington's house, now home to The Huntington Art Gallery and the family's European art collection, to the San Gabriel Mountains. In the early twentieth century, the fruits of the Gilded Age sprouted and took root in the Golden State's cultural and scientific institutions, not least in Huntington's extraordinary palm collection and the other gardens composed by William Hertrich, the first superintendent of the gardens.

MEMORY

right: At the de Young Museum, landscape architect Walter Hood redeployed a historic grove of palms (mostly *Phoenix canariensis*) from the old building's surroundings around the new building to quite different effect. Rather than signify—along with the original building's Spanish Colonial Revival architecture—a mild climate, the palms remind people of the site's past while interacting with the building's permeable and reflective surfaces, serving as objects of views from inside and acting as intermediary figures between humans and the edifice.

CITY BEAUTIFUL

left: A Beaux-Arts remnant of the California Academy of Sciences' 1916 building in San Francisco's Golden Gate Park is preserved in Renzo Piano's 2008 structure for the Academy and finds historically apt company in a fringe of kentia palms and two landmark Canary Island date palms, part of a design by SWA landscape architects. The Academy is built on the site of the 1894 California Midwinter International Exposition, a fair that aimed to promote California's mild climate, signaled by palms.

LOWCOUNTRY

The thrilling and hospitable garden of Alejandro Gonzalez and Jim Smeal on James Island, near the port city of Charleston, South Carolina, incorporates local natives such as palmettos, Spanish moss, and heritage live oaks on the wild, watery edge of the property. Japanese ferns hint at several exotic gardens closer to the house planted with bromeliads, cycads, succulents, palms, ferns, perennials, and conifers. The garden leans on palms for their aesthetic effects and exoticism.

SYLVAN

left: A clearing in the woods is a cozy setting for Mike Harris's extraordinary palm collection in Broward County, Florida. Somehow his woodsy house fits perfectly amidst palms, live oaks, and banyans.

JUNGLE

above: Palms and banyan trees (king palms and *Ficus macrophylla* in this case) together seem to distill a jungle essence at the Virginia Robinson Gardens in Beverly Hills, California.

JEWEL BOX

left: In the constant moisture of Hilo, Hawai'i, perched anthuriums and ferns go wild, adding to this tiered jewel-box composition at La Casa de las Palmas. Adult waggie palms (*Trachycarpus fortunei* 'Wagnerianus') are prime verticals, and a young Windamere palm (*T. latisectus*) radiates temporarily at mid-height over crinum lilies and bromeliads on lava-rock walls. Palms make some of the best epiphyte hosts, even in relatively dry climates such as California's.

TROPICAL COTTAGE

right: In Tom Piergrossi's Giverny of a garden on the Big Island of Hawai'i, foliage of *Areca vestiaria* (red form) harmonizes with the giant leaves of philodendrons, gingers, and flowering trees such as *Amherstia nobilis*. The big flower stalks and fruit clusters of the palms compensate in scale for what they lack in the potent colors of tropicals such as bromeliads, iresine, coleus, strobilanthes, vireya rhododendrons, and ti plants.

KEYS REGENCY

right: The long association of D'Asign Source with Punta Roquena in the Florida Keys includes the construction of this concrete screen in the 1970s, around which hybrid *Copernicia* palms were planted in a bed of ferns. The screen embodies a strain of Florida architecture akin to Hollywood Regency; absent the palms, the scene would lack the air of perfect mid-century ease.

SAVANNA

below: The Celebration Garden at The Huntington Botanical Gardens introduces visitors to a worthy landscape form rarely seen in California: the palm savanna. It is composed of trunked clara palms and young *Butia odorata* in a bed of grasses—*Festuca mairei*, *Muhlenbergia rigens*, *Sporobolus aerioides*—as well as succulents, shrubs, and perennials, and it satisfyingly evokes a wild terrain.

HACIENDA

above: Sherry Merciari's Oakland, California, garden forms an integral part of her house, built in the Mexican style around central courtyards. A reminder of those southerly climes, her prolific Guadalupe palms (*Brahea edulis*) owe their name to the Virgin of Guadalupe, the national symbol of Mexico. Paired with a hardy tapioca tree (*Manihot grahamii*), the palms magnify the ambiance she has created with art and decorative objects she has brought back from regular visits to family south of the border.

CLOUD FOREST

Nightly summer fog swirls,
condenses, and rains down
from the tree canopy into a
garden designed by Patrick
Lannan for Flora Grubb
Gardens in San Francisco's
Forest Hill neighborhood.
Himalayan Windamere palms
(*Trachycarpus latisectus*), tree
ferns, fuchsias, Chilean hard
ferns (*Blechnum chilense*),
and palm grass set the lush
scene.

PACIFIC FOREST

left: Roger Raiche's compositions for Planet Horticulture include bold monocots such as palms and succulents, with conifers, flowering rarities, and deciduous shrubs and trees in his home garden in Sonoma County, California. Whether you garden in British Columbia, Oregon, or California's Redwood Country, hardy palms such as *Trachycarpus fortunei* 'Wagnerianus' (left) and *T. takil* (center) add sculptural, evergreen energy to the quiet majesty of the Pacific forest.

JAPANESE

right: Clusters of windmill palms (*Trachycarpus fortunei*) and *T. fortunei* 'Wagnerianus' are planted regularly in classical Japanese gardens, as evoked here in San Francisco's Japanese Tea Garden, the oldest public Japanese garden in the United States and a legacy of the 1894 Midwinter Fair. From almost-subtropical Kyūshū to temperate Tokyo, palms grow among groves of deciduous plum, cherry, and maple trees. View them in dialogue with reptilian groves of native cycad, *sotetsu*, or sago (*Cycas revoluta*), at Kōraku-en Garden in Okayama. The grounds of the sacred Shinto shrine in Tokyo, Meiji Jingū, are carpeted with the radial leaves of thousands of windmill palm seedlings rooted beneath vaulting camphor and pine trees, beautiful weeds tolerated for a few years before removal, only for birds to sow another generation.

SOUTHERN CALIFORNIA IMPRESSIONS

Palms are ubiquitous in Southern California. Driving from San Diego to Santa Barbara and inland to Palm Springs, you're never out of sight of a palm, mostly the thin Mexican fan palm, *Washingtonia robusta*, a plant that reaches 100 feet (30 m) tall. You've seen them on television, in movies, in advertisements. They are more concisely emblematic of California (or "California," as we Northern Californians might air-quote) than redwoods, oaks, or eucalyptus. "Palms," as Jared Farmer writes in his book, *Trees in Paradise: A California History*, "are for the moment the signature trees of Los Angeles." In California, he says, "Palms have been planted for what they mean, not what they do. Or rather, what they mean *is* what they do." People have planted palms in California for their meaning from the beginning of European colonization, when Spanish missionaries grew date palms (*Phoenix dactylifera*) at Mission Basilica San Diego de Alcalá and beyond for fronds needed in religious ceremonies—the trees' fruit unlikely to ripen in the coastal climates threaded by the chain of Franciscan missions along El Camino Real.

One palm species, *Washingtonia filifera*, earns its common name, California fan palm, by growing wild in the Colorado Desert region of southeast California, particularly near Palm Springs. Few of that resort city's millions of annual visitors ever visit the magnificent native groves a few minutes away along the eponymous main street, Palm Canyon Drive. Ten miles south of the border in Baja California grow wild populations of *Brahea armata*, the Mexican blue palm, now a staple in low-water landscapes north of the border. Farther south on the Baja Peninsula is home of the ubiquitous palm symbol of Los Angeles, *W. robusta*, the Mexican fan palm. (A third *Brahea* species, *B. brandegeei*, that resembles a more gracile Mexican fan palm, is also native in southern Baja California.)

A hundred and fifty miles off the coast of northern Baja California, Guadalupe Island is home to the Guadalupe palm, *Brahea edulis*, a plant whose adaptation to maritime-influenced climates of California goes along with that of its island compatriots Monterey pine (*Pinus radiata* var. *binata*), sword fern (*Polystichum munitum*), pink-flowered currant (*Ribes sanguineum*), island oak (*Quercus tomentella*), toyon (*Heteromeles arbutifolia*), ceanothus, and California sagebrush (*Artemisia californica*). These familiar California natives form vegetation communities characteristic of the California Floristic Province. Thus, the biome of Mediterranean climate California has its own endemic palm, quite apart from the Sonoran Floristic Province's *Washingtonia filifera*.

As if to prove the division between the floristic provinces, the California fan palm does not thrive in areas of California where cool, moist ocean air infiltrates regularly, and where winters are long and wet, while the Guadalupe palm thrives and even self-sows in those regions. Meanwhile, Guadalupe Island's climate, latitude, and volcanic origins form an analog to the distant Canary Islands, home to the second- or third-most-common palm of California, the equally well-adapted (and disease- and pest-imperiled) *Phoenix canariensis*.

The rows of *Washingtonia robusta* that line Los Angeles streets strike some people as ridiculous, their small crowns hovering 60 to 80 feet (18 to 24 m) in the air on trunks that arc toward the south and the sun. I find them thrilling in their defiance of gravity and their flexibility, and I like the green shine and motility of their leaves. Many were planted in the lead-up to the 1932 Summer Olympics in perfectly spaced rows. They are allées along modest streets whose height extracts them from human-scale garden spaces, turning them into skyline features, "skydusters." Dead fronds tumble into the street, especially after windstorms, and are amassed into piles for disposal. Seedlings emerge from flowerbeds and cracks in the pavement. Along with their rustling sounds, these are reminders of the greenery high above.

The meaningfulness of palms poses a problem for designing with them in California, a puzzle-problem more than an obstacle-problem. Even ecologically well-informed figures of California landscape writing identify palms with morally and ecologically dubious land-scaping, attributing thirstiness and interloper status to all palms.

Mexican fan palms pop up everywhere on the skyline, from freeway crevices, out of backyards, in front of office buildings and hotels, along Beverly Hills avenues, beneath bird-festooned power lines in the Central Valley, and next to beach bike trails out of pure sand. They're not from the state, and botanical authorities deem them invasive, but they're not going away anytime soon.

Colors of slate and brick and the deep aqua of the pool marry with blue-gray pindo palm fronds, glossy green copper-backed Southern magnolia leaves, and the gray-green and white of *Pittosporum tobira* 'Variegatum' shrubs.

AMERICAN GARDENS

The following spaces, urban and rural and suburban, offer lessons on successful designs with palms. Some of the gardens are private, one is commercial, three are public. They are designed by home gardeners, landscape architects, horticulturists, botanical curators, landscape designers, collectors, and professional gardeners.

Delve into how it feels to be exploring these gardens—smell the fragrances of wet pavement and leaves and flowers; see light reflected off nearby windows and water; feel the quality of the air, dry, sticky, still, or breezy; hear the sound of leaves in movement; and watch the light change in the course of a few hours or a day. And learn how these places gain from the thoughtful use of palms.

A CHARLESTON CITY GARDEN

South Carolina is the Palmetto State, where palms grow wild and are welcome in cultivated landscapes, especially in the Lowcountry along the coast, where the city of Charleston sits.

This formal city garden we found while exploring the historic center of Charleston. Nosing over ancient brick walls, we could see how beautiful its pleasingly squared spaces were, flanked on the right side by the piazza (a Charleston term for a porch running the length of a house) of a grand nineteenth-century house. Silvery pindo palms (*Butia odorata*) anchor corners of two garden quadrants extending from the street between the house and neighboring two- to four-story residences. A traditional boxwood parterre garden centered on an ornate tiered fountain is protected by the brick wall from the street and connects through a pergola gate on the opposite side to a modern pool area. From the pool, the garden extends at a right angle, where it runs between the house and brick apartments converted from antebellum quarters for enslaved people. The garden, designed by landscape architect Robert Chesnut, balances comforting rigor, seclusion, garden flow, and views of neighboring historic architecture.

One of the exhilarating aspects of this garden was the familiarity of the plant palette and confined spaces to my San Franciscan eyes. Anchoring this very Southern garden, the pindo palm also tolerates conditions in the Pacific Northwest or tropical climates—sun or shade, droughty or rainy regimes. The species grows well in my hometown but is underused there, and seeing it in a garden that would work beautifully at home was a wish fulfilled. The Carolina Lowcountry's flat terrain and warm temperate climate get more than 50 inches (127 cm) of rainfall per year, with a wetter summer season and no month seeing less than 3 inches (8 cm), and occasional winter lows below 18°F (−8°C). All these familiar garden species could work in Mediterranean climates (with suitable soils) worldwide, and even in a mild temperate Central London or Tokyo location.

Among the familiar plants, roses clamber across brick dividing walls and Confederate jasmine (*Trachelospermum jasminoides*) smothers a pergola gate, both offering white bloom and the latter a spicy scent. Brush past boxwood clipped

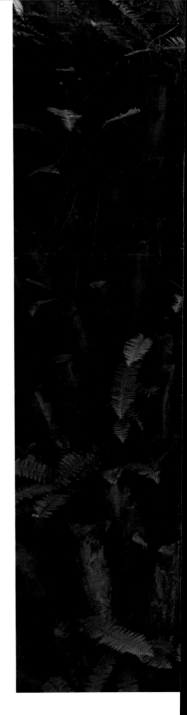

Viewed from the street, pindo palm (*Butia odorata*) leaves arch toward a parterre in the garden of a historic house in Charleston. Spiraling leafbases on the trunk and parallel-pattern leaflets overhead complement the geometry of ground plantings and porch shutters.

into globes and squared-off for perennial beds and pick up a counter note of its bitter odor. Along neighbors' brick walls bordering the property, tall *Podocarpus macrophyllus* hedges grow as dark green cladding, a soft backdrop for Southern magnolias, the latter a source of refreshing, almost ecstatic, summer fragrance for multigenerational family gatherings at the pool.

The blue pindo palms, along with the fountains, add dynamism to this formal garden. Their energy is caught in form—arching fronds, leaflets marching

semi-upright along the rachis—and in movement, as the leaves sway and recoil in breezes off Charleston Harbor. Alone among the plantings in this meticulously groomed garden, the palms host accessory plants on their trunks—kelly green sword ferns—as if to emphasize the vigor of their presence. Yet the corner-placed palms also make a cool, formal impression with their regular, repetitive forms of pinnate leaves, spiraling leafbases, and the simplicity of trunk and crown, common to most palm trees. It was a crucial feat to find a group of pindo palms so blue and matching in height for this serene effect. Perfectly matched, modest in size, judiciously placed, the pindo palms in this garden are the key to its mood, the element that enables a formal space to become a serene and relaxing one as well.

left: The presence of the surrounding city, one of the oldest in the United States, is palpable throughout the garden but does not intrude, thanks to placement of slow-growing pindo palms beyond the pergola gate.

THE RUTH BANCROFT GARDEN

On a former walnut ranch in the valley-flat suburbs of the eastern San Francisco Bay Area, Ruth Bancroft created an extraordinary low-water garden noted for its collections of succulents. Her landscape of aeoniums, aloes, cactuses, agaves, yuccas, and many other plants grow behind the concrete adobe-style walls that the city of Walnut Creek built to protect its growing subdivisions of single-family homes from its now busy thoroughfares—but here they preserve a fragment of the rural past.

Succulents store water in their swollen leaves and stems as a means of surviving drought, a trick useful in California's annual cycle of dry summers

133

and rainy winters, and one that produces picturesque, sculptural forms. It's a drought-evading strategy virtually absent from the palm family. The Ruth Bancroft Garden is now open to the public thanks to help from The Garden Conservancy. It serves as a place of instruction on drought-loving plants and inspiration for designers and home gardeners in making beautiful landscapes using plants that require much less water than the lawns, redwoods, and deciduous East Coast forest trees that characterize the surrounding neighborhoods.

The coastal valley climate of the garden exposes the plants to summers with high temperatures in the 80s F (high 20s C) and overnight lows in the 50s and 60s (mid-teens); a blanket of clouds will sometimes creep in from the Pacific Ocean

Aloe 'Creamsicle', lower left, a hybrid by garden curator Brian Kemble, and masses of *A. arborescens* have a monocot affinity with the larger, more complex crowns of *Trithrinax campestris*, *Chamaerops humilis*, and *Brahea armata* palms that step up toward the fine, irregular crowns of, left to right, *Pinus montezumae*, *Ceiba speciosa*, *Sequoia sempervirens*, and *Eucalyptus kitsoniana*.

at night, increasing humidity, and will evaporate in the morning. Summer heat waves have recorded temperatures above 110°F (43°C). Winters typically brings low temperatures in the 30s F (0–3°C) and high temperatures in the 50s and low 60s, though temperatures as low as 17°F (–14°C) have been recorded. Walnut Creek's average annual rainfall of 20 inches (51 cm) occurs from October to April, concentrated in December through March. Aside from infrequent nighttime overcast, summers are persistently sunny and rainless, with low humidity.

Key to the garden's enchantment are its trees and palms. An allée of veteran Canary Island date palms (*Phoenix canariensis*) attests to the history of the family property as a ranch. A blue-green Atlantic cedar, 80 feet (24 m) tall, casts its scribbled silhouette against the sky. Acacia, palo verde, brachychiton, ceiba, and eucalyptus trees add mass, veils, screens, height, and color. Punctuating the landscape as well are many other palms suited to the summer-dry Mediterranean climate conditions of Walnut Creek.

A closely set trio of 50-foot (15-m) *Washingtonia filifera*, the California fan palm, stands majestically unmanicured near the garden's most identifiable structure, Ruth's Folly, a celadon green gazebo. The palms' skirts of dead, straw-colored leaves hang in an even texture below their broad summits of fans held on rotors, all lively green with a hint of gray, the outer segments of the fans tasseled. The three close palms' long skirts leave enough room between them for corridors of light to appear, just as they do in their profusion in their native desert canyons near Palm Springs.

A Mediterranean fan palm (*Chamaerops humilis*) clump grows at a pond's edge. Around the pond, Mrs. Bancroft also planted two *Trithrinax* specimens, ferociously armed fan palms native to savannas in Argentina and Brazil. Like many of the palms in the garden, these South American palms were a gift from Dick Douglas, a friend with a garden of rare hardy palms a mile away. One of these, likely either *Trithrinax campestris* or *T. schizophylla*, has developed four major stems that now reach 15 feet (4.6 m) tall, with stiff, pewter leaves and warm cream flowers in fall. Like the nearby California fan palms, the much shorter trithrinax trunks are thatched with dead leaves, but they also reveal their unusual basket-weave leafbases armed with long spines underneath.

Pull back a few steps from the pond and the eye rises to the more distant washingtonias, with the trithrinax cluster a foreground foil—their orbs of foliage cast against the smooth thatch of the California fan palms. Metallic and rigid, the trithrinax leaves nonetheless echo the rustling rounds of the tall palms beyond. On a gray December day, an English oak lends its golden fall color to the jade-green and straw-colored towers of the washingtonias.

Move a few steps around the pond and the Mediterranean fan palm's several heads emerge from behind the trithrinax, the chamaerops's finer, softer, olive-green fans and autumn fruit clusters in yellow and auburn. Across the pond lives a single *Trithrinax* specimen, possibly a different species from the clustering one. Reflections of palms appear in the pond between lily pads.

The Mediterranean fan palm, one of California's ironclad ornamental plants, originates in rocky scrublands around the western Mediterranean Sea where fall rains break the annual summer drought. It's so adaptable that it succeeds in the wet heat of Miami as well as in the extended cool winters of Seattle.

Both the trithrinax and the washingtonia, like almost all palms, require permanent moisture for their roots to tap into. The trithrinax originates in a seasonally dry savanna, baking in one season, often flooded in another. The washingtonia's home is adjacent to permanent streams and seeps in the hot Colorado Desert of California, the Kofa Mountains of Arizona, and northern Baja California. The milder temperatures and accessible water table at the Ruth Bancroft Garden

A luminous Mexican blue palm brings the waxy reflectivity of ground-level xeric plants upward into arborescent form, a way station toward the culmination of blue Atlas cedar (*Cedrus atlantica*) in the distance.

reduce their need for irrigation, making them complements to a landscape that's conspicuously water-thrifty.

Mrs. Bancroft's careful mounding of earth through much of the garden to favor drainage for her succulents rumples the topographic plane, lifting and dipping key plantings in view of trees and palms in the midground and beyond.

A quick walk away from the palm-edged pond brings you to a realm of blooming aloes in winter. Spires of red, yellow, and orange punctuate fleshy, thorned rosettes perched on undulating berms. Unbranched arborescent species take on palmlike forms, as do tall yuccas.

From the northwest side of the blooming aloes is another palm-enriched composition. South of the aloe bed, with 80-foot (24-m) cedars and pines as their distant backdrop, Mrs. Bancroft planted pindo palms, *Butia odorata*, and Mexican blue palms, *Brahea armata*.

The Mexican blue palm's color is silvery, its stiff fans as reflective of light as any palm, its irregular skirt of dead fronds like straw. Through its emerging accordion folds, the leaf at the tallest palm's apex 20 feet (6.1 m) in the sky flashes spring green in its opening phase, while garlands of ripening fruit, like big green olives, hang outward from the silvery crown. Yellow-green, too, illuminates the live leaf stems at the center of the crown. Together they reveal the chlorophyllic vitality of a palm whose surface colors protect it against desert sun and heat (and perhaps even browsing animals). In summer, those garlands were ostentatious plumes of cream flowers. December's fruiting records the pollinators' feast of summer.

The pindo palm's flounce of gray-green feathers atop a short trunk makes a similar splash. The ribs of its leaves, the rachises, arch upward and then down, with leaflets like stiff ribbons. They flank a shorter Mexican blue palm. The pindo's tasty golden fruits form earlier in the year than the Mexican blue palm's yellowy ones.

Placing these palms just outside the aloe beds gave Mrs. Bancroft's design an intermediary between the grand, fine-leafed, idiosyncratic trees of the horizon, and the bold, regular, mid- and small-scale rosettes of the succulents. She understood their unique role, not to be confused with those of the woody trees or their fellow monocots, the aloes and yuccas. The trick is the palms' own larger, more intricate rosettes of leaves combined with their habit of rising to heights of 10 to 30 feet (3 to 9 m) on tree-thick trunks. Both the palms and the succulents share silvery, blue-, and gray-greens. So do many of the trees. Within the aloe beds, the tallest single-trunk species produce palmlike forms, another way station for the eye.

Off among the canopy trees, the ranch-era allée of Canary Island date palms gives the viewer another harmonious destination.

A FLORIDA BROMELIAD GARDEN

Patricia Bullis's young garden carved into the limestone of south Miami-Dade County creates a showcase for the colorful bromeliads her family nursery, Bullis Bromeliads, produces for export around the world. It also demonstrates the affinity palms and bromeliads have for each other in the landscape. The climate here is subtropical, with nearly 60 inches (152 cm) of annual rainfall. High temperatures stay in the 80s and 90s F (mid-20s to low 30s C) from May to October, with lows in the 70s F (mid-20s C). During the November-to-April dry season, still sprinkled with no less than 2 inches (5 cm) of rain per month, high temperatures reach the 70s and low 80s F (mid- to high 20s C) and lows average in the 50s and 60s F (low to mid-teens C). Annual dips into the 40s and even mid-30s F (2°C to 6°C) occur, and the record-low temperature is 26°F (–3°C). Plenty of heat and moisture, interrupted by winter spells of chilly, dry weather, enable many but not all tropical plants to thrive in South Florida.

Excavating the porous bedrock, Patricia invited a natural aquifer to fill a lobed quarry, added exotic fish, and used the pale stone to build an adjacent stepped platform under a canopy of feathery poinciana trees (*Delonix regia*). (Its scarlet bloom in early summer earns the tree another name, *flamboyán*.) In a region where vegetation devours the earth—and, in the case of coastal mangroves and

left: The leafy, red-centered bromeliad *Bromelia scarlatina* perches beneath a hybrid date palm clump.

above: Views of surrounding palm farms extend from an elevated platform reminiscent of a lost temple.

the Everglades, even some of the water—the sight of exposed rock is gratifying. Hewn here, as elsewhere in South Florida, for pavers and benches, it reveals ancient fossil shells and coral.

The rise of just a few feet over South Florida's flatness furnishes a view. In the distance between the clean boles of the poincianas, royal palms (*Roystonea regia*) on neighboring palm farms serrate the horizon under a billowing sky borrowed from an eighteenth-century French landscape painting.

Palms surround the pool and office. Patricia's favorite species, the native palmetto (*Sabal palmetto*)—braced for a year until securely rooting after

transplanting—swings out over springlike fountains that trickle down biomor-phic shelves in the walls of the pool; maidenhair ferns dance in the tinkle of water droplets. She uses palmettos' trunks with retained boots (leafbases) as perches for vivid vertical gardens of epiphytic bromeliads. A hybrid date palm (*Phoenix rec-linata* × *roebelenii*) grows near the waterline, a midscale centerpiece whose dense bouquet of leaning trunks echoes the larger, more open assemblage of palmettos around it. Fern and bromeliad accents add softness and color.

Beds of scarlet *Neoregelia* 'Maria', one of Bullis Bromeliads' patented introduc-tions, center-planted with silver *Alcantarea odorata*, flank steps and benches cut from stone excavated for the pool. Clumps of *Phoenix reclinata* rise from the right, counterposed with limestone-loving thatch palm. A clump of *Muhlenbergia dumosa* grass contributes a woolly coziness to the dramatic scene, while palmettos reach toward the poincianas' crowns.

Having obtained specimen palms from friends in the horticulture business, Patricia also loves planting young palms for the effects over time. A young

left: Foliage of a Key thatch palm, glossy above and matte below, catches those textures in underplanted bromeliads.

above: Feathery leaves of poinciana trees form a top deck over crowns of palmettos and a fringe of cabada palms behind a coral-rock retaining wall.

right: Large *Aechmea blanchetiana* bromeliads surround a young talipot palm destined for grandeur.

Leucothrinax morrisii, the native Key thatch palm used widely in South Florida landscapes, serves as a foliage element in its rosette phase, while beds of lightly rooting bromeliads such as the mottled vriesea and the small variegated *Neoregelia* cultivar can be rotated as the palm rises on its thin trunk over time.

Around the far side of the pool and platform, a path hugs rough slabs of coral rock, its chalky tone darkened by mosses, lichens, and algae. Feathering the elevated side of the slab wall are clumps of *Dypsis cabadae*, the charismatic cabada palm, whose neat stems will grow to resemble a thick blue bamboo, increasing the excitement of passing along the escarpment. Aroids and bromeliads accent the stonework while the inimitable heft of poinciana trunks takes the platform's weightiness upward.

Open beds away from the tree canopy are home to larger palms, including coconuts and a young talipot palm (*Corypha umbraculifera*) that will become a nimbus of enormous fan leaves, each the size of a small car, before it reaches flowering age in several decades. When flowering, it will develop a 25-foot-tall (8-m) conical

Color keeps attention on the bromeliads while palms define the volumes above with postlike trunks and swaying fronds.

inflorescence comprising millions of flowers atop a 50-foot-tall (15-m), or more, trunk; produce its only crop of seed; and die—a slow drama sure to match that of the seasonal poinciana bloom. In a touch reminiscent of the work of Brazilian landscape architect Roberto Burle Marx, a swath of purple *Tradescantia pallida* 'Purpurea' surrounds bromeliads whose pink, gold, and chartreuse tints bring attention to orange margins on the palm's older leaves and the fresh green on its newest frond.

Not least of the garden's charms is the building Patricia designed for her business in a welcoming tropical style. Sweet-smelling Madagascar jasmine (*Stephanotis floribunda*) vines climb up the posts around the deep veranda surrounding the office. Planted at the foot of a fragrant champak tree (*Magnolia champaca*) are specimens of another bromeliad cultivar introduced by Patricia's company, the dark-red *Alcantarea* 'Malbec', recalling her family origins in the wine-growing region of Argentina. Coral rock edges pathways and acts as finials, and upright palms—coconuts, a hurricane palm (*Dictyosperma album*), a pygmy date (*Phoenix roebelenii*), and palmettos—maintain a friendly, open viewshed for the office.

Even early in its growth, Patricia's garden borrows the heft of geological history and specimen trees to give the visitor a comforting sense of solidity. Her colorful bromeliads stimulate the eye in an atmosphere fragrant with champak and stephanotis and resonant with the trickling of water over coral walls and the rustling of palm fronds.

Balconies around the garden
bring visitors eye-to-frond with
tree ferns (*Cyathea cooperi*, top)
and palms and rare trees.

top right: Like many other palms,
pygmy date palms thrive in pots.

below right: A composition of
pygmy date palm foliage, timber
bamboo culms, variegated
spider plant, and a Tasmanian
tree fern (*Dicksonia antarctica*)
creates an aura of exoticism.

A COURTYARD GARDEN
IN SAN FRANCISCO

The first hint of Richard Gervais's compound full of decorative objects and furniture is the garden on the narrow alley sidewalk outside. Heavy containers planted with succulents, a red-flowering gum (*Corymbia ficifolia*) and queen palm (*Syagrus romanzoffiana*) grown as street trees dab greenery on his rapidly developing, formerly industrial-bleak South of Market neighborhood in San Francisco. The city's best-known concentration of new tech offices is three blocks away, surrounded by new and under-construction residential towers, while one of its nightlife centers is a quick walk in the other direction.

Through the passageway behind the alley door, a courtyard garden occupying the space equivalent to a small city house contains a wealth of plantings, sculptures, stone orbs, mirrors, pottery, flagstone pavers, a flowing koi pond, balconies, and a dining area among its patios and decks. But Richard's clever placement of a super-fragrant evergreen *Magnolia doltsopa* holds the experience of the whole space at bay, requiring the visitor to pass to the right to discover the extent of the garden. It unfolds further with minor rises and drops in grade, and peeks around plantings and groups of containers.

With Richard's showroom on the long left side of the garden, a separately owned clapboard cottage with balcony on the short street side, and walls of surrounding properties on the remaining two sides, the deep rectangle feels like a San Francisco twist on a Beijing hutong. Integrated with the double-height showroom on two floors are jewel-box apartments where Richard lives and shares with friends—including landscape designer Chris Jacobson, who, along with John Pierce, Davis Dalbok, and Dat Pham, have collaborated with Richard on designing the garden over its twenty-one years of existence. "I don't know plants, but I know what I like and I follow my instincts and get help from friends," says Richard.

Only a few palm species are included in his garden, but one, the pygmy date palm, native to Southeast Asia, is a motif, the plant repeated in an array of pots he obtained through his forty-five years doing business as the Richard Gervais Collection, through which he imports and sells art and antiques—especially from the Philippines and Southeast Asia, places he fell in love with after migrating from his native Massachusetts to Hawai'i and California. His favorite palm species, many *Phoenix roebelenii* morph from a low foliage treat, harmonizing with ferns, to an adorable miniature palm tree stretching out its limbs from a pot full of orange *Begonia boliviensis* and violet *Aechmea* 'Del Mar'. Out of a lower pot flows the rusty pink cloud-forest perennial *Oxalis spiralis* subsp. *vulcanicola* 'Sunset Velvet', while nearby gingers and taro (*Colocasia esculenta*) recall the landscapes of Richard's travels in tropical Asia.

Plants signify, especially when assembled into a legible grammar of associated plant varieties. Palms are wont to mean tropical, and, joined here by bamboo, they become a symbol of tropical Asia. Tree ferns, unusual to most North Americans, easily join the ideogram of exoticism. And objects all around restate the Asian theme. Richard says, "I love palm trees—and bamboo, which I have six kinds of." The palms, he continues, "are not so messy as the damn bamboo!" But his love for bamboos more than outweighs their drawbacks.

Color in the garden comes not just from flowers, but also from container glazes, glass objects, and even from the patina of metal cladding on a neighbor's enclosing

Seen from Richard's showroom, a pygmy date palm joins Mexican weeping bamboo (*Otatea acuminata* subsp. *aztecorum*), a *Bambusa oldhamii*, and tree ferns to structure a garden full of Asian art and garden decor.

walls. Space, sky, and intrigue expand in the fifteen mirrors hung around the garden perimeter, each in a decorative frame.

Along with a table for four in one corner, Richard has placed seats in several spots in the garden, and deck edges and stone objects offer casual places to sit and contemplate the scene when larger groups fill the garden.

A limbed-up 60-foot (18-m) coast redwood (*Sequoia sempervirens*) grew in the garden when Richard bought the property two decades ago. "How fabulous, I thought when I saw the place, a redwood tree in the heart of San Francisco!" It stayed until a few years ago, when its aggressive roots and dense shade proved too much for his patience, and he had it removed, allowing more light into his showroom as well.

Meanwhile, a queen palm he'd planted early on (a housewarming gift from Dalbok, garden-design maven and friend) had become the dominant vertical element in the small space, its trunk and animated leaves activating the volume above—call it cultivating the air rights—with all the advantages and none of the drawbacks of the redwood. A potted kentia palm (*Howea forsteriana*) and Mexican weeping bamboo fringe the base of the tree, with a bamboo ladder paralleling the palm's trunk rings.

Within San Francisco's mild but chilly, windy climate, Richard's frostless walled space on the warmer, downtown side of town not only welcomes outdoor living, but also lets him take maximal risks trying tropical plants. False aralia, *Plerandra elegantissima*, from New Caledonia, is normally used as a houseplant, but here it has grown into a substantial tree.

At the center of interlocking households, Richard's intricate garden serves as crossroads for friends and neighbors, a welcoming anteroom for his gallery, a party space, and a contemplative retreat offering an imaginative transport to tropical Asia. In this garden of diverse elements, the repetition of palms creates a coherent texture as they trigger memories and invite fantasy.

THE GARDEN OF THE SHEATS-GOLDSTEIN HOUSE

Visitors lucky enough to get into the garden of one of Los Angeles's most famous houses, the Sheats-Goldstein residence (recently deeded to the Los Angeles County Museum of Art), find themselves climbing down stairs and traversing trails through a jungle as painted by Henri Rousseau. Arrayed over 5 acres of very steep terrain and integral to architect John Lautner's masterwork on the city's Westside, the garden was designed to reward the explorer and to lodge in the unconscious, composed from an intensely palmy palette with no pretense of naturalism. Designer Eric Nagelmann, working with curator-owner James Goldstein over decades, has created a wonderland context for the space-age pavilion of the house, a surreal slice of life setting itself apart from the neighboring properties, yet a place still anchored unmistakably in Los Angeles.

Below the triangle-pleated entry gate, the driveway descends steeply through a thicket of giant birds of paradise (*Strelitzia nicolai*) held behind a low concrete wall regularly punctuated with trapezoidal knobs. The low, perched house remains hidden until the visitor reaches the parking court. Passing through the structure's minimal, glass-walled spaces—kept open-air most of the year—visitors find the triangular roofline opening upward to accept the view of the starry city carpet below. Kentia palms (*Howea forsteriana*) posed like bouquets of splaying tulips at the pool frame the scene.

Below the house, where the bulk of the garden grows, Easter eggs of art (among them pieces by James Turrell, Guy Dill, and Bernar Venet), places of repose, vertiginous view platforms, and thousands of extraordinary palms and other lush, evergreen, tropical-looking plants await discovery along the trails cast like a skein onto the topography.

"Inconsistency amongst the consistency is one of my themes," says Nagelmann, who creates gardens in Mexico, Hong Kong, Italy, Hawai'i, as well as Southern California. In his native Montecito, the garden-mad town near Santa Barbara, he created Lotusland's Cactus Garden, an equal and opposite dreamscape to Goldstein's garden, its spiny columns offering 300 species variations on the columnar form, all placed among faceted basalt and slate.

Scores of palm species and other bold monocots such as giant birds of paradise, dragon trees (*Dracaena draco*), bamboos, yuccas, and cordylines form the structure and texture of the Goldstein garden, the ground carpeted in subtropical foliage, including clivias, bromeliads, understory palms, and ferns. The garden's

The unmistakable texture of palm fronds is visible through layers of glass that open onto views of the Los Angeles Basin.

geometry of fronds dominates—always with a twist, thanks to the species diversity, as in the many double-pinnate Thai giant fishtail palms (*Caryota gigas*) from palm growers such as Sea Crest Nursery in Santa Barbara that Nagelmann had craned into the garden. The designer arranged encounters with wonder in the garden.

Within California's Mediterranean clime, the site's ultra-mild microclimate does not see below-freezing temperatures. Summers are rainless and balmy, with

a humid marine layer coming onshore at night, and average highs in the 70s and 80s F (mid-20s C) and lows in the 60s F (mid-teens C); winters see occasional episodes of rain amid sunny weather and an average daily range of 51°F to 67°F (11°C to 19°C). The garden's plants look tropical but range from extremely cold-hardy species such as the Chinese windmill palm (*Trachycarpus fortunei*), to those adapted to low-heat environments such as *Rhopalostylis* spp., to heat-loving subtropical plants that sail through the chilly weather that can descend upon Los Angeles.

Woody flowering trees, which in nature would join the macro-structure of most tropical forests, are focal points here (particularly flame of the forest, *Spathodea campanulata*) against the green theme of palms. Conifers such as Italian stone pines (*Pinus pinea*) and podocarpus (*Afrocarpus gracilior*), characteristic trees of the neighborhood, grow in the garden as backdrops for the flamboyance and as dividers from neighbors.

Integration of the concrete-and-glass, 1961-designed house with plant life gives the sense of discovering an interplanetary colony landed on a jungle world. Art

left: Drought-tolerant dragon trees and Canary Island date palms, plus unthirsty giant birds of paradise, sagos, and Chinese windmill palms, precede the expanse of the Los Angeles Basin.

center: An arch sculpture by Guy Dill marks a transition between a garden staircase close to the house and trails ranging deeper into the garden.

right: A group of *Syagrus ×montgomeryana* forms a space for reflection in the lower reaches of the garden that Eric Nagelmann created for Jim Goldstein.

A young Canary Island date palm destined to grow huge sends taut fronds over trapezoidal stairs, while moderate-size *Rhopalostylis* spp. and *Howea forsteriana* add soft, unarmed foliage to the surroundings.

installed deeper in the garden, secluded from the house, takes on intrigue, summoning echoes of Mayan ruins in the jungles of Mexico's Yucatán and Cambodia's Angkor Wat. Plantings of Mediterranean fan palm, bamboo palm, vriesea and alcantarea bromeliads, monstera, and mondo grass conjure the vigor of those distant settings.

Just as garden life makes itself felt inside the house, staircases extend house into garden. Trapezoidal steps repeat shapes and construction methods used in the house. Here carved into the hillside between poured-concrete walls, there hovering off the ground to maintain pitch and rhythm, embedded in a jungle, they are modernism as archaeological discovery.

The garden is planted all the way to the bottom of the property, to a road shaded by the walls of the canyon. Tucked into this lowest tier is a beautiful chapel-like space defined by plantings of *Syagrus ×montgomeryana*, a hybrid between the Brazilian species *Syagrus schizophylla* and *S. romanzoffiana* (queen palm). This sweet piece of architecture born of planting design is a good place to rest before taking the hike back up the slope, with more discoveries waiting.

HALE MOHALU ON THE BIG ISLAND

Davis Dalbok's home on the Big Island of Hawai'i is oriented to the sunrise and the mainland United States but draws its ingredients and inspiration from the tropical Pacific Rim. The owner of Living Green, the garden design treasure house and nursery in San Francisco, has, as he says, "one foot in the tropics," designing, living in, and gardening in wildly diverse properties in California and Hawai'i.

Davis acquired his property, Hale Mohalu, with his late partner, Michael Postl, in the 1980s as a botanical retreat and design playground. The two cofounded

center: A look up the curved drive to the house follows to their disappearance a line of thin-trunked Manila palms, *Adonidia merrillii*, and Alexandra palms, *Archontophoenix alexandrae*.

right: A rainbow shower tree (*Cassia ×nealieae*) forms a loggia for a palm collection including (left to right) *Areca vestiaria*, *Latania loddigesii*, *Sabal* spp., *Licuala spinosa*, and *Veitchia joannis*.

Living Green, which serves as a studio where Davis and his staff work on their designs, often palmy, for gardens and interior plantscapes.

Hale Mohalu collects the fruits of decades of Davis's design work. Entailing a vacation home rich with art of Hawai'i and the Pacific Rim, a compound of Balinese cottages, a litchi orchard and organic farm, rugged volcanic outcrops, and a forest of native island plants, the property is the apotheosis of an exotic tropical garden.

Growing up near Santa Barbara with a precocious love of plants, Davis discovered Ganna Walska's Lotusland while it was still her private home. Like many teenagers in the area, Davis jumped the washed-pink walls with a friend and breathlessly explored a rustic, overgrown universe of picturesque rarities. Comprising 37 acres and now open for public tours by appointment, the landscape includes a Japanese garden, an orchard, a lotus-filled water garden, a cycad garden, a tropical garden full of epiphytic plants, and an abundance of palms.

Davis's time in Santa Barbara as an estate gardener infatuated him with an enormous palette of exotic plants, many of tropical character or appearance. Palms were principal among these, yet his yen for seeking out new and unusual plants has

also scattered Hale Mohalu with jewels such as vireya rhododendrons, bamboos, bromeliads, tillandsias, orchids, gingers, bananas, flowering trees, and art.

The trek to Hale Mohalu starts in the most charming town in Hawai'i, Hilo, the principal city of the Big Island. The rainiest town in the United States and the county seat, Hilo sees 126 inches (320 cm) of annual rainfall that nurtures the abundant flora, even in its tight-knit downtown area, where blocklong awnings built to protect pedestrians from frequent showers sprout epiphytic ferns. Visitors encounter an abundance of produce and crafts at the farmer's market on the bayfront, a depot for the rich hinterlands to come.

Driving south up the slope of Kīlauea, visitors pass through the only significant native lowland rainforest remaining in the Hawaiian Islands, platted with residential communities. The forest of 'ōhi'a lehua trees (*Metrosideros polymorpha*), their crowns gray-green and twiggy with occasional red brushy blossoms, is rooted on lava flows varying in age from 200 to 2000 years, and in this rainy environment

left: Blue of the house plays on color in this clump of *Areca vestiaria.*

right: Taut palm trunks frame *Bismarckia nobilis* and *Beccariophoenix fenestralis* with a profusion of crinum, anthurium, and ti plants.

the exposed rocks under the trees carry tufts of lichens, ferns, moss, and exotic orchids, especially *Spathoglottis plicata* and *Arundina graminifolia.* Unlike the opulent greenery of a continental tropical rainforest, the dominant colors and textures of the Hawaiian-native forest are spare.

Half an hour drive south on a gently rising highway is Pahoa, the town whose wooden sidewalks, restaurants, and markets serve as a gathering spot for the Puna District in the eastern corner of the Big Island. The continuous eruption of Kīlauea in neighboring Hawai'i Volcanoes National Park and the jumbly black evidence of past lava flows engulfed in muscular growth on the roadside cast the possibility of disruption and renewal over the entire area.

Beyond Pahoa, the road ribbons over a summit and offers a glimpse down the slope of the dark-blue Pacific in the distance. After a left turn through a cleft in the young bedrock, the steep road levels out soon into a semi-agricultural area marked with burly mango trees, semi-wild coconut palms, horse paddocks, and a mysteriously formal allée of royal palms with clipped turf along the way.

Even against the exhilaration of arriving on the Big Island, the turn through the gate at Hale Mohalu feels like Dorothy's step from black-and-white into color as she goes from her tornado-thrown house into Oz. Intensely fragrant pua kenikeni (*Fagraea berteroana*) and tiare Tahiti (*Gardenia taitensis*) shrubs mark the gate. Enormous silver-backed green fans of low-dwelling elephant palm, *Kerriodoxa elegans*, greet visitors inside the fence, soon to be overtopped by a Thai giant fishtail palm planted in their midst. To the right, an asymmetrical pair of mauve-silver Bismarck palms (*Bismarckia nobilis*) shimmer in a bowl of giant timber bamboos. Screened by trees from the county road, a flow of green lawn expands beneath the gallery of extraordinary palms, bamboos, and trees. A red-cinder drive begins the ascent toward the house, past cinder islands in the lawn of wine-color bromeliads, scarlet ti plants (*Cordyline* spp.), chartreuse and gray succulents, peach vireya rhododendrons, and plots of the spiny, stilt-rooted palm *Verschaffeltia splendida* from the Seychelles.

The property's previous owners collected palms and flowering trees; some of the rare specimens on the land existed when Davis and Michael first saw it, and, along with the setting, inspired their purchase. Davis has transformed the house into a place of tropical comfort, filled with lavish flower arrangements culled from the garden. Its deck, a raft floating in the greenery, offers views of the Pacific Ocean glinting in the morning sun. Sunrises pour across the slate-decked lanai, the stone's colors intensified in rainwater from nightly showers. West Coast visitors' jet lag awakens them into the coolness of dawn to witness their own Hawaiian sunrise.

A palm allée, especially one composed of large species such as royal palms (*Roystonea* spp.) or Canary Island date palms (*Phoenix canariensis*), risks exceeding the significance of their destination. This line of palms, however, set on one side of the drive, serve the garden as much as the house or gate, for not only do they continually reframe views and set a rhythm of passage from the car, they also lure visitors to walk into the garden, offer orchids clinging to their moss-encrusted trunks, cast a note of wabi-sabi with their nightly drop of leaf or fruit, and change what might just be a humble dirt road into an invitation, even a seduction.

The road trails into the wonder of the garden. A dozen or so paces downhill from the house is a lava-stone garden dotted with sleek green shafts of young clinostigma palms from Western Pacific islands, their pale roots projecting into the black cinders from trunk bases, accompanied by the powdery silver rosettes of *Vriesea odorata* bromeliads. Platters of *Licuala grandis* fans swirl across feathery leaves of the Madagascar native *Marojejya darianii*. Tall Alexandra palms at the edge of the dark ʻōhiʻa forest scatter thousands of seeds for a crop of forked, grassy palm weeds.

On the other side of the road, a lava outcropping rises from the undulating lawn beneath an orange-flowering flame tree (*Spathodea campanulata*). One of several on the property, the pinnacle is planted with green ti plants, giant orange-tinted *Aechmea blanchetiana* bromeliads, a silver bismarckia palm, and ptychosperma palms thriving on plain rock. Davis has planted this dark mass to incite exploration of its side precipices, its improbably thriving rock-dwelling plants, and the parts of the garden that it hides.

Like an art gallery dedicated to giant sculpture, the spacious landscape at Hale Mohalu envelops plantings of an array of palms and titanic bamboos, enabling visitors to experience their full forms while still providing intimate corners and a larger rhythm of enclosure and openness beneath the flowering trees.

A trail through the restored native forest is manicured into a minimalist study in mossy stones and peeling bark. A sunken spiny-palm garden dedicated to the memory of Michael Postl becomes a place of contemplation beneath protective fans of the most silvery bismarckia palm I have ever seen. Tillandsia bowls on the lanai change colors with cycles of rain, sunshine, and bloom, rewarding the vacationing visitor's stillness and bringing close the colors of the garden beyond.

Most nights, after the sun has set and dinner is over, rain showers begin nurturing the garden, a phenomenon so fortuitous that it seems arranged for the pleasure of the guests. But the weather needs no one's skill to do its thing. It's Davis's garden that he has so artfully arranged for our pleasure.

Surrounded by heritage oaks, Edith Bergstrom's garden mixes cold-tolerant palms with flowering perennials, succulents, roses, and unusual trees, producing an atmosphere of California–Mediterranean eclecticism.

BERGSTROM GARDENS

Painter Edith Bergstrom grew up on a farm in the Imperial Valley of California, 25 miles north of the Mexican border, near groves of native California fan palms and orchards of date palms. Her love of palms didn't begin to emerge, however, until after college on a visit to a garden on the Southern California coast, where, in search of photo subjects, she says, "I began noticing patterns of palms' trunks—abstract, which was hip at the time, yet realistic." In addition to taking photos, Edith was painting in watercolor and had work accepted in the prestigious American Watercolor Society's 116th Annual Exhibition. Palms became a major subject of her paintings, and "my attention became kind of obsessive," she says.

Her paintings reveal the lovingly precise observation she gives to her subjects, an eye that few painters use when confronted with palms. "When I first had shows, people would say, 'I've never really looked at a palm tree before,'" continues Edith. "That made me feel good."

She gardens on nearly 2 acres in the town of Atherton, California, near Palo Alto, where large, level plots enable the substantial native oak woodland to envelop

the houses and gardens. Redwoods (*Sequoia sempervirens*), pines, and cedars (*Cedrus atlantica*, *C. deodara*) planted over the last century punctuate the oak canopy. The oak-conifer ambiance is particular to the Bay Area and the coastal valleys of Central and Northern California, but it shares the peculiar fullness of scrubby, summer-dry environments such as the French Riviera and older suburbs of Los Angeles. Rainfall is confined to the cool season, peaking in January, and averages 20 inches (51 cm) per year. The site sees winter temperatures occasionally plunge below 20°F (−7°C), but they remain above 26°F (−3°C) in most years. Spring starts in February, and summer and fall are warm, with average temperatures ranging from the mid-50s F (mid-teens C) to the low 80s F (high 20s C), with periodic dry heat spells peaking in the 90s F (low 30s C). Official all-time temperature extremes for the area are 16°F (−9°C) and 110°F (43°C). Edith has recorded 12°F and 17°F (−11°C and −8°C) in the two most extreme cold events over three decades.

Edith has become a collector of palms. She opens her garden for horticultural tours from the likes of the International Palm Society and the Conservatory of Flowers in San Francisco's Golden Gate Park. Her garden harbors 200 species of palms in eighty genera, a significant representation of the family's cold-hardy members, each recorded in a database and labeled in the garden. Eventually

left: Hardy palms, cactuses, stone, and heritage trees form a pleasing tiered composition.

center: *Trachycarpus martianus*, the Himalayan windmill palm, flanks *T. fortunei*, the Chinese windmill palm.

right: Hybrids of parajubaea with butia catch late-afternoon summer light. At left, Edith planted a pure *Parajubaea torallyi* var. *torallyi* from dry valleys in the Bolivian Andes for comparison with its hybrid cousins.

the site will become a botanical garden, preserving and developing the array of cold-hardy palms and companion plantings.

A drought-tolerant palette of plants accompanies the palms. Unthirsty flowering perennials such as lavender, verbascum, verbena, snow-in-summer (*Cerastium tomentosum*), erigeron, kniphofia, alstroemeria, and acanthus flow over mounds backed by spiraling palm crowns. Aloes, agaves, olives, nolinas, and cordylines in the mix bridge the color and softness of the perennials with the architecture of the rare palms.

Edith and her husband acquired the property next door two decades ago and tripled the size of the garden, altering the flat terrain by building up mounds of soil and transforming a swimming pool into a hollow. Serpentine paths and stairs make for great exploring, especially as trees become voluminous screens and palms' canopies rise above visitors who walk under them. Many of the palm plantings from the 1990s and early 2000s have reached this human scale, crowns still touchable, still yielding to close inspection, trunks still clad in the fascinating temporary armor of pruned leafbases.

Along the street, a rise planted in perennials, shrubs, succulents, and palms— shrubby Mediterranean fan palms (*Chamaerops humilis*); silver Mediterranean fan palms (*C. humilis* var. *argentea*); rosettes of bismarckia and sabals; pliable, shiny

Parajubaea torallyi; and a large blooming Mexican blue palm (*Brahea armata*)—serves as a showcase for Edith's painterly approach to planting design while bounding a peaceful front garden for the house. The topology of rise followed by basin repeats itself throughout the property. One saucer space fills with river cobbles and agaves; in another, Edith has created a flat lawn with stepping stones. Her Australian Valley holds a walk-through grove of *Livistona* species palms from that continent. Paths circulate, climb, and drop. In a dip, she uses the expansive crown of a single young *Sabal uresana* to create a chamber, an effect for which this grand (and cold-hardy) Sonoran species, with its long, smooth petioles and arcing fans, is well suited.

Stone integrated into the undulating landforms, stairs, and stacked walls helps set the garden apart from the natural alluvial and clay flats here, while their heft meets the heritage trees for an effect of age and weight. Neatly paved patios hug the house; an indoor pool building serves as a tropical conservatory.

The composition of plantings and mineral ground treatments in the expansive garden creates the changes of mood from desert to woodland required to incorporate the hundreds of palms Edith has collected; some come from forest environments, many from savanna, desert, or riparian places. Atop a mound, a *Butia* species, planted in a low dry-stack stone circle, curves over ocher-tinted posts of *Echinopsis spachiana* cactus; tiers of stiff *Brahea aculeata* and the tinsel shower of a *Livistona decora*, the ribbon palm, lead up to a tall tulip tree, *Liriodendron tulipifera*.

In grove plantings, visitors can compare individuals within rare species and see differences between species. In a moist, grassy spot, several Himalayan *Trachycarpus martianus*, one of my favorite medium-size fan palms for irrigated California gardens, stand in front of the widely used (and more cold- and drought-tolerant) Chinese windmill palm, *T. fortunei*. The differences in trunk texture—*T. martianus* having a tight burlap weave of leafbases versus the gorilla-hair effect of *T. fortunei*—and leaf structure and color are immediately apparent. The grove plantings also offer the experience of compression among the still nearly human-scale palm trees, followed by the expansion found in the open spaces of the garden next to the groves.

Experiments in new palm hybrids in the garden add to its value as a place of botanical introductions. *Parajubaea cocoides* crossed with *Butia odorata* grows vigorously in the local climate, combining the durability of butia with the shine, grace, and speed of growth of this finicky cloud-forest type of parajubaea. Paired with *Agave americana* 'Mediopicta Alba', the botanical experiment becomes a pleasurable composition. Such an experience characterizes the entire garden.

LA CASA DE LAS PALMAS

Palms make an impact with their colorful foliage, especially in tropical regions with an ample array of available species. Silver *Bismarckia nobilis*, green *Hydriastele beguinii*, and orange *Areca vestiaria* "red-leaf form" are shown, left to right.

In a garden on the Big Island of Hawai'i, a wet, tropical atmosphere seems to accelerate time. The garden is the record of one California nurseryman's exquisite botanical taste and an advent into a dreamscape of palms and tropical foliage plants collected from around the world. The late Jerry Hunter, trained as a landscape architect, founded Rancho Soledad Nurseries, a botanical treasure house near San Diego, and then continued his exploration and production of tropical plants here in Hawai'i.

Hunter's house, La Casa de las Palmas, presents its name on a signpost on a country lane outside the island's charming port town of Hilo. The sign is redundant, its message conveyed by the dense and complex allée of rare palms, ti plants (*Cordyline fruticosa*), monstera vines, and bromeliads aligned along the

159

left: Orchestrated plantings along the entry drive graduate from an embracing bosk of tropical color in the ground tier to a tasseled scaffold of tall palms, various and rare.

center: Teddy bear (*Dypsis leptocheilos*) and Alexandra (*Archontophoenix alexandrae*) palms are feathered staffs over elephant palm (*Kerriodoxa elegans*) and a foliage complex of bromeliads, cycads, and a native-Hawaiian tree fern, *Cibotium glaucum*, or *hāpu'u pulu*.

right: The vibrant green feathery leaves of the Madagascar native *Marojejya darianii* contrast with a rainbow of leaf hues.

entry drive, an animated fringe for surrounding cow pastures and a symphonic introduction for this house of palms. The road from Hilo gains elevation here and proximity to the cloud deck that offers its frequent showers to this exceptionally rainy flank of the Mauna Loa volcano.

Turning into the gate, the visitor sees bouquets of orange-crownshafted *Areca vestiaria* palms rising beneath towering pewter-trunked Alexandra palms (*Archontophoenix alexandrae*). They alternate in pulses with clusters of the Amazonian fan palm, *Mauritiella armata*, its chalky trunks armed with thorns—up-scaled, upright bramble canes. As one drives along the entry, with its jumble of vivid epiphytes clinging to the base of feather-topped palm stems, the diversity of planting reveals its rhythm, regularity, and its designers' foresight. The garden's design is the product of a years-long collaboration between Hunter and Big Island–based designer and green wizard Brian Lievens, a longtime family friend.

At a rise, the linear entry drive emerges and turns from the embrace of fronds and canes to become a sinuous road into the body of the property. Intimate decks of lawn in curving black-lava stone berms open around it, and then the road is bound by glossy hedges of the lady palm from China, *Rhapis excelsa*. The view between columnar palm trunks opens to the east and the Pacific Ocean. Blue seams appear from time to time in the misty sky.

On the way to the house, the road plunges back into a tunnel of foliage and cars ford a stream. A delicate arch of carved lava rock just upstream from the road enables walkers to keep their feet dry. The road branches to a circular black-paved parking loop pinned by a dense island of brilliant red sealing-wax palms, *Cyrtostachys renda*, over massive *Dioon spinulosum* cycads, and the corrugated-platter leaves of licuala palms. Surrounding pools of lawn go chartreuse in the passing glare of the tropical sun and provide both relief from the welter of large-scale foliage and a flat counterpoint to the insistent verticals of palm trunks and bamboos.

Hunter's moody retreat is a two-story rectangular house surrounded by deep lanais on all sides, floored in Mexican tiles. On the left flank, where tile stairs reach the second-floor lanai from the parking loop, groves of the small licuala palm (*Licuala grandis*) and the pygmy date palm (*Phoenix roebelenii*) enclose these open galleries, the former palm's rumpled, apple-green circles at second-floor eye level corresponding with the perfect corrugated wedges of trunkless joey palms' (*Johannesteijsmannia altifrons*) leaves on the ground below, and contrasting with the fine, thready fronds of the miniature dates. These framed close-ups render details of flower, fruit, and texture that would wash away in the grander scale just beyond.

Pygmy date palms cluster at the waterline and a clump of *Arenga undulatifolia* unfold above a stream that defines the property's edge.

right: *Allagoptera arenaria*, the trunkless Brazilian seashore palm, shimmers next to a *pōhaku* stonework koi pond, a feat harmonious with the nearby lava-rock streambed.

From the face of the house, a lanai overlooks a descending lawn to the gigantic silver-mauve crowns of *Bismarckia nobilis* in the distance. At right, a populous grove of the same orange-crownshaft palm of the entry drive, *Areca vestiaria*, shows off red and gold pigments to balcony visitors. Grassy pools surround islands of leaping trees. Vales of lawn, chambers in the planted forest, connect to stone walkways through the trees.

Out in the garden, past the pools of lawn, rare palms from Madagascar and Thailand, Samoa and New Caledonia, planted scarce decades ago, already loom tall.

A waterfall carves a pool into the basalt bedrock. Emerging from this basin, the stream—which the car forded on the drive in—descends in cascades over which the variegated fingers of *Schefflera pueckleri* trees flutter on upslope airflow. Nurtured by daily showers riding the tradewinds from the Pacific, moss grows quickly over dry-stack lava-rock staircases and walls, while ferns expand on black masonry and tan aralia trunks, casting an ancient air of Machu Picchu over these young works.

Atop charcoal mounds of lava rock near a pond, rosy *Alcantarea imperialis* bromeliads perch like artfully upturned hats, and young palms push out their nude root tips. Even asphalt paving—a practical surface where more than 125 inches (318 cm) of yearly rainfall spawns rampant growth—holds a lavalike space between trees and shrubs and opens views to the giant plumes of the tropical American canopy palm *Iriartea deltoidea* and the blue-marbled cloud deck above.

The far side of the property seems to fall off into the rocky cleft of Waiakea Stream, 40 feet (12 m) below the house. From the edge of this canyon next to the house rise two handfuls of the small Australian palm tree, *Laccospadix australasica*, planted as an emissary between fearsome heights and the residents. Its stiff, upright, feather leaves—rosy felt on the midrib—gently leaning stems, and finger spikes of flowers give comforting distraction as well—that is, after one gasps at the vertiginous river view and the festival of vegetation on the far side.

Layers of miniature ferny palms and giant leaf litter–collecting species in the understory, with clusters of palms at moderate scale and towers of canopy palm trees, plunge the visitor into a benevolent, surreal museum of burgeoning world palm flora—an ever-growing gallery of trunk fibers, spines, smooth leaf sheaths, colorful fruits, and foliage spinning variations on fan, feather, fishtail, pleating, gathering, ribbing, edging, mottling.

Against these fascinations, the garden's plateau of lawn and rock become chambers for catching one's breath and runways for views outward and up. This exceptional garden on a slope of the volcanic giant Mauna Loa envelops the visitor in an encyclopedic array of plants, a coaxing atmosphere of exploration, and a soundscape of rushing water and rustling palms.

Radial fronds of Mexican blue palms (*Brahea armata*) contain an explosive energy amid oozing agaves and coralline prickly pear cactus in the blue garden at Lotusland.

GANNA WALSKA LOTUSLAND

Nothing else is like Ganna Walska Lotusland. The Montecito garden, near Santa Barbara, is one of the wonders of California. It's both one woman's masterwork and a showcase of successive designers' visions—a collection of wildly different gardens cohering into a singular wonderland, a private estate open to the public, a botanical garden with no visible aesthetic compromises, an exotic, pink-walled sanctuary knitted into native trees and terrain, and a harmonious paradise of palms that compete for salience with other charismatic plant groups.

Lotusland is situated in a benign climate in a south-facing belt of land between the Santa Barbara Channel, an arm of the Pacific Ocean, and the Santa Ynez Mountains. Oceanic influence and topography make frosts rare and add night-time humidity, while comfortable days peak at 65°F (18°C) in January and 77°F (25°C) in August, the hottest month. Annual (if erratic) rainfall of 18 inches (46 cm) sustains a rich native chaparral on mountain slopes and extensive coast live oak (*Quercus agrifolia*) woodlands.

First planted in the 1880s by nurseryman Ralph Kinton Stevens, and passing through the stewardship of more than a dozen designers, architects, master craftsmen, and owners, the gardens bear the imprint of age, rare in California. A surreal cactus garden designed in the late 1990s by Eric Nagelmann comprises plants grown over seven decades by Merritt Dunlap, a friend of Madame Walska. (Nagelmann's latest project at Lotusland is a palmetum showcasing and augmenting the rich palm collection by scores of species.) A research collection of palms in the genus *Chamaedorea* brought by palm expert Don Hodel is a study in theme and variation. Madame Walska allocated gifts of flowery plants to a potager-like plot now becoming the insectary garden; as if to underscore the rule of the exotic on the property and her iconoclastic bent, her palms hold sway behind the neat hedges, an effect repeated with Hodel's chamaedorea palms behind the hedges of the theatre garden designed by Isabelle Greene.

Dozens of monumental Chilean wine palms (*Jubaea chilensis*) propagated by Stevens in the nineteenth century seem imported from the Jurassic period and form the largest concentration of specimens in cultivation in North America. The

left: Jubaea palms line the milky blue pool in the aloe garden at Lotusland, with sidekick Chinese windmill palms (*Trachycarpus fortunei*) growing beneath them and a sole Canary Island date palm (*Phoenix canariensis*) at right.

right: The uber-Californian pattern of meandering oak branches anchors the plantings of agaves, Chilean wine palms, and Mexican blue palms at Lotusland.

left: Among coast live oaks, *Phoenix reclinata* clusters (including larger, hybrid specimens at left and right) swan upward beside the great lawn, dormant for the dry season.

right: Blue-green slag glass edging leads like bread crumbs through the greenery of a grove of Guadalupe palms toward the blue garden. A Chilean wine palm, about 3 feet (1 m) thick, stands at right.

climate of their central Chilean home resembles closely that of California, and they take to the gardens of California like natives. At Lotusland their giant-pinwheel crowns share sky with ancient coast live oaks native to the site. Their massive, bulging trunks—the thickest of all palm species, source of the sugary syrup *miel de palma*, and undoubtedly key as water storage to their survival through annual summer droughts in habitat—stand like moai assembled among the sinuous trees and eccentric succulents.

The grandest strokes belong to landscape designers, for no artistic medium other than architecture employs such large-scale elements. (Even the biggest buildings cannot so effortlessly take as essential ingredients a borrowed view of mountains or the surrounding ecology.) Madame Walska's design ambitions encompassed preexisting elements such as Chilean palms and the nearby Santa Ynez Mountains, while she painted with an expanding array of other exotic plants (especially palms), sculpture, stone, and building materials.

For her blue garden, she used the monumental Chilean palms' gray-tinted foliage as glaucous overstory for an array of other blue-cast plants and materials. Key to visitors' sense of absorption in the color are the Mexican blue palms (*Brahea armata*) she used in profusion among blue-gray agaves (*Agave attenuata* 'Nova'), cactuses, blue Atlas cedars (*Cedrus atlantica* [Glauca Group]), aqua slag glass path edgers, and blue oat grass, *Festuca glauca*. The Mexican blue palms' radial crowns add a feeling of frozen fireworks, stopping time in the serene, blue-gray moment. Marine fogs from the Santa Barbara Channel regularly turn the atmosphere from a golden lucidity to a muted light that biases the eye toward blue and silver.

167

Two palms flanking an entrance to a property is a traditional ornamental use. A pair of magnificent Chilean wine palms serves this function at Lotusland. Often in rural California, these gateway sentinels are the only palms in the vicinity.

Lotusland being full of palms, a witty reversal of this tradition occurs in the blue garden. Ganna Walska placed two stone finials at its entrance. Over the modest ball-topped posts, lavish plantings loom. Young blue Atlas cedars form a screen between silvery agaves (*Agave beauleriana* [syn. *A. franzosinii*]) edging the lawn and heritage oaks, araucaria trees, and Queensland kauri pines (*Agathis robusta*). Stout Chilean wine palms gather like a meeting of elders, their jutting silhouettes pleasingly spaced among the larger woody trees.

Nearby, around a curve, hedgerows composed of live oak and two varieties of Senegal date palm form an edge to the vast lawn that declines from the pink 1920 house to the blue garden. The clustering habit of *Phoenix reclinata* and its larger hybrid serves the purpose of massing among the dense crowns of the oaks, while adding tangerine-colored fruit clusters and flexile, feather-pattern foliage. A peninsular bed pointing between lobes of the great lawn and comprising floppy *Agave beauleriana*, stiff *A. americana*, and tall, skirted *Furcraea parmentieri* pulls the colors from the tucked blue garden into a focal point for viewing from the house and a counterpoint to the hedgerow beyond.

The blue garden is a drought-tolerant landscape, as are many of the gardens at Lotusland. A path behind it leads to the main driveway, no longer in use for entry, through a grove of Guadalupe palms (*Brahea edulis*) (and a couple more heritage Chilean palms—it feels profligate not to honor each one of these reverend jubaeas in wandering the gardens, as it would to become inured to Botticellis at the Uffizi). Native to Guadalupe Island, a part of the California Floristic Province 150 miles (240 km) west of northern Baja California, the brahea performs like a native plant in coastal Alta (upper) California. Century-old Chilean palm trunks stand like massive pillars among the smaller scale, younger braheas. Leaf scars on the trunks record the life history of each tree; brown and monolithic, the trunks nonetheless emanate the vitality of sleeping elephants. Here the Guadalupe palms gather under the shade of taller trees in a multigenerational ensemble that compresses the walk in verdancy and shadow before opening to the glaucous gallery of the blue garden.

Along the driveway toward the house from the blue garden, an Emerald City of columnar cactuses, including *Echinopsis spachiana* and *Cleistocactus hyalacanthus*, gathers behind radial tufts of bromeliads. Taller candelabras of *Euphorbia abyssinica* (syn. *E. obovalifolia*), a cactus-mimicking succulent tree from Africa, are planted across the driveway from the New World cactuses. Amassing big plants

left: Spines of columnar cactuses transmit silver and copper, while phoenix palms culminate in orange fruit. Colors at Lotusland emanate from foliage, spines, and fruit as much as flowers.

right: A clump of Everglades palm (*Acoelorrhaphe wrightii*) rises to the left of the main drive over a shrubby Mediterranean fan palm while a Chinese windmill palm (*Trachycarpus fortunei*), Mexican fan palm, and Canary Island date palm cut profiles into the sky, the last above fellow Canary Island–native dragon trees at right.

the way other designers plant perennial beds, Madame Walska used Senegal and Canary Island date palms to make up the tallest layer of the composition. Magnifying the forms of the bromeliads, the palms' crowns add movement to otherwise rigid plants, while their trunks return the cylindrical forms of the cactuses and euphorbias. A texture unique to the palms is their curving pinnate leaves.

Wizened (by California standards) dragon trees (*Dracaena draco*) stand among diverse palms close to the house. Their broccoli profiles, balloon-sculpture branches, and dark understory alternate with the scattered towers of palm trunks—alternately thick, smooth, furry, thorny, thin, flexible, and immobile.

Lotusland's main drive—now a walkway—proceeds like parade of palmy exoticism introducing the wonders within, starting with the pair of nineteenth-century Chilean palms at the original gate. It proceeds past swaths of kentia palms (*Howea forsteriana*), Jurassic araucaria trees, and the palms and succulents of the blue garden and the gardens near the house.

Few places in California, natural or cultivated, approach the intoxicating magic of Ganna Walska Lotusland in as many acres. Its extraordinary vegetation and style are unmatched in public gardens in California. Without Madame Walska's profuse use of palms, it would fall short of its place.

PAT TIERNEY'S KEY WEST GARDEN

Key West, established in the 1820s, is the oldest city in South Florida. It's far enough from the peninsular land mass (famously closer to Havana than Miami) and sufficiently insulated by the warm seas around it that its lowest recorded temperature is 41°F (5°C). With southwest progress down the island chain, you encounter landscapes that are increasingly hospitable to the most tender tropical plants such as breadfruit trees (*Artocarpus altilis*) and habitats for native palm species not found on the mainland. The long drive lulls you into a mellower attitude. When you're beginning your 165-mile (266-km) trek in the contemporary sprawl and rising cranes of mainland South Florida, switching from four-lane expressway to two-lane road, island-hopping through native woodlands and mangroves and past strip malls, making increasingly spectacular crossings over turquoise and aquamarine water, the island's Victorian architecture, density, and heritage gardens give the impression of arriving in a New England port town run aground in the Caribbean.

Caitlin and I arrived in Key West after nightfall. We had spent the day photographing gardens and palm habitat along the Overseas Highway. When I gave Pat Tierney a call to check in about shooting his garden the next morning, he invited us for dinner. Soon seated on his veranda under a fan—welcome on this warm November night—we learned about his career in landscape design. Beginning in his native Miami, where he started designing and building landscapes for friends from school, his work expanded during the 1980s boom years. A desire for a slower pace took him to Key West, where he now works out of the home he shares with his husband, Victor, for residential and hospitality clients in Florida and the Caribbean.

An exceptional plantsman and seasoned designer, Pat uses his home garden not only as the place of relaxed outdoor living that we experienced, but also as showroom, lab, and mini-nursery.

"I try to make my gardens very informal," says Pat. For a garden proposal, he prefers not to make an exact site plan, "since I do the whole thing: I design, and I install. And, if I like the garden, I maintain it. I really enjoy what I do.

"The biggest thing about a tropical garden is you have to maintain it. You have to cut things back so they'll flourish." Irrigation is crucial in the Keys; rainfall—significantly lower than on the mainland—can be erratic, soils are sharply draining limestone or sand, and three seasons of hot weather put high demands on the plants.

top left: A blue latan palm (*Latania loddigesii*) is the keystone of a color composition with burgundy-rust ti plants (*Cordyline fruticosa*), gold crotons (*Codiaeum variegatum*), ceramics, and pool tile in Pat Tierney's home garden.

top right: Tall palms raise the perspective into the space above the garden, increasing its volume and giving the illusion of greater distance.

below left: A dark glazed pot rests between the feathery leaf of a clustering, upright arenga palm species, possibly *Arenga ryukyuensis*, and the glossy fan leaves of the Keys native thatch palm, *Thrinax radiata*.

below right: Lures into the garden include stone-paved pathways, outdoor shower, pool, seating steps to the veranda from the pool deck, and a gazebo-shaded poolside table flanked by an arenga palm and banana clumps, pruned for the apt balance of space and green companionship.

Pat's long experience with palms makes questions of species selection second nature to him. "You can plant a palm, but you have to imagine how it's going to grow into itself. You could plant a bamboo palm—a chamaedorea—in the place of a large latan palm, and you're not going to get the same thing." For designers not accustomed to living with an array of palms, the lesson of choosing the right species is crucial.

Pat's hand with color is liberal but precise. In the house paints, garden and house decorations, and flower and foliage, the garden's combinations respond gratifyingly to the island's subtropical sunlight and dawn glow alike. He makes masterful use of variations in his palms' foliage, flower, and fruit colors. The blue latan palm next to his pool is a contained radial explosion in powdery blue-gray and pink-rust tomentum, the premier color focus of the garden thanks to its association with the violet, aqua, and teal accent tiles in the pool and the complex mix of pink, red, and beige in underplanted ti.

The corner house occupies about half the property; its footprint is pulled slightly toward the neighboring property on the longer side of the rectangular plot, with a pool area bound by the shorter property line and tucked into a corner formed by two wings of the house. A fence surrounds the garden, with plantings as bounteous outside on the street as within. A shady garden on the back property line is planted with mix of tall, thin feather palms, including *Veitchia winin* and *Ptychosperma elegans*; a meandering path threads through them, leading to an outdoor shower. "I always do a garden path around the properties, just so, for myself and the people who live there, they can do their garden tours," says Pat. "People really enjoy that." The thin palms expand the sense of space upward, but, more importantly, seen from the pool area they stilt up behind the house. (From the street, their crowns peek out from behind the mix of fan and feather palms planted on the street.) Their elevated presence expands the scale of the landscape by raising the perspective, giving the illusion of lateral distance. The massiveness of a woody tree and its continuous canopy in this small space would have very different effects—darkening, roofing, and stilling the garden.

Details in the understory of the garden include plantings that thrive in the partial shade cast by palm crowns, such as bromeliads, crotons, and bananas (*Musa* spp.), and decorative objects Pat has imported from his regular travels.

The picture Pat paints for his clients with his garden is of a relaxed life spent outdoors as much as possible, caring for his surroundings and his circle of friends and loved ones.

Palmettos and dwarf palmettos surround a fountain pool at the entrance to the Walled Garden at Riverbanks Botanical Garden.

RIVERBANKS BOTANICAL GARDEN

Columbia, South Carolina, is the Palmetto State's capital and on a par with more well-known Charleston in population. Its Riverbanks Zoo and Botanical Garden straddles the Saluda River, a 10-minute drive from the center of the city. Deciduous woodlands envelop the area. Here in the middle of the state (the Midlands), average temperatures of 34°F to 56°F (1°C to 13°C) occur in January, and 72°F to 93°F (2°C to 34°C) in July. All-time records range from –1°F to 107°F (–18°C to

42°C). As in Charleston nearby on the coast, rain amounting to 49 inches (125 cm) falls amply throughout the year, with a peak in July and August. It's a warm temperate climate with rare arctic outbreaks.

Riverbanks truly comprises zoological gardens, with botanical features integrated into animal exhibits, but a significant portion of the park is dedicated to gardens alone, under the direction of Andy Cabe. A centerpiece is the beautiful Walled Garden, the first portion of the Botanical Garden to open, in 1995. Plantsman Jenks Farmer, a South Carolina garden designer, nurseryman, crinum expert, and author (and our generous guide in South Carolina) worked on the Walled Garden. He took inspiration from the historic Siebels House in Columbia and its elegant plantings of perennials and flowering shrubs with native palms—palmettos (*Sabal palmetto*), dwarf palmettos (*S. minor*), and shrubby saw palmettos (*Serenoa repens*)—in designing the beautiful combinations at Riverbanks.

The first sight on entering is a balustrade that encloses a brick walkway angling down into the Walled Garden around a fountain. Canted trios of the state tree, *Sabal palmetto*, peek above the balustrade from a bed of trunkless dwarf palmettos. On the outside flank of the walkway, saw palmettos and hellebores form a chartreuse and silver understory for calico-bark crape myrtles.

The Walled Garden, traditional as it may appear, is not static, either through the seasons or over the years. The gardeners are continually experimenting with hardy, half-hardy, and annual plants. The effect is of an English garden tapped into

left: The blues and purples of alliums and larkspur (*Delphinium* spp.) glow against the gray-green foliage of dwarf palmettos and yellow cole flowers.

center: In a combination outside the Walled Garden that would work even in New York City, Saint Louis, or Baltimore, majestic ginkgos stand over mounds of needle palms (*Rhapidophyllum hystrix*) and dwarf palmettos.

right: *Nannorhops ritchiana*, the Mazari palm of Afghanistan, Pakistan, and the Arabian Peninsula, splays its silvery fan leaves in a shrub composition of *Forsythia* 'Golden Times', (from left to right) *Morella cerifera* 'Lane', *Ilex latifolia*, and *Elaeagnus pungens* 'Clemson Variegated'.

the botanical resources of a hot-summer climate. In the United States, too much is made of the stereotypical palette of plants in the celebrated English perennial border; a set list of plants at their best in someone else's climate does not lead to a thrilling combination or succession in one's own. The adventuresome, whether in the Old World or the New, create with the widest palette they can find for the most beautiful effects. Palms make their unique contributions here.

The low palms in these borders function in the realm between shrubs and evergreen grasses. Some will eventually become treelike, but as with any young palm, their service begins as foliage. In addition to the palmetto trees, most plants here are permanent ground-dwellers.

Riverbanks is a showcase for the hardiest palms, plants that can work in gardens where temperatures (rarely) drop as low as 0°F (–18°C). American natural habitats from North Carolina to Louisiana and Texas (and even California), rich in winter-deciduous and winter-dormant plants, are home to palms. You'll see green on a winter walk in the swamps of Barataria Preserve outside New Orleans, mostly in the leaves of dwarf palmettos, live oaks (*Quercus virginiana*), and Southern magnolias (*Magnolia grandiflora*); in May, the fresh canopy of red maples, bald cypress, and other deciduous trees over resurgent green perennials transforms the place. And with their clever palm uses, the gardeners and planting designers at Riverbanks defy the received notion that winter-deciduous plants and palms don't go well together.

WINE COUNTRY PALM GARDEN

On an oak-wooded crest in the Sonoma County Wine Country north of San Francisco, Hélène Morneau and Kris Sunderlage of Exteriors Landscape Architecture designed a contemporary California–Mediterranean garden with palms. The clients, whose previous garden the firm helped create, just down the hill at a house where they lived part-time, were settling full-time in their modern new house (designed by architect Michael Cobb). After spending much of their lives in colder climates, they wanted to have palm trees in this landscape.

I consulted with Exteriors and their clients on the palms that would succeed in their thermally favored Northern California microclimate—warm and dry in summer, chilly and wet in winter—and supplied the specimens from Flora Grubb Gardens. January can bring temperatures ranging from 37°F to 57°F (3°C to 14°C), while July brings highs of 90°F (32°C) and cool, sometimes overcast mornings

averaging 53°F (12°C). Extremes of 110°F (43°C) and 17°F (−8°C) have occurred in the area, but the site's slope, southerly exposure, and elevation above winter inversions protect it from hard freezes. Rains limited to the cooler half of the year accumulate to 42 inches (107 cm) per year, on average.

The garden's pool and entertaining areas extend along the sunnier, downhill side of the house on tiers that maximize views of the forested hills beyond the valley vineyards. Hélène and Kris sited date palms (*Phoenix dactylifera* 'Medjool') to frame views, cast reflections, add movement, and intermediate between the human scale and the two-story stucco house. Beds of agaves, aeoniums, and aloes; grasses and low-water perennials; and herbs and shrubs such as lavender and rosemary delight the eye and contribute scent to the atmosphere as family and friends brush past them. Gravel surfaces away from the limestone pool deck give gently underfoot and, along with tan stone, evoke traditional Mediterranean lands in this distinctly modern California setting.

It's often useful when introducing a palm—or just a new palm species—into a landscape that previously lacked palms to repeat the species. The second plant can be at a different height or phase of development, but twins or triplets may work, too. The repetition creates a context and relationship that buffers the exclamation-point effect of a solitary palm tree.

In this garden, a trio of pindo palms (*Butia odorata*) was placed at the top of a slope in the curve of the driveway as it rises up the hill near the house. The clump changes as you climb the driveway and around the palms. Seen at first from below, the palms arch energetically outward amid solemn Italian cypresses (*Cupressus sempervirens*); then, closer to eye level, their gray-green foliage stands out against the washed-peach walls of the house. Finally, a close pass enables you to inspect the detail of trunk, flowers, and fruit. Nowhere else in the garden does this species occur, but it works as a triple.

Date palms underplanted with aloes, *Agave* 'Sharkskin', and *A. desmetiana* 'Variegata', emerge above billowing privet and olive trees, their diamond-cut leafbases and pinnate leaves contributing to the plantings a regularity of pattern befitting the clean lines of the house and pool terraces beyond. As Hélène says, the date palm provides "that wonderful punch with so little effort. All parts of it are spectacular. Every part of that tree I feel has something to offer, like the sway of the fronds in the breeze. There's something that's alive about them."

It can be comforting to interrupt a panorama with trees; often vertical elements can render an overwhelming space picturesque. Fastigiate woody trees will (often bulkily) serve this function. The designers placed date palms just beyond the edge of the pool. These palms will keep their form while slowly gaining height, and thus will serve indefinitely as frames for the view with no effort to shape them beyond occasional pruning of fronds. A woody, branching tree would ramify in the space, eventually blocking more than desired.

Another phenomenon, elusive and subtle: the palms activate the volume and bound the space beyond the pool. It's as though our attention to the trees' animated crowns transits the space, making us conscious of its dimensions, even rendering the air more palpable in their yield to the breeze.

A single-trunk Mediterranean fan palm (*Chamaerops humilis*), almost anthropomorphic, leans from the house into a casual gathering space, softening the impact of the house; a second chamaerops repeats the texture of the primary palm for a naturalizing effect.

At the same time, the palms' trunks limit downhill and outward movement from these terraces, lending security to what might otherwise be a vertiginous garden.

A hedge of Mediterranean fan palms forms a first layer in the *mille-feuille* foliage horizons expanding out from the pool. The fan palms conceal the base (and thus the true height) of the date palms, enhancing the levitating quality of the date palms' crowns. The two species' forms and scale complement each other, and their cultural requirements are compatible.

The landscape architects' use of palms in this Wine Country garden is gracious and sensual, but unsentimental. They cast palms in roles for which they're perfectly suited.

The hardiest palms, limited in scale, add their energetic charisma to the mix of ground shrubs, cycads, and small trees in this warm temperate garden.

MARY ALICE WOODRUM'S SOUTH CAROLINA GARDEN

The first garden with palms that Caitlin and I visited in South Carolina was at Mary Alice and Bear Woodrum's home in a woodsy neighborhood in North Augusta. What luck. We received the warmest of welcomes from Mary Alice (and Jenks Farmer, our South Carolina guide), and felt immediate ease in exploring the extensive and enchanting garden. The well-drained Sandhills soil of the Woodrums' neighborhood allows Mary Alice, a painter, sculptor, gardener, and jewelry artist, to grow an enormous range of plants, from conifers and deciduous trees to perennials, cactus, succulents, cycads, and, you guessed it, palms.

Mary Alice's homey palace of a garden exemplifies the possibilities of using the hardiest of palms for their aesthetic effects, integrating them with the inherited and native landscape, and combining them with diverse plant groups, sculpture, water features, built landscape, and architecture.

Out front on the fence we saw the first sign of Mary Alice's artistic bent: a bottle tree—or bottle arbor variation, blue and olive-colored glass bottles frozen in flight over a garden gate sculpted in waving vertical bands of rust-colored metal. Festooning it, white clematis opened in perfect bloom. Down a bit, sprawling between fence and road, a bluish prickly pear cactus grew fresh sprouts and flower buds on the margins of its pads. Behind the cactus, three staggered young Chinese windmill palms (*Trachycarpus fortunei*) rose within an intentional but not-quite-manicured composition including sculpted and weeping conifers and

left: The garden's intimate corners are composed with the same care given to the sweeping, arboretum-scale front garden.

right: Shrubby needle palms are the most cold-hardy of all palm species, and furry-trunked Chinese windmill palms the most cold-hardy of tree palms.

broadleaf evergreens. Into the garden behind the fence, up the land's gradual tilt from the road, the pointy white bracts of Chinese dogwoods (*Cornus kousa*) gleamed that last morning in April beneath native pines and oaks. Amethyst sparks of allium blooms and wine-colored eucomis sprouts decorated the pine-oak duff.

The driveway, opening through a wider version of the sculpted garden gate, makes a gentle curve as it seeks and then veers to the right of the house. Leaf-and-needle duff showered from canopy trees carpets most of the garden and softly edges the drive. Flowering yuccas, mounds of needle palm (*Rhapido-phyllum hystrix*), jagged silver saw palmetto (*Serenoa repens*), and dwarf palmetto (*Sabal minor*) add linear, digitate forms to the mix of bristly conifers and herbs near ground level. A klatsch of Chinese windmill palms catches the eye where the drive veers right, conspiring with small, limbed-up trees to delay a full view of the house. Big pines and oaks posted throughout the land help enclose chambers of lawn lined with midstory trees and shrubs—holly, loquat, redbud, Japanese maple, boxwood, juniper—and perennials and ferns. These spaces, connected by passages and tunnels in the wood, invite rambling.

In the grouping at the curve of the driveway, Mary Alice plays with the tension between like-leaved palms of differing growth habits. The shiny, articulated fan leaves of needle palms cartwheel from multiple growing points; this is a true shrub palm, mostly seen foliated from ground to peak, never quite achieving a recogniz-able trunk. Next to them, Chinese windmill palms carry flatter, duller, less articu-lated but still deeply divided fan leaves on single stems that become furry posts. Their head-and-trunk form is legible, almost apelike. Placed incorrectly, they'd be awkward or lost in the needle mounds. By planting the windmills out from the needle palms, and keeping the needles clear of the trunks of the dominant pines to allow the pines' verticals to rhyme with the windmills', she has allowed the assemblage to fluctuate in the eye between contrast and similarity. Beneath them, plum yews and sagos maintain continuity with the broader garden palette.

To the rear of the house, palms become more populous around the patio, pool, and water features. Big palmettos (*Sabal palmetto*), their trunks covered in lattice-work leafbases, stand between the house and a lawn. Dwarf palmettos and Chinese windmill palms dominate beds mounded on the pool deck between retaining walls and blue-bottle edging. A waterfall planted with a mix of perennials—autumn fern (*Dryopteris erythrosora*), pitcher plants (*Sarracenia* spp.), acorus—is backed by Mediterranean fan palm and Chinese windmill palm.

Palms as perennials, shrubs, and trees all play roles in the Woodrums' gar-den. In the pool deck beds, dwarf palmettos function as showy foliage elements

(and screening), accented by their intricate, upright inflorescences turning from asparagus-like stalks in bud, to plumes of cream in flower, to staffs of black berries in fruit. Chinese windmill palms serve the more traditional function of palm trees around the pool.

When I entered the house and admired the impression of windmill palm fronds on the wall over a fireplace, Mary Alice told me about her husband's encouragement to try out the effect, not to be bound by fear of failure. The story stood for the nature of their mutually encouraging relationship and the freedom they had found with each other. Mary Alice describes their home as "a garden of love fulfilled—two nurturing souls together."

The Woodrums' garden is a place of artistic self-expression, family gathering, and shared effort and achievement infused with memory and future plans. Born of rigorous horticulture and discerning eye, it's a place of tender beauty that brought me to the brink of tears.

left: *Sabal minor*, the dwarf palmetto, waves its glaucous, sheltering fans beneath a limbed-up camellia in a bottle-edged poolside bed.

right: Leaves of *Trachycarpus fortunei*, the Chinese windmill palm, impressed into a wall in the Woodrums' home

Las Palmas, the garden designed by Steve Martino, features color block walls—an admiring echo of the work of Mexican architect Luis Barragán.

LAS PALMAS

Gardens are made up of two worlds, the man-made and the natural world. I try to juxtapose these two worlds. I've described my garden design style as "Weeds and Walls"—Nature and Man.

—STEVE MARTINO

Phoenix-based landscape architect Steve Martino interlocks his designs with the delicate desert environments in which he most often works. Considering himself more of a garden designer than landscape architect, he writes on his blog that he likes "to solve problems and create interesting places that my clients love to be in and that are grounded to the natural processes of the site and region." Native plants, local geology, and water sources draw insects, birds, and other wildlife into the gardens he designs, concentrating the life of the desert in the places where

people gather. His precise, emphatic use of planar surfaces delight the eye, focus views, cast shade, enhance depth in the garden, serve as backdrops for planting tableaux and surfaces for lounging and partying, and preserve privacy.

In the Palm Springs neighborhood of Las Palmas, Martino created for a former fashion-industry entrepreneur a garden tied to the desert fan palm (*Washingtonia filifera*) canyons for which the getaway town is named. Drawing perennial streams off the mountains to the west, the canyons provide habitat for the palms and other water-loving trees such as cottonwoods and willows and are an important place for the Agua Caliente band of Cahuilla Indians. The palms played a big role in their economic lives, providing shelter, food, clothing, and tools, and indicating the availability of permanent water.

Martino says, "I really like the *Washingtonia filifera*s that are native to Palm Springs. The Las Palmas house had ninety-eight palms on site that we reused." He continues, "[They] had to go into a storage area in the corner of the property. The storage area was really neat; it looked like a palm canyon." Palms not often playing a role in his Arizona projects, he says, "Typically when people ask me if I like palms, I say yes, I like their hearts in my salad. That's because in Phoenix, people always want [non-native] *Washingtonia robusta* palms" (a ubiquitous Baja California native I've deemed the cockroach of palms—not wholly disrespectfully—for its indomitable vitality and weediness).

At Las Palmas, Martino developed a desert pleasure ground amidst framed beds of succulents—Joshua tree–like beaked yucca (*Yucca rostrata*), agaves and furcraeas, columnar prickly pear and barrel cactuses, Sputnik-y dasylirions, wiry ocotillos, and snaky pedilanthus. Those ninety-plus repositioned native palms preside over the level ground, their heavy, organic verticals and wind-tossed crowns drawing eyes into voluminous skies and toward stony mountains plunging to the valley floor four blocks away. Feathery palo verde trees change with seasons, blooming gold in spring, dropping their tiny leaves in drier times, their smooth bark staying green all year against pigmented walls. After a rain, the occasional brushy creosote bush (*Larrea tridentata*) in the garden emits the unmistakable odor that gives it its name and by which it signals distant showers occurring out in their mercilessly dry surrounding habitat. It is the apt counterpoint to the charismatic palm, signature of the desert's few perennially watered places.

Dramatic, even architectural, plantings in rubble mulch (evoking the mountain slopes in view) are the wild counterpoint in this civilized, sybaritic space. Squared-off cactus beds evocative of trays of *fruits de mer* float in pools and tuck at the base of glass walls, vitrine displays for people inside and spiny companions for those lounging in chaises half-submerged in the pool: look but don't touch—desert plants must defend themselves. Even the palms are armed.

Expanding on the mid-twentieth-century–inspired limestone- and glass-clad house designed by architect Don Boss (a former associate of A. Quincy Jones), Martino casts his signature color block walls in tomato, putty, mustard, and pale sage. Translucent forms in fiberglass and frosted glass add brighter color notes and glow in sunshine and night lighting. Every surface—matte masonry and stone, luminous glass and fiberglass—is flawlessly finished. Warm, muted colors prevail in the limestone house and paving; the teal pool, green lawn and hedging, blue sky, rust-tinted palm trunks, and tan granite slopes complete the landscape's palette.

Screened from the street on two sides by hedges of *Ficus microcarpa* var. *nitida*, the corner property opens through a driveway on the left of the house. The drive leads to a parking court and garage beyond the front door and continues to another planting bed–flanked parking area in the far corner of the rectangular site next to the tennis court. Translucent butter-color fiberglass panels fence the tennis court, reminiscent of a brise-soleil.

Rising a couple of steps to the front door patio, you reach the dominant elevation of the residence. It is a subtle plane composed of shimmering rectangles of water and solid paving, both elements interrupted only by planting beds. A primary axis begins at a fountain on the property line across the driveway from the front door. It passes through the front door and glass-walled foyer, and then outside again across the pool and pool deck; along with the driveway, two main cross axes intersect it. Martino explains that by matching the house elevation to the pool deck, he intended to create "absolute convenience of the indoor and outdoor space seamlessly flowing together; the doorways [to the outside] do not even have thresholds, the tile runs right under the glass doors. The site has 5 feet of slope across it. I have the slope transitions beyond the pool to keep the house and pool on the same level."

The pools mirror the palms; nothing else compares as narcissistic subject (if they could only see themselves); nothing else reaches their height with such a distinct shape to cast.

Martino's use of the California fan palms at the edge of the central platform emphasizes the transition to the lawn area a couple of steps down, the heft of their trunks shared in the posts supporting the golden-shaded pavilion. Frosted glass walls intermittently block sight between the elevations as you wander.

The predominant California fan palms are joined by a lofty trio of Mexican fan palms emerging from an atrium at the center of the house and a natural-style date palm (*Phoenix dactylifera*) cluster between the main house and the guest house. Mediterranean fan palms (*Chamaerops humilis*) and Senegal date palms (*Phoenix reclinata*) are also used in the garden; they're smaller than the other palms, relating to the arborescent yuccas and columnar cactus (including *Stetsonia coryne*). Desert trees such as palo verde add soft, sinuous shapes to the cutout silhouettes of the iconic succulents and palms.

Numerous gathering spots—some with fire features, tables, and chairs; some upholstered in bright fabrics in key colors; some sheltered under eaves of the

The depressed elevation of the lawn around the central platform, and its proximity to the hedge, create a sense of seclusion and separation from the house and pool.

house—are placed throughout the garden. Lawn surrounding the center offers the intimacy of retreating from the action and the luxuriant feel of grass against bare feet. The ficus hedge blocks neighboring houses while preserving higher-angle perspectives. Views of the mountains quickly turn shadowy and flatten as the sun progresses to the west; Mount San Jacinto's summit is 10,000 feet (3048 m) high and less than 10 miles (16 km) west and blocks the sun earlier than anywhere else I've been, a boon in a climate that metes out hot days eight or nine months of the year.

Every detail in the garden is assured. Martino has precisely orchestrated the colors, textures, perspectives, plant combinations, movements, and natural cycles. Nowhere does the stamp of human artistry get lost amid the displays of desert vitality, the context in which this patch of civilization exists. The tension between "weeds and walls—nature and man" reaches its culmination here in the palms of the garden, the preeminent signs of water and its availabilty to people in the desert.

TRANSBAY TURNING POINT

When my interest in palms blew up into a fixation, even obsession, at the end of my high school years in San Francisco, they were a curiosity here, a bone of contention burdened by their association with Los Angeles (opponent in a city rivalry in which only San Franciscans rattled their sabers), but not generally seen as plants worthy of consideration for garden use or public planting. Then I went off to college in New England and started to learn about trees and plants there. I nurtured my palm love on visits to California and Florida and Hawai'i, and in reading palm publications—and wished for tastes to change on visits home.

Before leaving for college, I joined the International Palm Society and its Northern California Chapter—as perhaps the youngest member at that time—and my new palm gurus, such as Davis Dalbok and Garrin Fullington, showed me the range of species they had planted in the gardens they designed and in particular at the chapter's Lakeside Palmetum in Oakland. To my primed eyes, this obscure place was a thrilling, dreamlike trove of new palm varieties for the Bay Area. Its design was effective for display of a collection of rare plants, but otherwise unremarkable.

So much has changed. Now a new park designed by PWP Landscape Architecture and under construction on the roof of a transit center in downtown San Francisco exemplifies new attitudes toward designing with palms and points toward a shift in understandings—especially local, Western ones—of public life, humans, and nature.

Years after my New England stint, living back in San Francisco, I encountered the park's future designer, a friend from college, Adam Greenspan, in Bay Area horticulture circles. A native of Los Angeles, Adam shared my love of palms and other bold, unusual plants such as cycads and succulents and was using many of them in designing gardens in the Bay Area and Los Angeles. We nerded out together, comparing notes about our experiences with different species and about our sightings of rarities, and I sold him plants I propagated as

left: *Nīkau* palms (*Rhopalostylis sapida*) thrive in the cool climate of the San Francisco Botanical Garden in Golden Gate Park.

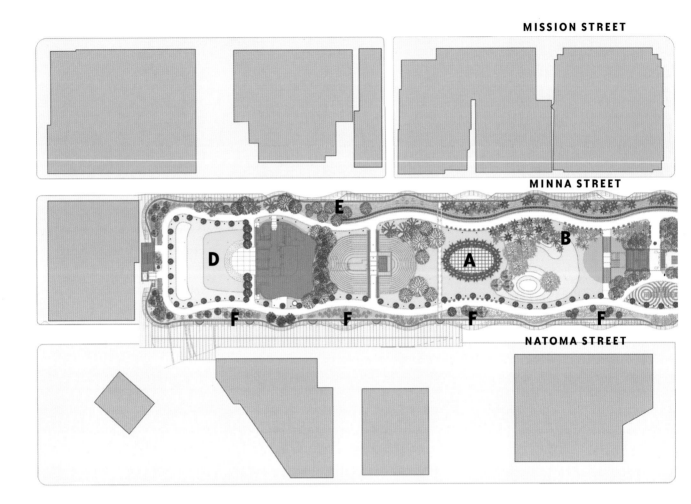

MISSION STREET

MINNA STREET

E

B

D

A

F   F   F   F

NATOMA STREET

a volunteer at the San Francisco Botanical Garden (then Strybing Arboretum). Things were changing in the Bay Area landscape in the 1990s, with new avenue plantings of palms in San Francisco and beyond, and greater openness among home gardeners, landscape architects, and designers to the range of fascinating plants adaptable to our unusual climate.

One of the sources of inspiration for those garden designers, the Lakeside Palmetum, is beginning to grow into prominence, three decades after I first visited. Oakland and its heart, Lake Merritt, get more visitors now, and the Palmetum and its neighboring gardens have become the Gardens at Lake Merritt under the dynamo supervision of Tora Rocha. The maturing array in particular of cool-climate palms first planted in 1982 are now rivaled only by new plantings at the San Francisco Botanical Garden in Golden Gate Park—where my own propagation of, and lobbying efforts for, palms were inspired by the Palmetum. Specimens that were young when I first visited the Palmetum are reaching flowering age

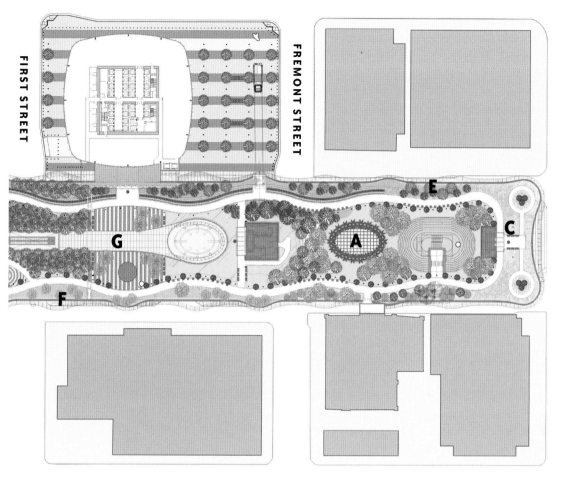

FIRST STREET

FREMONT STREET

The plan for the Transbay
Transit Center Park
by PWP Landscape
Architecture

A. Skylights with
palms

B. Palm garden

C. Graywater
garden

D. Amphitheater

E. California native
garden

F. Mediterranean-
climate gardens

G. Central Plaza

and pushing their crowns against the horizon. Second- and even third-generation seedlings are appearing where irrigation allows.

The moment a palm tree, especially a rare one, starts showing its trunk is an occasion. The revelation of the cylinder's surface as older leaves detach from the base of the rosette is the beginning of that plant's "treehood," its crowning. Growing amidst the veteran canopy of trident maples at the Palmetum is the tallest of all palms—and thus of all monocots—*Ceroxylon quindiuense*, the wax palm of the Andes, or *palma de cera*. For wax palms, the wait for the trunk can take decades. In the last ten years, waxy white internodes broken by rings of dark leaf scars have become visible on the adolescent ones; eventually the huge feather-duster crowns will become skyline elements, like the old Mexican fan palms around town. Perhaps someday the ceroxylons will approach the 200-foot (60-m) heights they reach in habitat.

Under maple shade, bamboo palms (*Chamaedorea* spp.) form lovely thickets, their flowers exuding a clean, pleasing scent. Cool weather–loving nīkau palms, *Rhopalostylis sapida*, and umbrella palms, *Hedyscepe canterburyana*, share the shade, where their hundreds of flowers feed bees. Nearby, grouped Chinese fan palms, *Livistona chinensis*, barely beginning to show trunks after thirty years in this cool climate, splay their broad fans. The delicate, vining rattan palm from Australia, *Calamus caryotoides*, lashes its barbed threads onto surrounding plants to climb upward. Freeze-scarred king palms (*Archontophoenix cunninghamiana*) lord over the edge of the maple grove.

In the sunny section, Quito palms (*Parajubaea cocoides*) planted in 1984 now tower overhead; their miniature coconuts provide a tasty feast for the squirrels. A young Chilean wine palm, *Jubaea chilensis*, perches on a mound, its obese trunk an elephant among gazelles, its dense, vinyl-texture leaves a bonfire of dark green. This tree will endure any extremity of drought or cold the Bay Area can throw at it, produce copious delicious coquito nuts, and, with the potential to live for centuries, mature into the most majestic of palm species.

There won't be a wait to see a majestic jubaea at the Transbay Transit Center Park. Having searched California for specimens—with some help from me and my Palm Broker

Rosettes of palms create vivid patterns among the softer textures of greensward and canopy trees. Image by PWP Landscape Architecture.

colleagues—my friend Adam Greenspan, now partner at PWP Landscape Architecture, will see his botanically rich design for the roof of San Francisco's new transit hub realized with large jubaeas and a garden of unusual palms among many themed gardens in the park. Imagining palms prominently placed in the middle of San Francisco exceeds any hope I had as a teenager for public palm plantings. Seeing them deftly integrated into a deeply considered park at the intersection of people's sightlines, a gathering place for thousands, gratifies me in my hope for the future of design with palms.

A new park built 70 feet (21 m) up from the earth—the ground of which is a nineteenth-century fill that raised bay floor to dry land—the Transbay Transit Center's rooftop City Park epitomizes the artifice of designing a landscape in a century of global urbanization and climate change. The constraints of designing with palms (and all plants) in the twenty-first century can expand the designer's freedom and increase the joy, fascination, and utility of a landscape. Transbay's heat-sink position brings advantages for growing a broad array of plants—especially palms—and their fibrous root systems are a plus in on-structure planting beds. Meanwhile, the changing climate, new technologies, the global rush into city living, new pests, new palm species—there's a lot to contend with.

There are few parks in the area. The neighborhood grid consists of large blocks threaded by alleys between broader streets. Four blocks long, the four-story, million-square-foot transit building arches over major streets as it runs midblock between skyscrapers. It is built to serve regional bus systems, San Francisco's Muni buses, as well as commuter and high-speed rail. A quick walk will take travelers to a station of Bay Area Rapid Transit (BART), the regional heavy-rail commuter system.

A half-block wide, the 5.4-acre rooftop park's rectangular envelope is comparable in proportions to Golden Gate Park. But it borrows its scale and midblock position from South Park, a historic park nearby that forms an intimate oblong of similar width but measures one-third Transbay's length. (Also in the vicinity is Yerba Buena Gardens, a popular park with skyline views, which opened in 1993.)

Reached by spectacular escalators and a gondola, the new park will give visitors a view of privately owned public open spaces (POPOS, in San Francisco parlance)—mostly roof gardens—required by the planning code and scattered on adjacent buildings and throughout the central business district. A bridge connects the park to a new POPOS. The Transbay park is likely to increase consciousness and use of these under-the-radar perches and add a sense of permeability to the skyscraper village.

The park will beckon though the Light Column, a well of natural light reaching from below ground, with a glass roof fringed in timber bamboo (*Phyllostachys bambusoides*). Tall, hybrid washingtonia palms evenly spaced around an oval skylight will draw eyes from the bus level without sacrificing light. Such skylight spaces recall atriums at the center of San Francisco's Beaux Arts department stores such as City of Paris and The Emporium, where rooftop fairs with a Ferris wheel were a cherished annual event.

The park's South Park and Golden Gate Park antecedents are part of San Francisco's Victorian heritage—the former a longtime urban haven, the latter a lush site of horticultural innovation transmuted from sand dunes. The new park combines haven and ingenuity in a composition hovering at the foot of some of the city's tallest towers. Adam notes, "Many people will look down on this park, and the palms are like super-graphic succulents or flowers [seen] from high above." He compares the effect to a mosaic of succulents in a vertical garden, or to Roberto Burle Marx's similar use of giant bromeliads, agaves, and palms. As Adam anticipates, the palms' "rosettes in varied colors and scales are vivid and unique when looked down upon from above (in a way that is different, more intricate, more designed, than broad-leaved tree canopies or even conifers)."

Once the visitor reaches the roof, Adam's horticulturally intense gardens, inspired by the botanical adventuring of the nineteenth century and its living legacy, will unfurl along a sinuous path that traces the park's perimeter. Along it, a line of water jets designed by artist Ned Kahn shoots up in response to the passage of buses on the level below, animating the function of the facility.

The enfilade of perimeter gardens along the path is organized by thematic and geographic community: A wetland processes graywater and runoff; California native plantings culminate in theme gardens but recur throughout, attracting pollinators and emanating local scents. Other gardens include a grassland community, a flowery zone, and gardens of the world's Mediterranean and arid zones. Specimen trees, cycads, and succulents accent the collections. A palm garden comprises a range of both mesic (*Rhopalostylis baueri*, *Howea belmoreana*) and more drought-tolerant (*Brahea clara*, *Butia odorata*) specimens. This garden alone spills over the path, onto a central picnic meadow, palms reaching to the oval of *Washingtonia ×filibusta* around the skylight.

The portion of the park inside the perimeter path is spacious. It includes an arrival grove of lophostemon trees into which visitors step from the grand escalator, flat areas for lounging, an amphitheater, a children's play area, undulating sections providing a sense of seclusion from the towering city, a bamboo grove, and a paved plaza with a café. Any structures on the park level are vine-covered or glass.

Adam used a beautiful array of palms in the park because they are aesthetically useful, with bold, attractive forms that are legible from ground level and from high above. They are practical for their ease in transplanting, fibrous roots adaptable to planting beds, and flexibility and wind-resistance. And they have historical resonance, tying San Francisco's early horticultural verve to park-making that serves the city's densest new neighborhood

Water spouts up whenever a bus passes underneath the palm garden in Ned Kahn's art piece for the Transbay Transit Center Park. Image by PWP Landscape Architecture.

and the throngs of passengers below who need a green breather from their low-carbon commutes.

Here in California, John Muir's Mecca, the conventional romance that humans despoil a pristine nature reaches its peak. Humans lived in and managed this place for millennia before any European felled an oak for firewood. And the reality is that we humans as an agrarian and industrial species have begun to determine through climate change the conditions for most of the rest our fellow organisms living on the planet. Everything is now subject, however marginally, to our choices of stewardship. It's exciting that we can create spaces in the most unlikely places for other organisms to join us in the built environment, our urban habitat. They'll join us anyway, and not just pigeons—look at the coyotes now roaming San Francisco, and the native coyote bushes and exotic New Zealand Christmas trees sprouting in cracks in the concrete. We might as well design for our needs and theirs, and enjoy the process and the results of stewarding the urban ecosystem.

Palms are another source of joy and nectar. They are a family of plants embedded in a dense web of ecological associations, occupying an exceptionally dense node of relationships with our species, and offering exceptional beauty and fecundity for making and remaking our garden Earth.

Pseudophoenix sargentii at the Bait Shack garden designed by Nicholas D'Ascanio for D'Asign Source in the Florida Keys

PALM
SPECIES

Guides to the palm family naturally possess a
preponderance of tropical species,
for palms are most abundant in tropical
regions. Presented with the plethora of
cultivated palm species—some quite rare and
not obtainable in quantity or large sizes—
one might get lost trying to design a landscape,
unable to see the palms for the jungle.

For the designer or gardener outside the tropics, finding the more cold-hardy species amidst the abundance is another hurdle. My effort in these species portraits is to help focus the search.

The bias for the species portraits is toward palms suited to gardens outside tropical regions, both commonly available and rare. I have included a good number of those frost-tender, tropical species most commonly encountered in landscapes in tropical and subtropical areas; I've also included a few rare and exciting tropical species. But, being a Californian, I've favored the rare species and new introductions that are most promising for the West Coast of the United States and similar climates.

Scientists and lay researchers regularly introduce new or obscure palm species to the awareness of enthusiasts and specialty growers. Occasionally, new plants from cooler habitats such as tropical cloud forests enter the market, finding welcoming extratropical climates not only along the US West Coast, but also in Hawai'i; New Zealand; Australia's southeastern and southwestern corners; Western Europe; the Canary Islands, Madeira, and the Azores; South Africa; southern Brazil; Chile; and various tropical cloud forest regions.

The key groupings of palms are used in the text. Feather (pinnate) and fan (palmate) are the two primary forms of leaves in the palm family. Among the feather palms, significant subforms of the leaf occur: plain pinnate (flat), with leaflets arranged in a single plane, as in the flying feathers of most birds; plumose leaves, which look fluffy like ostrich feathers; undivided leaves, with leaflets fused together like a banana leaf; and bipinnate leaves, limited to the genus *Caryota*, which have a primary rachis (leaf stem) from which secondary rachises diverge and to which wedge-shaped leaflets are attached. I note which among the pinnate palms have crownshafts; they are not seen in the fan palms.

Among the fan palms, the main groupings are palmate and costapalmate, often included here in the species portraits. The segments of the fan-shaped leaf blade may be divided entirely to the meeting point with the petiole (*Rhapis* species), the blade may be entirely undivided (some *Licuala* species), or it may be variously deeply or shallowly divided (most others).

Each of the palm portfolios includes information regarding appearance, growing culture, heat and cold tolerance, uses and effects, and availability, as well as alternative species that serve similar functions in the landscape.

» APPEARANCE Genus descriptions are omitted for genera comprising only one species. Dimensions are for mature cultivated plants—those that are of flowering and fruiting age—within a surmised lifespan of the plant in a managed landscape.

» CULTURE Cold-hardiness figures are estimates for the lowest temperature that an established plant with a mature-diameter trunk can survive and return to a reasonably good appearance. Longer and more repeated exposure to this temperature will produce more damage, or death. Climate adaptations are listed from optimal to marginal.

» TOLERANCE Drought tolerance is indicated—low, moderate, high—for established plants and will vary according to soil conditions, air temperature, humidity, and wind conditions. Palms exposed to lower humidity, higher light levels, and more wind will require more water to thrive. Even plants with high tolerance for drought require regular moisture in their establishment phase, and established plants able to tolerate a short cool-season dry stretch such as in South Florida cannot necessarily endure without supplemental water a long, rainless Mediterranean climate summer like California's or a hot, monsoonal climate winter and spring like Mumbai's.

> Low: These plants require consistent soil moisture and tend to prefer higher humidity.

> Moderate: These plants can remain healthy through rainless stretches but not through extended drought without irrigation; some but not all of them may also tolerate lower humidity and higher wind exposure.

> High: These plants can survive multiple-month rainless periods once established. Almost all drought-tolerant palms need to be able to reach a permanent moisture source with their roots. Few palms can survive long in completely dry soil. Many drought-tolerant palms also tolerate low humidity or windy sites.

Salt tolerance is generally defined into three zones, or belts, according to salt and wind exposure. These concepts come from Edwin A. Menninger's 1964 book, *Seaside Plants of the World*. A high salt exposure occurs in Belts I and II. Moderate occurs in Belt III. Low is where salt exposure is minimal or negligible, farther inland or in a more protected area than Belt III.

> Belt I is the closest to the ocean, where regular salt spray and occasional wave overwash occur. Coconut palms tolerate this belt.

> Belt II is protected from the full onslaught of salty winds by larger trees, dunes, and structures.

> Belt III is where some salt accumulates in the soil but the site is not under chronic exposure, and plants can be helped by irrigation and rinsing with fresh water.

» HEAT REQUIREMENT A requirement for heat is assumed for palms.

> Low, 60°F–70°F (16°C–21°C) days and 50°F–55°F (10°C–13°C) nights: These palms can grow in cooler conditions such as coastal California and Chile, New Zealand, the Atlantic shores of Europe, and high altitudes in the tropics. A species may have low or high tolerance for heat or it may *require* cool conditions. In either case, it can grow without much heat and succeed.

> Moderate, 70°F–80°F (21°C–27°C) days and 55°F–65°F (13°C–18°C) nights: These palms can live where uncomfortably hot weather is uncommon and can survive a cool season.

> Moderate-high, 80°F–90°F (27°C–32°C) days and 65°F–70°F (18°C–21°C) nights: These palms enjoy long seasons of warm weather but may not tolerate a long season of cool weather.

> High, 85°F–115°F (29°C–46°C) days and 70°F (21°C) and higher nights: A few species need sustained hot weather to thrive, tolerating only a season or two of moderate temperatures.

» USES AND EFFECTS These lists indicate the best ways to highlight the aesthetic appeal and cultural aspects of a plant. When a species fails to thrive in conditions such as drought, wind, saltiness, or extremes of sun or shade, I indicate those conditions to avoid in using it. Estimates for cold-tolerance and warnings to avoid frost are listed separately from climate categories. Cold damage affects different plants in different ways in different regions.

» ALTERNATE SPECIES Listed alternate species partly resemble the described species and can serve similar functions in the landscape, though they may have different climate requirements or different market availability.

» AVAILABILITY These ratings—rare, uncommon, and common—apply to areas within North America in which the plant is suited to the climate.

Acanthophoenix

A genus of three species, all of them spiny, native to the islands of Réunion and Mauritius in the southwest Indian Ocean, *Acanthophoenix* includes moderate-size to tall feather palms with crownshafts. The most commonly grown, *A. rubra*, named for its reddish brown crownshaft, originates from lowland rainforests and is suited to tropical and warm subtropical climates. All species' trunks meet the ground in an elephant's foot bulge that enlarges over time.

Acanthophoenix crinita

BRISTLE PALM, *PALMISTE ROUGE*, SPINY FOG PALM

This feather palm from Réunion, a palm-rich French island in the Indian Ocean, resembles a smaller kentia palm (*Howea forsteriana*) from a distance, but it makes a powerful impression at an intimate scale, with soft and spiny black bristles that coat its bulging crownshaft, tuft its leaves and trunk rings, and catch light like the coat of a bear. The bristles would seem as useful in capturing moisture from fog as in defending against hungry predators.

A slow-growing tree that originates in moist montane rainforest and cloud forest habitat at an altitude of 2600–6000 feet (800–1830 m) above sea level, *A. crinita* is a curious and intriguing species for small gardens in cool, mild climates such as the California Coast. Where adapted, it tolerates high light levels but can also grow in shade, especially as a young plant. Average annual temperatures in its habitat rate below 63°F (17°C), and at the highest altitudes it may experience frost on rare occasions. This medium-size to small, single-stem palm has a crownshaft covered in spiny bristles that are more like stiff hairs than needles. Its leaves, also dotted with bristles, have pendulous leaflets that respond readily to breezes and resemble those of the kentia palm. The trunk, ranging from 4 to 8 inches (10 to 20 cm) in diameter and reaching as tall as 30 feet (9 m) in habitat, splays out conspicuously at the base, meeting the soil in a mound. Leaf scars lined with spiny hairs ring the brown trunk. The crownshaft bulges with budded inflorescences that open after the leafbases containing them peel off. Like many crownshaft palms, its large and branching inflorescence, ivory-colored and spiny, resembles a pendulous sea creature once it emerges from its unarmed bracts. The internodes between leaf scars are smooth on upper portions of the trunk but develop vertical cracks farther down.

APPEARANCE *leaves*, 6.5–7.5 ft. (2.0–2.3 m) long; *crown span*, 13–15 ft. (4.0–4.6 m); *trunk*, 26–33 ft. (8–10 m) tall and 4–8 in. (10–20 cm) thick

CULTURE *hardiness*, 29°F (–2°C); *exposure*, full sun or part shade; *soil*, well-drained; *climate*, cool tropical, mild warm temperate, Mediterranean

TOLERANCE *drought*, low; *salt*, low

HEAT REQUIREMENT low

USES AND EFFECTS small tree palm, groves, focal point, containers, floral design (leaves, inflorescences, infructescences); *effects*, jungle, tropical, cloud forest, cabinet of curiosities; *special uses*, cool, windy, humid locations; *avoid* hot, immediate coast, desert conditions

ALTERNATE SPECIES *Aiphanes lindeniana, Archontophoenix cunninghamiana, Deckenia nobilis* (tropical, warm subtropical), *Howea forsteriana*

AVAILABILITY rare

Acoelorrhaphe wrightii

EVERGLADES PALM, PAUROTIS PALM

This slow- to medium-growing, medium-size, densely clumping fan palm resembles a cross between a lady palm (*Rhapis* spp.) and a Mexican fan palm (*Washingtonia robusta*) in gestalt. Shiny green fan leaves with waxy gray undersides resemble small washingtonia leaves, down to the thorns on the leaf stalk. They grow atop 4-inch-thick (10-cm) trunks covered in fibrous leafbases that resemble large rhapis stems. Lower leaves pass through a golden phase before dying off to straw color, hanging on briefly, and then breaking off near the base. Petioles (leaf stalks) as

Acoelorrhaphe wrightii grows beside a freshwater pond at Fairchild Tropical Botanic Garden, Miami.

long as the fans allow plenty of light through the crowns. Flower stalks project out from the crowns, creamy green in flower, ripening to golden orange with black fruit. Combined with golden leaves, chestnut-to-gray trunk fibers, and the verdant foliage, these staffs of fruit bring paurotis palms to a peak of color in season.

Properly groomed, the palm's effect is of a rambunctious rhapis in macro, with its leafbase stubs poking out from burlap-fiber sheaths on the trunk and its crowns sharp-edged in silhouette. Although normally upright, or leaning subtly outward from a central point in the clump, stems can take on wandering, sinuous curves, especially in larger, older clumps and shaded specimens. Like all clumping palms, the paurotis can be pruned of unwanted stems to maintain a neater, daintier, or more sculptural cluster, or even to a solitary stem—although the chief appeal of the species is its colonial growth habit.

Native to wet areas of South Florida (hence the common name, Everglades palm), the Yucatán, the Bahamas, Cuba, and the Caribbean coast of Central America, this sole species in its monotypic genus tolerates a surprising amount of cold, with foliage damage appearing when temperatures dip into the mid-20s F (around –4°C). It does not require standing water or even constantly wet soil in cultivation, but it must have access to constant subsurface moisture. It's known to tolerate seasonally brackish and seaside conditions as well as standing, but not stagnant, water.

APPEARANCE *leaves*, 5–6 ft. (1.5–1.8 m) long; *crown span*, 9–12 ft. (2.7–3.7 m); *clump span*, 20 ft. (6.1 m) at base and 30 ft. (9 m) at crown; *trunk*, 20 ft. (6.1 m) tall and 3–6 in. (8–15 cm) thick

CULTURE *hardiness*, 24°F (–4°C); *exposure*, full sun or part shade; *soil*, moist, neutral to acid; *climate*, tropical, subtropical, Mediterranean, desert

TOLERANCE *drought*, low; *salt*, moderate to high

HEAT REQUIREMENT high

USES AND EFFECTS focal point, hedge, screen, water marginal, floral design (leaves, inflorescences, infructescences); *effects*, jungle, tropical, savanna, oasis; *special uses*, swampy, wet locations; *avoid* parched soils

ALTERNATE SPECIES *Mauritiella armata* (tropical), *Rhapis humilis*, *Zombia antillarum* (tropical, warm subtropical)

AVAILABILITY common

Acrocomia

A small genus of moderate-size to large single-stem feather palms—one trunkless, two arborescent—these viciously armed plants are rare in cultivation. Leafbases do not form a crownshaft. The uncommonly available Cuban belly palm, *Acrocomia crispa* (tropical, warm subtropical), is a peculiar but attractive tree with its swollen middle trunk.

Acrocomia aculeata, A. totai

GRUGRU PALM, MACAW PALM, COYOL

This medium- to fast-growing, completely spiny feather palm ranges from Cuba, across the Caribbean, to eastern and southern Brazil, Paraguay, and Argentina. *Acrocomia aculeata* encompasses a number of ecotypes that show different tolerances to cold. The southernmost and most cold-hardy of these has been categorized as *A. totai*. I have seen an acrocomia looking pristine in New Orleans even in the wake of a colder than normal winter that damaged queen palms (*Syagrus romanzoffiana*), and I've seen them dotting cattle pastures in tropical Costa Rica. From a distance, its fine, plumose leaves and slightly bulging trunk give it the look of a queen palm, but closer inspection reveals the beautiful and daunting aura of 1- to 3-inch (3- to 8-cm) spines emerging from the trunk, inflorescences, leafbases, petioles, and leaves. The moderate-size palm's crown ranges from rich green, to yellowish, to silvery green. Its trunk, most often clear of leafbases at maturity, is pale gray, but spines often add a black contrast or shadowing to the color impression.

APPEARANCE *leaves*, 10–12 ft. (3.0–3.7 m) long; *crown span*, 17–22 ft. (5.2–6.7 m); *trunk*, 15–35 ft. (4.6–10.7 m) tall and 9–16 in. (23–41 cm) thick

CULTURE *hardiness*, 22°F (−6°C); *exposure*, full sun or part shade; *soil*, well-drained, intolerant of saturated soils; *climate*, tropical, subtropical, Mediterranean, desert

TOLERANCE *drought*, moderate; *salt*, moderate

HEAT REQUIREMENT moderate

USES AND EFFECTS focal point, security planting, formal lines, staggered-height grouping, savanna planting, floral design (inflorescences, bracts, infructescences); *effects*, jungle, pastoral; *special use*, discourage access; *avoid* locations near walkways and active play areas

ALTERNATE SPECIES *Aiphanes minima, Syagrus romanzoffiana*

AVAILABILITY uncommon

Acrocomia aculeata in the Kapnick Brazilian Garden, designed by Raymond Jungles, Naples Botanical Garden, Florida

A group of three *Adonidia merrillii* curve above a fence in Pat Tierney's garden in Key West, Florida.

Adonidia merrillii

MANILA PALM, CHRISTMAS PALM

The Manila palm is the perfect little (often medium-size) palm tree. It appeals to almost everyone who sees it—its flouncy crown of unarmed, arching feather leaves, tidy green crownshaft, and pert, branched stalk of pale, fluffy flowers and lipstick-red fruits create a cartoonishly cute picture of a palm. Its kawaii character is noticeable especially in its younger phases, when, with its trunk tapering from a swollen base, it possesses the garden equivalent of baby fat while already flowering and fruiting. A medium to fast grower, its stem inclines readily toward the sun, an effect noticeable in clustered specimens that lean gracefully away from each other to reach maximum light levels. *Adonidia merrillii* comes from the Philippines (islands near Palawan) and Malaysian Borneo (islands near Sabah).

APPEARANCE *leaves*, 6–8 ft. (1.8–2.4 m) long; *crown span*, 10–16 ft. (3.0–4.9 m); *trunk*, 25–50 ft. (7.6–15.2 m) tall and 4–12 in. (10–31 cm) thick

CULTURE *hardiness*, 32°F (0°C); *exposure*, full sun or part shade; *soil*, adaptable, well-drained, tolerates calcareous soils; *climate*, tropical, warm subtropical

TOLERANCE *drought*, low; *salt*, high, low soil

HEAT REQUIREMENT high (intolerant of long stretches of cool weather)

USES AND EFFECTS accent, focal point, street tree, groves, uniformity, interior (bright, warm), floral design (leaves, inflorescences, infructescences); *effects*, tropical, tidy, surreal; *special uses*, small, sunny spaces and salty winds; *avoid* cold

ALTERNATE SPECIES *Areca catechu, Hedyscepe canterburyana, Ptychosperma elegans*

AVAILABILITY common

Aiphanes minima, from the
Greater Antilles, at the Naples
Botanical Garden, Florida

Aiphanes

Occurring in montane tropical Andean forests from Venezuela to Bolivia, as well as Panama, Costa Rica, the Antilles, and Brazil, this beautiful genus of very spiny pinnate palms has ruffly leaves with short, wide segments ending in jagged, ripped-looking (praemorse) tips. Leafbases do not form a crownshaft. Mostly moderate in size, they can be single-stem tree palms, trunkless foliage plants, or clustering shrub palms. Several very rare species reach such a high altitude in habitat that they are likely to be adaptable to frost-free, mild Mediterranean and mild temperate climates. Other worthy cultivated species in the genus include *A. horrida*, with plumose leaves, from drier habitats as high as 5300 feet (1615 m), and rare *A. lindeniana*, a suckering species from cloud-forest habitat as high as 8858 feet (2700 m). All are viciously spiny.

Aiphanes minima

MACAW PALM

A medium-size, single-trunk feather palm that defends itself with cruel black spines on its trunk and leaves, this species occurs in the Carribean islands Hispaniola, Puerto Rico, and the Antilles. The effect of the voluptuous crown with slender trunk makes it (and several of its cousins in the genus) one of the thrillingly gravity-defying palms. It vaguely conjures a fishtail palm (*Caryota* spp.) with its broad, rich green, jagged-tipped leaflets typical of its genus, but it is not bipinnate, and its armature sets it apart from the closer likes of plants in the *Ptychosperma* and *Veitchia* genera as well. Best in shade as a young palm, the macaw palm grows well in full sun as it begins its trunking ascent. It looks best when planted in numbers and must be sited where its piercing parts won't impinge on casual enjoyment of the landscape—keep it away from paths and a sufficient distance from seating areas to lessen the risk of the spines hurting people.

APPEARANCE *leaves*, 6–8 ft. (1.8–2.4 m) long; *crown span*, 12–15 ft. (3.7–4.6 m); *trunk*, 20–50 ft. (6.1–15.2 m) tall and 2.5–8.0 in. (6–20 cm) thick

CULTURE *hardiness*, 32°F (0°C); *exposure*, full sun or part shade; *soil*, rich, well-drained; *climate*, tropical, warm subtropical

TOLERANCE *drought*, low; *salt*, low

HEAT REQUIREMENT moderate–high

USES AND EFFECTS groves, focal point (cluster), scattered accent tree within a viewshed or under canopy, floral design (leaves, inflorescences, infructescences); *effects*, jungle, curiosity; *special use*, security; *avoid* frost, heavy and poorly draining soils, prolonged drought, sun at early stages

ALTERNATE SPECIES *Ceroxylon* spp. and *Howea forsteriana* (cooler, mild climates); *Ptychosperma elegans*, *Veitchia joannis*, and other *Veitchia* spp. (tropical, warm subtropical)

AVAILABILITY uncommon

Allagoptera

These small to medium-size feather palms, most clustering and trunkless, occur in Brazil and adjacent Argentina, Bolivia, Paraguay, and Uruguay, in seasonally dry woodland and scrub, including along the seashore. They are useful as foliage and informal hedge plants. Leaves of most species are plumose, emerging from a subterranean to subaerial stem. Leafbases do not form a crownshaft. One species, *A. caudescens*, is a moderate-size, slow-growing tree palm suited to subtropical, tropical, and the mildest Mediterranean climates. In form it is quite unlike its cousins in the genus: it has flat leaves and an upright trunk revealed by the abscission of its leafbases in maturity. Not detailed here are other worthy cultivated species in the genus: *A. campestris* and *A. leucocalyx* (both inland, more cold-hardy species with similar growth habits and size, subtropical, Mediterranean, tropical), and *A. brevicalyx* (similar to *A. arenaria* in habit, habitat, and requirements, with better fruit production).

Allagoptera arenaria

SEASHORE PALM

The seashore palm is called *coco de praia* (coconut of the beach) in its native Brazil, where it occupies dunes and sandy soils along the Atlantic coast from the states of Paraná and São Paulo in the subtropical south to Sergipe in the tropical north. Usually branching underground into multiple growing points, it lacks aboveground stems and forms a mass of plumose, shiny green leaves with white-silver, waxy undersides, edges, and upper-surface midribs of leaflets. Notes of yellow mark older, senescing leaves, leaflet midribs, and the inside of the peduncular bract. The bract surrounds a spike-shaped inflorescence that develops into a cob-shaped cluster of edible green and orange fruits.

Allagoptera arenaria in the Kapnick Brazilian Garden, Naples Botanical Garden, Florida

This slow-growing species makes a lively, elegant foliage plant or hedge, not only in the salty, beachside conditions to which it's eminently suited, but also, along with its hardier cousins in the genus, in inland gardens.

APPEARANCE *leaves*, 3–8 ft. (0.9–2.4 m) long; *crown span*, 13–15 ft. (4.0–4.6 m); *trunk*, mostly subterranean, branching, occasionally barely above ground

CULTURE *hardiness*, 25°F (−4°C); *exposure*, full sun; *soil*, sandy or heavy; *climate*, subtropical, tropical, warm temperate, Mediterranean

TOLERANCE *drought*, moderate; *salt*, very high

HEAT REQUIREMENT moderate–high

USES AND EFFECTS informal hedges, focal point, containers, floral design (leaves, inflorescences, infructescences); *effects*, beach, grassland; *special uses*, sandy, salty, beach locations; *avoid* shade, cool-summer climate, poorly draining soils

ALTERNATE SPECIES *Arenga engleri*, *Brahea moorei* (multiplanted)

AVAILABILITY uncommon

Archontophoenix

Australia's eastern coastal rainforests are home to this genus of six elegant crown-shaft palms, moderate to large, two of which are very popular in tropical, subtropical, warm temperate, and Mediterranean landscapes. The bangalow, or king palm, *A. cunninghamiana*, ranging into the temperate zone as far as the southern coast of New South Wales, is one of the more cool-tolerant tree palms with a crownshaft.

Undescribed here but worthy cultivated species in the genus include *A. maxima*, *A. myolensis*, and *A. tuckeri*, all similar in requirements and function to *A. alexandrae*.

Archontophoenix alexandrae

ALEXANDRA PALM

A clean, elegant, unarmed, moderate to tall palm tree from tropical coastal rainforests of Queensland, Australia, the Alexandra palm thrives in warm, moist subtropical and tropical regions and can be cultivated in warm, frost-free Mediterranean climates. Rich green, flat feather leaves, twisting from horizontal close to the stem to vertical toward their tips, present a more coherent crown than its southerly, more cold-tolerant cousin *A. cunninghamiana*. All members of the genus are self-cleaning, with beautiful crownshafts; *A. alexandrae*'s is pale green, marrying nicely with the pale undersides of its leaves, and matching the green of the first several internodes of the trunk below. White flowers on white-branched, pendulous inflorescences emerge from kayak-shaped bracts below the crownshaft, attract honeybees, and develop into bright red fruits.

Archontophoenix alexandrae at Hale Mohalu, Big Island, Hawai'i

APPEARANCE *leaves*, 10–15 ft. (3.0–4.6 m) long; *crown span*, 15–25 ft. (4.6–7.6 m); *trunk*, 60 ft. (18 m) tall and 8–11 in. (20–28 cm) thick, with a swollen base to 20 in. (51 cm)

CULTURE *hardiness*, 29°F (–2°C); *exposure*, full sun or shade; *soil*, well-drained, moist, undemanding of fertility; *climate*, subtropical, tropical, mild warm temperate, Mediterranean

TOLERANCE *drought*, low to moderate; *salt*, low

HEAT REQUIREMENT moderate

USES AND EFFECTS allées, groves, focal point, canopy, floral design (leafbases, inflorescences, infructescences); *effects*, forest, jungle, formal, elegant; *special uses*, shade, streamside, steep slopes; *avoid* frost, drought, windy (especially coastal) sites

ALTERNATE SPECIES *Ceroxylon alpinum*, *C. echinulatum*, *C. parvifrons* (cool, mild climates); *Dictyosperma album* (tropical, subtropical)

AVAILABILITY common to uncommon

Archontophoenix cunninghamiana

KING PALM, BANGALOW PALM, PICCABEEN PALM

Known as the king palm in the United States (a literal translation of the botanical name) or, in Australia, bangalow palm (for its leafbases' use as a water carrier) or piccabeen palm, *A. cunninghamiana* is the hardiest member of this widely culti-vated small genus from eastern Australia. Its natural range reaches moist forests, from Durras Mountain, at 35°S latitude, on the Pacific coast east of Canberra, to 21°S in Queensland. Its midlatitude origins enable it to grow in mild temperate areas with long, cool winters and less-than-torrid summers, as long as its roots get consistent moisture and it sees only light frosts. It also grows in those hot-summer climates where winter brings stretches of cool weather, such as central Florida.

The king palm is a medium- to fast-growing stately tree with a tropical air, its languid crown of green feather leaves arranged in a crownshaft at the top of the smooth, ringed trunk. The soft, gently arching leaves, green on both surfaces, twist their orientation from horizontal near the base to vertical at their tips, the upper leaflets folding and flopping over and contributing to the palm's somewhat informal look. Undersides of the leaflets have scattered short, brown, hairlike scales called ramenta.

Starting as a swelling hidden inside the oldest leaf on the crownshaft, the flower cluster progresses to a green, squid head–shaped sheath revealed beneath the crownshaft when the lowest leaf peels off. It splits open suddenly, unleashing showy amethyst blooms that hang straight down in chains on the branches of the flower cluster. Round, deep red fruits form thereafter, adding even more color. The fleshy, army-green crownshaft, subtly textured with fine brown scales, reveals not only developing flower clusters in its pregnant swelling, but also sometimes rings of developing trunk, as if it were melted, thick and precise, onto the summit of the trunk.

Like many crownshaft palms, *Archontophoenix* species begin to develop a ringed, woody trunk—often deceptively thin—at an early age, before fully mature leaves have developed. The upper few internodes on the trunk are often green but quickly turn to a brown-gray that fades on older trees in sunshine to a pale silvery gray. Young plants can fit nicely into narrow spaces before the trunk thickens and crown expands, at which point the tree's height clears pathways and living spaces. Young plants will reach toward brighter light, producing a leaning trunk; seedlings planted close together become clusters picturesquely curving outward from a mutual center point.

APPEARANCE *leaves*, 6–10 ft. (1.8–3.0 m) long; *crown span*, 12–16 ft. (3.7–4.9 m); *trunk*, 25–60 ft. (7.5–18.0 m) tall and 6–12 in. (15–31 cm) thick

CULTURE *hardiness*, 25°F (−4°C); *exposure*, full sun or shade; *soil*, moist, adaptable; *climate*, mild warm temperate, subtropical, Mediterranean

TOLERANCE *drought*, low; *salt*, low

HEAT REQUIREMENT moderate

USES AND EFFECTS accent, focal point, street tree, allées, groves, canopy, floral design (leafbases, inflorescences, infructescences); *effects*, tropical, tidy, formal; *special uses*, in clusters, groves; *avoid* drought, windy (especially coastal) sites

ALTERNATE SPECIES *Dictyosperma album*, *Satakentia liukiuensis*

AVAILABILITY common to uncommon

Archontophoenix purpurea

MOUNT LEWIS KING PALM

Archontophoenix purpurea is the most colorful member of its small Australian genus. The color of its crownshaft can be deep purple-red or a subtle gray-mauve; the crownshaft bulges slightly at the base without tapering upward, further setting apart the pigmented cylinder from the slightly thinner trunk below. The moderate to slow grower is a robust and gross-textured palm with flat pinnate leaves with pale undersides that have conspicuous ramenta. Its budded flower cluster is very conspicuous after appearing under the cast-off lowest leafbase but before emerging from the sheathing bracts, and its fruits are large—1 inch (3 cm) in diameter—and showy red. Its low-mountain origins—up to

4000 feet (1219 m)—give it a slight advantage in cooler climates over its cousin *A. alexandrae*, but it is less hardy than *A. cunninghamiana* and prefers shade as a young plant.

APPEARANCE *leaves*, 6–10 ft. (1.8–3.0 m) long; *crown span*, 15–20 ft. (4.6–6.1 m); *trunk*, 40 ft. (12 m) tall and 12–18 in. (31–46 cm) thick

CULTURE *hardiness*, 28°F (−2°C); *exposure*, shade when young, then sun; *soil*, well-drained, moist, undemanding of fertility; *climate*, subtropical, tropical, warm Mediterranean

TOLERANCE *drought*, low; *salt*, low

HEAT REQUIREMENT moderate

USES AND EFFECTS allées, groves, single or grouped focal point, canopy, floral design (leafbases, inflorescences, infructescences); *effects*, color, forest, jungle, formal, elegant; *special uses*, shade, streamside, steep slopes; *avoid* frost, drought, windy sites

ALTERNATE SPECIES *Ceroxylon alpinum*, *C. echinulatum*, *C. parvifrons* (cool, mild climates); *Dictyosperma album* (tropical, subtropical); *Satakentia liukiuensis*

AVAILABILITY rare to uncommon

Areca

A large genus of tropical crownshaft palms from India and Southeast Asia through Malesia to the Solomon Islands includes a few commonly available ornamentals.

Areca catechu

BETEL-NUT PALM

The plant for which the palm family, Arecaceae, is named, the vibrant betel-nut palm occurs as a plant in wet tropical regions of southern India, Southeast Asia, the Malay Archipelago, Melanesia, and Micronesia. This fast-growing palm is planted or semicultivated for use of its fruits as a stimulant chewed in combination with the leaf of *Piper betle*, lime, and sometimes other ingredients such as spices or tobacco. The extensive practice is akin to tea drinking, tobacco smoking, or khat chewing. The plant's appearance marks a wet tropical landscape in that wide swath, in a manner not unlike that of *Bactris gasipaes*, the peach palm, in Central and South America.

The normal form is a luscious, single-stem tree palm reaching up to 50 feet (15.2 m), with arching, dark green feather leaves. The crownshaft and white-ringed, relatively thin trunk are equally green. Leaflets rise off the rachis in a V-shaped cross section and are broad and often fused in young plants, especially at the far end of the feather. The inflorescence bursts out of its casing of bracts below the crownshaft, a stiff, brushy cluster of fragrant flowers leading to attractive 1- to 2-inch (3- to 6-cm) bright red fruits. Cultivars include dwarf forms and color forms with yellowish or reddish crownshafts, trunks, and even foliage. Plural planting suits its scale—slender and tall.

APPEARANCE *leaves*, 6–10 ft. (1.8–3.0 m) long; *crown span*, 12 ft. (3.7 m); *trunk*, 50 ft. (15.2 m) tall and 8–12 in. (20–31 cm) thick

CULTURE *hardiness*, 34°F (1°C); *exposure*, sun or part shade; *soil*, well-drained, moist, fertile, acid; *climate*, tropical, warm subtropical

TOLERANCE *drought*, low; *salt*, moderate

HEAT REQUIREMENT high

USES AND EFFECTS allées, groves, grouped

focal point, floral design (leaves, inflorescences, infructescences); *effects*, Asian, Southeast Asian, pastoral, color; *special use*, medicinal; *avoid* frost, drought

ALTERNATE SPECIES *Adonidia merrillii*, *Geonoma undata* (cool tropical, mild warm temperate, Mediterranean), *Hedyscepe canterburyana*, *Ptychosperma elegans*

AVAILABILITY common to uncommon

Areca vestiaria, orange-crownshaft form, at Hale Mohalu, Big Island, Hawai'i

Areca vestiaria

Use this fast-growing palm in the tropics, warm subtropics, and even mildest warm Mediterranean zones for its breathtaking foliage patterns, its colors (green, orange, red, and burgundy), its clustering habit and moderate size, and as a permeable, less-aggressive alternative to bamboo. It can also be maintained with careful attention indoors. One cultivar with darker red crownshaft coloration produces burgundy-colored new leaves. Intermittently fused leaflets emphasize the pleated nature of the leaf blade.

APPEARANCE *leaves*, 3–5 ft. (0.9–1.5 m) long; *crown span*, 5–8 ft. (1.5–2.4 m); *clump span*, 20 ft. (6.1 m); *trunk*, 20 ft. (6.1 m) tall and 3–4 in. (8–10 cm) thick

CULTURE *hardiness*, 32°F (0°C); *exposure*, sun or part shade; *soil*, well-drained, moist, fertile, acid; *climate*, tropical, warm subtropical, warm Mediterranean (tolerates cool spells)

TOLERANCE *drought*, low; *salt*, low

HEAT REQUIREMENT moderate

USES AND EFFECTS focal point, shrub, screen, hedge, bamboo alternative, floral design (leaves, inflorescences, infructescences); *effects*, Asian, Southeast Asian; *special use*, medicinal; *avoid* frost, drought

ALTERNATE SPECIES *Chamaedorea costaricana*, *C. tepejilote* (multiplanted; tropical, subtropical, mild warm temperate, Mediterranean), *Cyrtostachys renda*, *Ptychosperma macarthurii*, *P. schefferi* (tropical, subtropical)

AVAILABILITY uncommon

Arenga

Related to palms in the genus *Caryota*, the fishtail palms, this group of twenty feather-palm species ranges from northern Australia to Japan's Ryukyu Islands, China, and India. Leafbases do not form a crownshaft. The stems of both the clustering and solitary species in the genus are monocarpic, producing flowers and fruit at maturity at the leaf internodes, a process that can take years to play out; clustering species continue to produce new stems and thus persist after the demise of a fruiting stem. Other worthy cultivated species in the genus include *A. micrantha*, with a larger growth habit and lovely coppery and mauve foliage tones, which thrives in cool-summer conditions as well as seasonal heat; *A. pinnata*, a tall (to 50 feet, or 15.2 m), single-trunk species with a shuttlecock crown that is a key source of sugar and alcohol in the Malayan Archipelago, amenable to subtropical and warm Mediterranean conditions; and the large, mesmerizing, clustering *A. undulatifolia*, with wavy leaflets, suited to tropical and subtropical conditions.

Arenga engleri

Defying the iconic and regular form of the palm tree, *A. engleri* forms a multistem shrub and foliage cluster, not a symmetrical tree. Its flat, feathery leaves are rich matte green above and silvery beneath, emerging from short trunks clothed in black fibrous leafbases, the broad leaflets ending in an irregular (praemorse) apex, like strips of thick paper with a deckle edge. Leafbases on older stems peel off, especially in wetter climates, to reveal a gray, ringed trunk. Rendered in green, silver, and black, this slow-growing palm makes an impression as a single specimen, dotted as clusters under high canopy, grown in a container, or even as a dynamic hedge.

The most memorable use I've seen of the hardy Taiwan sugar palm was in a planter tucked between a small swimming pool and a courtyard wall at the Hotel Le Marais in the New Orleans French Quarter. Its eruption of large leaves against brick brought vivid life (and the pleasing fragrance of its flowers) to a formal, urban space in daylight and left mesmerizing shadows from pool lights on the walls at night. Clusters of gold-yellow flowers start to develop at the top of older trunks and progress downward from each leafbase scar until fruit ripens on the lowest cluster. The flowers' fragrance carries on the breeze. Preceded by diminishing size leaves at the top of the stem, these inflorescences signal the end of the trunk's lifespan, but not that of the plant—it continually produces new stems from the base.

APPEARANCE *leaves*, 5–7 ft. (1.5–2.1 m) long; *crown span*, 10–15 ft. (3.0–4.6 m); *clump span*, 10–30 ft. (3–9 m); *trunk*, 2–4 ft. (0.6–1.2 m) tall and 4–8 in. (10–20 cm) thick

CULTURE *hardiness*, 18°F (−8°C); *exposure*, full sun or part shade; *soil*, moist, well-drained; *climate*, tropical, subtropical, warm Mediterranean

TOLERANCE *drought*, low; *salt*, moderate

HEAT REQUIREMENT moderate

USES AND EFFECTS informal hedge, focal point, foliage accent, mixed border, in containers, floral design (leaves, inflorescences, avoid handling fruit); *effects*, jungle, tropical; *special use*, fragrance; *avoid* chilly, immediate coast, desert conditions

ALTERNATE SPECIES *Allagoptera* spp., *Arenga micrantha*, *A. ryukyuensis*, *Serenoa repens*

AVAILABILITY uncommon

Attalea

Many similar species occupy this tropical and subtropical genus of mostly huge, mostly solitary tree palms with upright, shuttlecock crowns of feather leaves. Leafbases do not form a crownshaft. Cultivated species include *A. butyracea* (yagua palm), *A. cohune* (cohune palm), *A. dubia* (bacuacu palm), and many others.

An unidentified *Attalea* species at the Naples Botanical Garden, Florida

A genus of (mostly) massive, solitary feather palms with upright, often enormous, leaves in feather-duster crowns, the attaleas are plentiful (with nearly seventy species) in warm tropical areas of Mexico, Central America, the Caribbean, and, especially, South America. One attractive species, *A. dubia*, the bacuacu palm, occurs naturally in the coastal rainforest of southern Brazil from the state of Rio de Janeiro to the subtropical state of Santa Catarina, and has proven reliable in cultivation in warm Mediterranean climate and subtropical parts of the United States, areas where summers are warm and winters rarely dip below freezing. Slow-growing, attaleas produce long, upright leaves well before forming trunks, contributing their tall, arching ladders of foliage to gardens for many years before taking on the form of a palm tree with hefty trunk and shuttlecock crown. Leaves vary from stiff and flat to soft and plumose (*A. dubia*). Flat leaf planes of *A. butyracea* and *A. cohune* twist from tangent to the trunk axis at their bases to perpendicular at their nodding tips. Some species never form aboveground trunks, remaining fountains of foliage for their lifespan. Paddle-like leafbases of most species remain attached to the trunk for many years. Groomed trees display bold patterns below the crown before leafbase stubs peel to show the naked trunk.

The transition of attaleas from a monumental upright fountain of leaves to a grand feather-duster of a palm tree exemplifies the need for designers to plan for the long-term metamorphosis of tree palms. In the case of attaleas, the upright growth of the leaves, however tall, enables designers to fit them into spots narrower than many other large tree palms will fit.

APPEARANCE *leaves*, 10–30 ft. (3–9 m) long; *crown span*, 20–35 ft. (6.1–10.7 m); *trunk*, 20–60 ft. (6.1–18.3 m) tall and 10–25 in. (25–64 cm) thick

CULTURE *hardiness*, 28°F (–2°C) (*A. dubia*); *exposure*, full sun or part shade; *soil*, well-drained; *climate*, tropical, cool tropical, subtropical, mild warm temperate, Mediterranean

TOLERANCE *drought*, low; *salt*, varies

HEAT REQUIREMENT moderate to high

USES AND EFFECTS foliage drama, large tree palm, focal point, hedgerow, avenue planting, grove, canopy; *effects*, jungle, tropical, savanna, formal; *special use*, monumental planting for less-than-spacious spots; *avoid* containers, chilly, frosty, dry conditions

ALTERNATE SPECIES *Ceroxylon quindiuense* and *C. ventricosum* (cool regions), *Parajubaea torallyi*, *Raphia* spp. (tropical)

AVAILABILITY uncommon

Beccariophoenix

Three solitary-trunked, unarmed species rather new to cultivation make up this feather-leaf genus of large trees from Madagascar. Leafbases do not form a crownshaft. Another worthy cultivated species in the genus is *B. madagascariensis* (similar scale and function to *B. fenestralis*, but less cold-tolerant).

Beccariophoenix fenestralis

MADAGASCAR WINDOWS PALM

This large, slow-growing feather palm resembles a beefed-up coconut palm, but without the huge coconuts. Especially in youth, many of its glossy leaflets cling to one another toward their outer points while separating closer to the rachis, making linear windows. It's a majestic tree for spacious landscapes in tropical and warm subtropical climates.

APPEARANCE *leaves*, 15 ft. (4.6 m) long; *crown span*, 25–30 ft. (7.6–9.1 m); *trunk*, 40 ft. (12.2 m) tall and 12 in. (31 cm) thick

CULTURE *hardiness*, 30°F (–1°C); *exposure*, full sun or part shade; *soil*, well-drained; *climate*, tropical, warm subtropical

TOLERANCE *drought*, low; *salt*, low

HEAT REQUIREMENT high

USES AND EFFECTS foliage drama, large tree palm, focal point, hedgerow, avenue planting, grove, canopy, floral design (leaves, inflorescences, infructescences); *effects*, beach, tropical, jungle, formal; *special use*, foliage; *avoid* containers, chilly, frosty, dry conditions

ALTERNATE SPECIES *Cocos nucifera*, *Parajubaea* spp.

AVAILABILITY uncommon

Beccariophoenix fenestralis at Hale Mohalu, Big Island, Hawai'i

Beccariophoenix alfredii

HIGH PLATEAU COCONUT PALM

Palm fanciers making gardens in cooler or frost-prone climates are always looking for coconut mimics that will grow beyond the tropics, because the beautiful and iconic *Cocos nucifera* haunts our dreams yet requires near-tropical and warmer conditions to thrive. Most of the best look-alikes, such as species of *Parajubaea* and *Jubaeopsis*, are cousins of the coconut. This fellow member of the tribe, the high plateau coconut palm from the central plateau region of Madagascar, may bear the closest resemblance to the coconut palm of all. Like the coconut, its flat, bright green leaves with yellowish leafbases divide into regularly arranged leaflets with prominent midribs. The feathery leaf blade twists from horizontal as it arches outward to near-vertical at the apex, another coconutty characteristic. Its thin, densely ringed, gray-brown trunk (neatly revealed after a juvenile period of clinging leafbases) resembles the coconut's in proportion to crown, stature, texture, and color. How does the high plateau coconut palm differ from the real thing? It makes no coconuts, to be sure: Inflorescences shaped like a drum brush occur beneath the leaves and produce small, red-purple, mandarin-shaped fruits. Rather than an eccentric, leaning habit, *B. alfredii* takes an upright stance, and instead of producing a spherical, languid crown, its leaves drop off once they fall much below the horizontal, resembling only the manicured coconut palms of public landscapes (where frequent pruning removes not only the big coconuts, but also the lower third of the leaves). Our mimic also diverges from the true coconut palm in being unlikely to tolerate nearly the same intensity of coastal exposure.

The high plateau coconut grows slowly in sandy soil along river courses in a seasonally dry habitat at an altitude of about 3400 feet (1036 m) above sea level, an origin that confers tolerance of mild frosts, fluctuating humidity, and cool weather in cultivation. New to cultivation, young plants are succeeding in Southern California, South and Central Florida, Hawai'i, and Australia.

APPEARANCE *leaves*, 12–15 ft. (3.7–4.6 m) long; *crown span*, 25–30 ft. (7.6–9.1 m); *trunk*, 40 ft. (12.2 m) tall and 12 in. (31 cm) thick

CULTURE *hardiness*, 26°F (–3°C); *exposure*, full sun or part shade; *soil*, well-drained; *climate*, tropical, cool tropical, subtropical, Mediterranean

TOLERANCE *drought*, low; *salt*, presumed low

HEAT REQUIREMENT moderate

USES AND EFFECTS foliage drama, focal point, hedgerow, avenue planting, grove, canopy, floral design (leaves, inflorescences, infructescences); *effects*, beach, tropical, savanna, formal; *special use*, monumental planting for less-than-spacious spots; *avoid* containers, chilly, frosty, drought conditions

ALTERNATE SPECIES *Cocos nucifera*, *Parajubaea* spp.

AVAILABILITY uncommon

Bismarckia

Native to savanna environments on the seasonally dry western side of Madagascar, bismarckia palms thrive in full sun from a young age and tolerate some drought once established. A dioecious palm, it requires two individuals of different sexes grown in proximity to produce viable seed.

Bismarckia nobilis

BISMARCK PALM

Huge, thick-textured, silvery blue fans attract almost everyone who comes across this grand native of Madagascar. It serves as a gateway to palm love for many people and becomes a prime subject of zonal denial for those outside the warm, mostly frost-free climate it prefers. Many very young plants in full sun display purple-red tones, and a less often cultivated (and less cold-hardy) green form cannot be left out. But the dominant impression is of silvery blue gigantism. Leaf segments remain stiff to their ends, and the deeply undulate costapalmate leaves render the crown a pleated, labyrinthine space—an Alice in Wonderland fascination to gardeners and visitors for years before forming a trunk, the leaves resonant in wind with rising age. Powerful, unarmed, fleece-tufted, mostly smooth-edged petioles connect the heavy fans to the trunk, at which point the leafbase splits, opening into a triangular pattern.

In warm-summer climates, established plants can regrow from rare freezes to the mid-20s F (–5°C), but the species reaches its pinnacle in subtropical and tropical areas, including the wet tropical parts of Hawai'i. In California, it's best to avoid transplanting, but in more humid areas, progressive root-pruning of trunked plants allows for wholesale field-growing and transplanting. In marginal climates, its enemies are long, cool, moist winters and cold soils as much as frosty temperatures. In California, plants in semiarid, well-drained Inland Valley locations with long, hot summers have survived damage from nightly freezes occurring over weeks, while plants tried in cool-summer, mild-winter locations grow slowly, if at all, and often succumb to fungal diseases. The popular silvery blue form is more cold-hardy than the green form.

APPEARANCE *leaves*, 8–10 ft. (2.4–3.0 m) long; *crown span*, 18–22 ft. (5.5–6.7 m); *trunk*, 20–70 ft. (6.1–21.3 m) tall and 12–18 in. (31–46 cm) thick

CULTURE *hardiness*, 23°F (–5°C); *exposure*, full sun or part shade; *soil*, well-drained; *climate*, tropical, subtropical, desert, warm Mediterranean

TOLERANCE *drought*, moderate to high; *salt*, moderate

HEAT REQUIREMENT high

USES AND EFFECTS focal point, monumental stands, canopy, containers (as juvenile), floral design (leaves, inflorescences, infructescences); *effects*, savanna, tropical, desert, grandeur; *special use*, warm desert gardens; *avoid* heavy, wet, cold soils and deep shade

ALTERNATE SPECIES *Brahea armata*, *B. clara*, *Latania loddigesii* (more gracile, less hardy), *Sabal uresana* (more cold-hardy)

AVAILABILITY common to uncommon

Borassus

Five species of large to very large, solitary, armed, costapalmate palm trees range from tropical and southern Africa to Madagascar, South Asia, Southeast Asia, and the Malesia region. *Borassus aethiopum* is a massive tree with a thick trunk worthy of use in the grandest of spaces in tropical and subtropical landscape design. *Borassus flabellifer* is one of the most economically important palms.

Borassus flabellifer

PALMYRA PALM

The palmyra palm, or toddy palm, *B. flabellifer* is cultivated widely in South and Southeast Asia and is one of the most useful and celebrated of palm species. A big, brutish tree adapted to frost-free tropical and subtropical monsoonal climates and thriving at the seacoast, it is rarely used in ornamental landscapes. It's often seen in photographs of Cambodia's Angkor Wat. Its often golden petioles; husky trunk with persistent dark, thorny leafbases split at the base; and large black fruits accented with yellow lend a rough, muscular air to a garden. Over time, these moderate-growing trees become more graceful, leafbases sloughing off to reveal a dark trunk that rises to dominate their scene at heights of 40 to 60 feet (12.2–18.3 m) or more.

APPEARANCE *leaves*, 12–15 ft. (3.7–4.6 m) long; *crown span*, 22 ft. (6.7 m); *trunk*, 20–60 ft. (6.1–18.3 m) tall and 3 ft. (0.9 m) thick

CULTURE *hardiness*, 30°F (–1°C); *exposure*, full sun or part shade; *soil*, well-drained; *climate*, tropical, subtropical, desert

TOLERANCE *drought*, moderate; *salt*, high

HEAT REQUIREMENT high

USES AND EFFECTS focal point, monumental stands, skyline tree, floral design (leaves, inflorescences, infructescences); *effects*, savanna, tropical, desert, grandeur; *special use*, warm desert gardens; *avoid* wet, cold soils and shade

ALTERNATE SPECIES *Brahea clara, Sabal uresana, Washingtonia filifera* (all more cold-hardy)

AVAILABILITY common to uncommon

Brahea

Brahea is a genus of armed, monoecious fan palms of Mexico and Central America. Most are medium-size to large solitary tree palms. Many are drought-tolerant and originate in desert, semiarid, and seasonally dry regions. Their leaves are costapalmate, most species have beautiful teeth on the petioles, and their trunks are thick and heavy in relation to their crowns. Transplanting most *Brahea* species from the field requires extra care—larger root balls, digging in phases—and field-dug plants take extra time to become established in their new sites.

The genus name *Erythea*, a synonym of *Brahea*, conjures an image from Greek mythology of nymphs secluded on remote western islands—and this is the situation of *B. edulis* (syn. *E. edulis*), the species endemic to Guadalupe Island, a volcanic island 150 miles (240 km) west of northern Baja California.

Brahea armata at Bergstrom Gardens, Atherton, California

Brahea armata

MEXICAN BLUE PALM

Brahea armata, the best-known species in the genus, possesses a crown of silvery blue, thorny stalked leaves atop a thick trunk. Dead leaves stay attached for many years on younger trees, forming a thatch skirt on some and a subtly spiraling pattern of leaf stubs on those that are pruned. With age, leaves detach spontaneously, revealing a finely ringed trunk surface with regular leaf-stub detachment scars. Foliage color ranges from nearly white to blue-green to olive-green, but most cultivated plants have been selected from the silvery end of the spectrum. Contributing to the color is a waxy coating on the leaves; brush the surface and a powdery residue lingers on your fingertips. Slow-growing, the Mexican blue palm makes an outpouring of flower clusters when it reaches maturity—usually with several feet of trunk. The soft, cream-colored stoles arch deftly out of the glaucous foliage in unison and hang straight down, reaching well below the leaf crown, even to the ground in shorter plants.

With its heft and conspicuous bloom, the Mexican blue palm serves well as a solitary tree and focal point in the landscape. It's spectacular as well in trios, duos, and groves amid greener plants, or as scattered punctuation in a desert garden. Its slow growth recommends it for container growing and use as a foliage element. At the Los Angeles International Airport, a planting of young

Mexican blue palms with birds of paradise (*Strelitzia reginae*) greets travelers, the silver-blue fans setting off the orange-and-indigo flowers and army-green foliage of the city's official flower. Its cold-hardiness (plants have survived 14°F, or –10°C, with minimal damage) enables it to succeed throughout inland California, southern Nevada, and Arizona up to 2000 feet (610 m) in elevation, and some veteran trees even grow at Locarno on Lake Maggiore in Switzerland. Plants in hot, rainy summer regions falter, and the species isn't useful in humid subtropical and moist tropical areas.

I speculate that the unusual drought-tolerance of *B. armata* (facilitated by its bluish leaf veneer, heavy trunk, and fleshy roots) is an adaptation to competition with other trees and arborescent plants in its oasislike habitat. Native to desert canyons of northern Baja California almost up to the California border, the Mexican blue palm cohabitates with the California fan palm along certain creeks, occupying drier upslope sites and yielding the moister creekside to *Washingtonia filifera*. Meanwhile, its slower growth and shorter stature may also have arisen from a reduced need to compete with other shadowing vegetation in sites at a remove from permanent water.

APPEARANCE *leaves*, 6 ft. (1.8 m) long; *crown span*, 15 ft. (4.6 m); *trunk*, 40 ft. (12.2 m) tall and 2 ft. (0.6 m) thick

CULTURE *hardiness*, 15°F (–9°C); *exposure*, full sun; *soil*, well-drained; *climate*, desert, Mediterranean, warm temperate

TOLERANCE *drought*, high; *salt*, high

HEAT REQUIREMENT moderate

USES AND EFFECTS foliage element, flowering focal point, avenue tree, container plant, floral design (leaves, inflorescences, infructescences); *effects*, desert, color; *special uses*, desert gardens, foliage compositions, companion to succulents and spiny plants; *avoid* shade, moist soils, heavy fertilizing

ALTERNATE SPECIES *Bismarckia nobilis, Brahea clara, Chamaerops humilis* var. *argentea, Sabal uresana, Washingtonia filifera*

AVAILABILITY common

Brahea clara

CLARA PALM

The clara palm is a botanically indistinct but horticulturally important sister of the Mexican blue palm. Its habitat is the eastern side of the Gulf of California, in Sonora, Mexico, where monsoonal rains and humid gulf air regularly rake the landscape in the summer and fall months. This plant, with softer, more sonorous and animated fans held on longer petioles than its sibling, grows faster than the Baja race, produces shorter though still conspicuous flower clusters, and tolerates moister, cooler conditions than its brother across the gulf, and it may be nearly as cold-hardy. It's also rarer in nurseries and landscapes. Rather new to

Brahea clara at The Huntington
Botanical Gardens, San Marino,
California

the commercial trade, it tends to be more varied in form and color, although many nearly match the most brilliant Baja California plants.

For the first few years, this moderate-growing palm will need regular dry-season irrigation to get established, but after a while it will require only occasional deep watering to look good.

Spent leaves may remain attached to the trunk in the manner of the familiar *Washingtonia robusta* (Mexican fan palm), or they can be pruned off as they fade from blue-green to yellow and finally to straw color. Leafstalks connecting the big fans to the trunk are armed with curved teeth along a yellow margin—menacing to the eye but less painful than most roses' thorns.

At Flora Grubb Gardens, we're bullish on claras. We hope they'll become popular additions to the landscape in the years to come. They're easy to care for and add a sensuous silvery tone to the garden.

APPEARANCE *leaves*, 7 ft. (2.1 m) long; *crown span*, 16 ft. (4.9 m); *trunk*, 50 ft. (15 m) tall and 18 in. (46 cm) thick

CULTURE *hardiness*, 18°F (−8°C); *exposure*, full sun or part shade; *soil*, well-drained; *climate*, desert, Mediterranean, subtropical

TOLERANCE *drought*, high; *salt*, high

HEAT REQUIREMENT low

USES AND EFFECTS flowering focal point, avenue and grove tree, floral design (leaves, inflorescences, infructescences); *effects*, desert, color, sound; *special uses*, warm desert tree, foliage compositions, coastal gardens; *avoid* shade, wet soils

ALTERNATE SPECIES *Bismarckia nobilis, Brahea armata, Chamaerops humilis* var. *argentea, Sabal uresana, Washingtonia filifera*

AVAILABILITY uncommon

Brahea brandegeei

SAN JOSÉ HESPER PALM

The San José Hesper palm comes from the southern third of Baja California. It's a tall tree (to 50 feet, or 15.2 m) with a thinner trunk than most other species in the genus, tolerant of extremes of desert heat plus high humidity and temperatures to 25°F (−4°C) and below, and one of the few *Brahea* species successful in Florida and similar climates. Its green leaves with glaucous undersides and inflorescences shorter than the leaves make a dense crown; old leaves hang onto the trunk in a skirt for many years before sloughing off with age. Compared to its compatriot, *Washingtonia robusta, B. brandegeei* is a neater looking, smaller, more elegant species for similar functions in the landscape.

APPEARANCE *leaves*, 7 ft. (2.1 m) long; *crown span*, 15 ft. (4.6 m); *trunk*, 50 ft. (15.2 m) tall and 12 in. (31 cm) thick

CULTURE *hardiness*, 25°F (−4°C); *exposure*, full sun or part shade; *soil*, well-drained; *climate*, desert, subtropical, Mediterranean, tropical

TOLERANCE *drought*, high; *salt*, high

HEAT REQUIREMENT moderate

USES AND EFFECTS grove tree, street tree, floral design (leaves, inflorescences, infructescences); *effects*, desert, color, sound; *special uses*, to pierce a volume, Hollywood skyline tree at half scale, oasis sentinel, canyon dweller; *avoid* shade, wet soils

ALTERNATE SPECIES *Brahea calcarea, Coccothrinax barbadensis, Pritchardia maideniana, P. remota, Trachycarpus fortunei, T. martianus, T. takil, Washingtonia robusta*

AVAILABILITY uncommon

Brahea calcarea

WHITE ROCK PALM

Brahea calcarea, the white rock palm, at The Huntington Botanical Gardens, with *Phoenix reclinata* behind it

Brahea calcarea is better known by its synonym, *B. nitida*. Slightly daintier and much more shade-tolerant than *B. brandegeei*, the white rock palm's shiny, unarmed leaves, frosted atop and on the undersides in reflective wax, are exceptionally attractive, and its trunk offsets the crown nicely. Slow-growing, shiny, and bright green as an understory plant, it's equally charismatic in full sun, where it grows upward more steadily, presents more graphically folded fans, and reveals its whitish, waxy counterpoint more readily. Densely packed flowers along branched inflorescences emerge as sculptural elements from the crown at maturity.

APPEARANCE *leaves*, 7 ft. (2.1 m) long; *crown span*, 15 ft. (4.6 m); *trunk*, 50 ft. (15.2 m) tall and 12 in. (31 cm) thick

CULTURE *hardiness*, 20°F (−7°C); *exposure*, full sun or part shade; *soil*, well-drained; *climate*, desert, subtropical, cool tropical, Mediterranean, warm temperate

TOLERANCE *drought*, high; *salt*, unknown, likely moderate

HEAT REQUIREMENT low

USES AND EFFECTS foliage element, container plant, grove tree, hedgerow element, street tree, floral design (leaves, inflorescences, infructescences); *effects*, color, shine, sound; *special use*, alkaline conditions; *avoid* wet soils

ALTERNATE SPECIES *Brahea moorei* (as foliage; it's trunkless), *Coccothrinax* spp., *Livistona chinensis* (as foliage), *L. fulva*, *Trachycarpus princeps*, *T. takil*

AVAILABILITY rare

Brahea edulis

GUADALUPE PALM

The Guadalupe palm lives on Mexico's westernmost outpost, Guadalupe Island, where green crowns atop curving trunks pepper steep slopes overlooking the Pacific Ocean to an altitude of 3280 feet (1000 m) above sea level. This foggy volcanic island, a biosphere reserve 150 miles (240 km) from the coast of northern Baja California, also anchors along with Cedros Island the southernmost flank of the California Floristic Province, the realm of plants characteristic of California. This winter-dominant precipitation zone runs between the deserts and the ocean from southwestern Oregon to northwestern Baja California. The endangered Guadalupe palm, a California native in the biogeographical sense, grows in habitat alongside plants familiar to many California gardeners and naturalists, such as Monterey pine (*Pinus radiata* var. *binata*), ceanothus, red-flowering currant (*Ribes sanguineum*), sword fern (*Polystichum munitum*), leather fern (*Polypodium scouleri*), dudleyas, lavateras, California sagebrush (*Artemisia californica*), California juniper (*Juniperus californica*), and several California poppies (*Eschscholzia* spp.)—including one endemic. An endemic cypress (*Cupressus guadalupensis*) joins the endemic palm among about thirty other plants known only from the island. Many other species limited to Southern California's Channel Islands, such as the island oak (*Quercus tomentella*), also occur there. I like to call the Guadalupe palm California's true native palm, not only for its ecological origin but also for its horticultural affinity with lowland California landscapes, and because our state's political native, *Washingtonia filifera*, the California fan palm, from the Sonoran Floristic Province, performs poorly in the heavily populated coastal climates of California (though it thrives and even naturalizes inland).

To be accurate, the extant Guadalupe palms on the island used to grow with these plants, but many became endangered or were extirpated: Sailors left goats on the island in the early nineteenth century to ensure future meat supplies, and over the decades, the prolific beasts devoured all the vegetation they could reach. The destruction ended in 2007 when the goats were removed as part of a restoration project, and, in a heartening development, plants are responding with rapid growth and seedlings are showing up around mother plants and from long-suppressed seed and rootstocks.

Okay, its native-ness is a technicality, but a fun one to contemplate (palms with pines and oaks and cypresses—oh my!). What matters, though, is that the Guadalupe palm is a lovely species that thrives in Mediterranean climates, as long as it has some decent drainage and irrigation for the first several years of its life until it's

The Guadalupe palm, *Brahea edulis*, at Sherry Merciari's garden, Oakland, California

established. Along with climate compatibility, it offers a nice scale—it stays below 30 feet (9.1 m) tall, mostly below 15 feet (4.6 m)—performs well in a container, and looks clean and green, thanks to its tendency to shed old leaves. No nasty thorns, either.

Brahea edulis also proves difficult to cultivate outside Mediterranean climate zones, adapting to mild temperate areas such as New Zealand but not to areas of seasonal tropical heat and copious summer rainfall, such as the US Southeast. Drought-tolerant, even drought-loving in marine-influenced parts of California, it falters when heavily sprayed with lawn irrigation.

This palm serves beautifully where planting a more common palm is a mistake. It remains more intimate to people in the landscape than does the skyduster Baja California native, *Washingtonia robusta* (Mexican fan palm), or the massive, towering California desert native, *W. filifera* (California fan palm). The Guadalupe's speed of growth to walk-under height as a young plant is satisfying, but it slows with age, taking a long time to progress from a trunk measurement of 10 feet (3 m) to the ultimate 35 feet (10.7 m) at one hundred years.

As it approaches that walk-under height, it begins to shed its unarmed leaves spontaneously as they die off, leaving a naked, elephantine trunk—another point in its favor for those who resent the thorny, adhering leaves and leafbases (and costly maintenance) of washingtonias. Its broad green foliage, more generous and animated in youth than that of the Mexican fan palm, if less shiny, approaches the scale of jade-green California fan palm foliage, as does its heavy trunk. Unlike washingtonias, Guadalupe palms thrive in shade as well as sun, becoming larger and more luxuriant, and readily leaning toward light—such as when close-planted in clusters. Inflorescences are a fascinating feature, with thick, soft tomentum on the sheaths enclosing the flowers in the early phase, and then becoming intricate branched structures in palest creamy green, followed by round, green-dotted fruits resembling the largest olives that turn to yellow and black at maturity. In tidy landscapes or paved areas, it's best to remove the heavy infructescences before fruitfall.

Beneath an oak canopy they are stupendous, rising as vertical counterpoint to the hardwood tree's coiled branches, the Guadalupe's green complementing the range of California oak colors, the water needs of both in harmony. Guadalupe palms also perform beautifully beside the sea. They remain green and healthy looking where Mexican fan palms can look stunted and resentful, especially in cool-summer areas. Their foliage also flexes and bounces in the wind, vanes registering the beauty of blustery weather.

APPEARANCE *leaves*, 8–10 ft. (2.4–3.0 m) long; *crown span*, 16 ft. (4.9 m) in sun to 20 ft. (6.1 m) in shade; *trunk*, 15–35 ft. (4.6–10.7 m) tall and 14–17 in. (36–43 cm) thick

CULTURE *hardiness*, 18°F (−8°C); *exposure*, full sun to shade; *soil*, well-drained; *climate*, Mediterranean, warm temperate

TOLERANCE *drought*, high; *salt*, high

HEAT REQUIREMENT low

USES AND EFFECTS foliage drama in shade, containers, coastal element, focal point, hedgerow, avenue planting, groves, leaning cluster, canopy, floral design (leaves, infructescences); *effects*, tree palm in human scale, tropical; *special uses*, California-native and Mediterranean themes; *avoid* excessive heat, wet soils, spray irrigation that wets the trunk or bud

ALTERNATE SPECIES *Brahea calcarea*, *Pritchardia beccariana* (tropical, cool tropical, mild warm temperate, Mediterranean), *P. pacifica*, *Sabal* spp., *Washingtonia filifera*

AVAILABILITY common

Brahea moorei

DWARF ROCK PALM, POWDER PALM

The trunkless dwarf rock palm grows beneath oak canopy at altitudes from 5249 feet (1600 m) to 6234 feet (1900 m) in the Sierra Madre Oriental of northeast Mexico, where seasonal rainfall can be erratic and paltry. An unarmed foliage plant with shiny green leaves edged in chalky wax on top and completely dusty-white on the bottom, *B. moorei* is lovely as a large-scale groundcover, companion to perennials and shrubs, container plant, or focal point at ground level. This palm dwells on limestone in habitat but tolerates a range of well-drained soils and light levels in cultivation. Young plants, with their deeply divided, soft, unarmed fans, resemble members of the gracile Caribbean genus *Coccothrinax*. As with many ground-dwelling palms, its stem trundles along semiburied in soil. Flower stalks rise upward from the foliage to bloom and then arch over with small yellow ripe fruit.

APPEARANCE *leaves*, 4 ft. (1.2 m) long; *crown span*, 7 ft. (2.1 m); *trunk*, subterranean, overall height 5 ft. (1.5 m)

CULTURE *hardiness*, 15°F (−9°C); *exposure*, full sun to shade; *soil*, well-drained; *climate*, warm temperate, Mediterranean, subtropical

TOLERANCE *drought*, high; *salt*, unknown

HEAT REQUIREMENT low

USES AND EFFECTS foliage, containers, alkaline soils, floral design (leaves, inflorescences, infructescences); *effects*, woodland, tropical; *special use*, understory planting; *avoid* wet soils

ALTERNATE SPECIES *Brahea calcarea* (when young), *Coccothrinax argentata*, other *Coccothrinax* species in youth, *Sabal minor*, *Serenoa repens*

AVAILABILITY rare

Butia

The *Butia* genus comprises a group of feather palms mostly from Brazil, whose members generally have recurved leaves with upward-angled leaflets that create a V-shaped cross section. Leafbases do not form a crownshaft. Many are solitary trees, and some are trunkless foliage plants, sometimes suckering. The identity of plants in cultivation in the United States can be difficult to pin down because of hybridity and nomenclature confusion. By far the most common are the species included here. Not detailed are worthy cultivated species in the genus, including *B. eriospatha* (from cool elevations of 2300–3900 feet, or 701–1189 m, in Brazil's southernmost, temperate states), *B. catarinensis* (from seaside habitat in the southerly state of Santa Catarina), and *B. paraguayensis* (a hardy, low-growing palm from grasslands in northern Argentina, Paraguay, southern Brazil, and Uruguay).

Butia odorata

PINDO PALM, JELLY PALM

Among the most versatile of species is the pindo palm, *B. odorata* (formerly *B. capitata*, a separate species from Brazil). The moderate-size feather palm has an

arched olive-green or blue-green leaf whose leaflets are angled upward, forming a V-shaped trough along the rachis. Leaflets may be attached at the same angle on each side of the rachis, for a regular, architectural form, or they may emerge at slightly different angles from the midrib, for a more ruffled, grassy impression. On every pindo palm an energetic, bouncy effect arises from a crown of leaves that appears to leap upward and curve outward from the apex of the trunk. Young plants crouched at ground level produce a grassy, structured effect, while modest-size older trees, some leaning, most growing upright, hang onto spiraling leafbases for a reptilian girded appearance, a trace of science-fiction costuming. Wine-colored flower buds pop out of cylindrical baseball bat–shaped bracts. Flowers open to a rich cream color and fruits ripen to a gold or deep orange and become delicious eaten out of hand.

A range of climates suits pindo palms. From the hot, humid summers and balmy winters of South Florida, to the occasional deep freezes and year-round moisture of South Carolina, to the desert climates of Las Vegas, to the long, wet winters of Northern California and even mild spots in the Pacific Northwest, *B. odorata* grows well and looks good.

It will tolerate container growing for decades, especially in cooler climates, and established plants in the ground can endure drought. Sun-loving, it also grows well in shade, and it tolerates seaside conditions remarkably well. It's not happy with highly alkaline soils, however, such as those found in Miami's rocky limestone or the alkaline clays in Austin, Texas.

APPEARANCE *leaves*, 4–7 ft. (1.2–2.1 m) long; *crown span*, 10–15 ft. (3.0–4.6 m); *trunk*, 30 ft. (9.1 m) tall and 12 in. (31 cm) thick

CULTURE *hardiness*, 15°F (−9°C); *exposure*, full sun to shade; *soil*, well-drained; *climate*, warm temperate, Mediterranean, subtropical

TOLERANCE *drought*, high; *salt*, high

HEAT REQUIREMENT low

USES AND EFFECTS containers, seaside, street tree, focal point, groves, edible fruit, floral design (leaves, inflorescences, infructescences); *effects*, savanna; *special use*, container subject; *avoid* wet soils

ALTERNATE SPECIES *Dypsis decaryi*, ×*Jubautia splendens*, *Ravenea glauca* (recurved form), *R. xerophila* (desert, tropical, warm subtropical, Mediterranean)

AVAILABILITY common

Butia yatay

A modest-size tree from Argentina, southern Brazil, and Uruguay, this palm has more sculptural leaves than *B. odorata*, thanks to regularly arranged leaflets and a more neatly arrayed crown. It's equally cold-hardy and heat-tolerant.

APPEARANCE *leaves*, 4–6 ft. (1.2–1.8 m) long; *crown span*, 8–12 ft. (2.4–3.7 m); *trunk*, 40 ft. (12.2 m) tall and 9–14 in. (23–36 cm) thick

CULTURE *hardiness*, 12°F (−11°C); *exposure*, full sun to shade; *soil*, well-drained; *climate*, warm temperate, Mediterranean, subtropical

TOLERANCE *drought*, high; *salt*, moderate

HEAT REQUIREMENT low

USES AND EFFECTS containers, street tree, focal point, groves, edible fruit, floral design (leaves, inflorescences, infructescences); *effects*, savanna; *special use*, container subject; *avoid* wet soils

ALTERNATE SPECIES *Butia odorata*

AVAILABILITY rare

×*Butiagrus nabonnandii*

MULE PALM

The mule palm is the most common hybrid palm, a product of hand-pollinating the female flowers of *Butia odorata*, the pindo palm, with the pollen of *Syagrus romanzoffiana*, the queen palm. The product is a variable, fast-growing, mostly sterile plant that offers good qualities of both parents. Leafbases do not form a crownshaft. It is reliably hardy to 16°F (−9°C) and will tolerate drought once established. The matte foliage is medium green, closer in color to the queen and in luminosity to the pindo. Minimally plumose fronds recurve broadly, making a well-formed crown covering three-quarters the span of a healthy queen palm (whose crown can lack structure). Fibers cling to leafbases in the crown, but once the tree reaches maturity, lower leaves peel off readily upon dying, cleanly revealing the trunk. (Butia palms tend to retain a spiraling pattern of leafbases on the trunk far longer into maturity.) The trunk is thick, but not as stout as the pindo's, and makes a pleasing proportion to the crown. In California landscapes, plants have a tendency to show micronutrient deficiencies on older leaves—yellow spotting—unless carefully fertilized.

above: Mule palms (×*Butiagrus nabonnandii*) at the Gardens at Lake Merritt (Lakeside Palmetum), Oakland, California

left: *Butia yatay* in the late Richard Douglas's garden, Walnut Creek, California

APPEARANCE *leaves*, 9 ft. (2.7 m) long; *crown span*, 15–20 ft. (4.6–6.1 m); *trunk*, 40 ft. (12.2 m) tall and 15–20 in. (38–51 cm) thick

CULTURE *hardiness*, 16°F (−9°C); *exposure*, full sun to shade; *soil*, well-drained; *climate*, subtropical, warm temperate, Mediterranean, tropical

TOLERANCE *drought*, high; *salt*, moderate

HEAT REQUIREMENT moderate

USES AND EFFECTS street tree, focal point, groves, canopy, floral design (leaves, inflorescences, infructescences); *effects*, tropical, savanna; *special use*, container subject; *avoid* wet soils

ALTERNATE SPECIES *Parajubaea* spp., *Dypsis decaryi*

AVAILABILITY rare

Caryota

FISHTAIL PALMS

The fishtail palms are largely single-trunk tree palms, with a few clustering species, including a common interior plant, *C. mitis*. They range from India through Malaysia, Indonesia, the Philippines, and New Guinea to Vanuatu and Australia. *Caryota* is the only palm genus to produce bipinnate leaves: first, a primary axis of petiole and rachis supports the leaf, and then secondary ribs branch off, bearing the leaflets. The quasi-triangular or fan-shaped leaflets with ragged outer edges and straight margins are shaped like the fins (not so much the tail) of a fish. Leafbases do not form a crownshaft. They are unmistakable, most often used in cooler climates as houseplants; they are less common in mild-climate landscapes because they are thirsty, short-lived, and require frequent pruning. The species have bright green leaves, the essential color of tropical foliage, with soft cream felt on their leafbases and nearly black, contrasting fibrous scales and hairs on the leafbase, rachis, and secondary rachis branches. Upon leaf opening, numerous dark threads detach from the edges and sections. Most species produce a single trunk with wide internodes between the rings of leafbase scars. Like many agave species, all caryotas are hapaxanthic, meaning the stem grows to maturity, produces inflorescences, sets seed, and then dies. Large pendulous flower structures begin at the top, proceeding downward, like giant tassels on a decaying tree. Occurring often within decades from planting these moderate-size to enormous palms, the phenomenon demands careful placement and planning for removal.

Caryota gigas

THAI MOUNTAIN GIANT FISHTAIL PALM

The Thai mountain giant fishtail palm, *C. gigas* (whose name is often cited as a synonym of *C. obtusa*), resembles a huge tree fern. It features a few (three to eight) enormous leaves to 30 feet (9.1 m) long and 12 feet (3.7 m) wide, articulate arching canopies atop a trunk approaching 3 feet (0.9 m) in diameter, especially where it swells like a cigar above ground level, and 20 to 60 feet (6.1 to 18.3 m) tall. The gaze reveals the tree's color counterpoint as you look from the almost glossy, fine green foliage onto the sooty petiole and bulky black fibrous leafbases—quite conspicuous on younger plants. The leafbases and ringed trunk fade in time to a concrete gray. Originating in montane rain forests, at 4600–5900 feet (1402–1798 m), in northeast Thailand, the allied species *C. obtusa* is from eastern India through northern Burma, southern China, northern Thailand, and

Caryota gigas at Hale Mohalu, Big Island, Hawai'i

Vietnam. The species tolerates light frosts and extended cool weather, but it also thrives in mild tropical Hawai'i.

APPEARANCE *leaves*, 30 ft. (9.1 m) long; *crown span*, 5–20 ft. (4.6–6.1 m); *trunk*, 20–60 ft. (6.1–18.3 m) tall and 3 ft. (90 cm) thick

CULTURE *hardiness*, 28°F (−2°C); *exposure*, full sun to shade; *soil*, well-drained, moist; *climate*, cool tropical, tropical, Mediterranean, warm temperate

TOLERANCE *drought*, low; *salt*, low

HEAT REQUIREMENT low

USES AND EFFECTS focal point, Jurassic groves, canopy, floral design (leaves, avoid handling fruit); *effects*, tropical, jungle, surreal; *special use*, canopy tree; *avoid* drought, wind

ALTERNATE SPECIES *Caryota no, C. kiriwongensis*

AVAILABILITY uncommon

Caryota maxima 'Himalaya'

HIMALAYAN FISHTAIL PALM

Growing like a pagoda composed of feathers, the Himalayan fishtail palm has a narrower and more upright silhouette than the Thai mountain giant (*C. gigas*) and does not achieve the same massive proportions. Like the Thai mountain giant, it tolerates frosts and long stretches of chilly weather and can grow where summer heat is lacking. Bright green, tan, and cream predominate on its stem and leaf-bases. It's an excellent treelike element for a small urban garden, where its tiered canopies of foliage allow plenty of light to penetrate into narrow spaces. This cultivar originates in the Himalayan foothills of Nepal and eastern India, where it grows at altitudes of 6000 feet (1830 m) and higher. The *C. maxima* species ranges eastward to China, Southeast Asia, Sumatra, and Java, occupying altitudes from 656 to 5900 feet (200 to 1798 m) above sea level in rainforest and semicultivated in disturbed areas for its edible bud and useful stem and fibers.

APPEARANCE *leaves*, 10–15 ft. (3.0–4.6 m) long; *crown span*, 20–25 ft. (6.1–7.6 m); *trunk*, 20–40 ft. (6.1–12.2 m) tall and 12 in. (31 cm) thick

CULTURE *hardiness*, 28°F (–2°C); *exposure*, full sun to shade; *soil*, well-drained, moist; *climate*, cool tropical, tropical, Mediterranean, warm temperate

TOLERANCE *drought*, low; *salt*, low

HEAT REQUIREMENT low

USES AND EFFECTS focal point, groves, street and avenue tree, floral design (leaves, avoid handling fruit); *effects*, tropical, jungle, Asian theme; *special use*, pagoda-shaped tree; *avoid* drought, wind

ALTERNATE SPECIES *Caryota rumphiana*, *C. urens*

AVAILABILITY uncommon

Caryota mitis

CLUSTERING FISHTAIL PALM

For tropical and subtropical regions where water is plentiful (and for heavily irrigated locations in the warmest Mediterranean climates), the clustering fishtail palm, *C. mitis*, grows multiple 6-inch-thick (15-cm) stems from the base, producing a dense cluster of broad leaves. Several plants in a line make a lovely fast-growing screen. It can also be useful as single dense cluster and in containers. Individual stems reach maturity, flower, fruit, and die while younger stems continue to develop from the base; without regular pruning of dead leaves and removal of dead trunks, the clustering fishtail palm quickly becomes unkempt.

Caryota mitis at the Miami Beach
Botanical Garden

APPEARANCE *leaves*, 8 ft. (2.4 m) long; *clump span*, 18 ft. (5.5 m); *trunk*, 12 ft. (3.7 m) tall and 8 in. (20 cm) thick

CULTURE *hardiness*, 30°F (−1°C); *exposure*, full sun or part shade; *soil*, moist; *climate*, tropical, subtropical, mild Mediterranean, warm temperate

TOLERANCE *drought*, low; *salt*, low

HEAT REQUIREMENT moderate

USES AND EFFECTS hedge, bamboo alternative, focal point, floral design (leaves, inflorescences, avoid handling fruit); *effects*, tropical, jungle, Asian theme; *special use*, interiors; *avoid* drought, wind

ALTERNATE SPECIES *Arenga tremula*, *Ptychosperma schefferi*

AVAILABILITY common

Ceroxylon

WAX PALMS

Hundreds of palms with smooth, white, wax-coated columns ringed with dark leafbase scars rise out of the patchwork of remaining cloud forests of the Andes in South America. Crowns of glossy green, pinnate leaves shimmer in the cloudy skies, their silvery satin undersides alternating with rich green. Their leafbases do not form a crownshaft. These tallest of the world's palms—and monocots—the genus *Ceroxylon* comprises twelve species of solitary tree palms limited to the wet foothills and cool, misty slopes of the world's second highest mountains. They are scattered from Venezuela through Colombia, Ecuador, Peru, and Bolivia. The premier species, *C. quindiuense*, has been measured at a record height of 190 feet (58 m) and was designated in 1985 the national tree of Colombia, where it grows gregariously in the Valle de Cocora National Park. One of the smallest (to 40 feet, or 12.2 m) species, *C. parvifrons*, occupies the highest altitude habitat of all palms—11,480 feet (3500 m) above sea level in Ecuador—so high that a perpetual chill prevails in its mossy equatorial habitat and frost occurs upslope on nearby exposed pasture.

For landscapes in places with mild, humid climates such as New Zealand, the coasts of California, Australia, Chile, South Africa, the western coast and islands of Europe, and cool tropical highlands worldwide, the genus offers extraordinary beauty for designers willing to hunt down seedlings, irrigate, and wait. Here in San Francisco, few palms perform so perfectly in our perpetually cool climate. Several of the species might have been at home with Jazz Age skyscrapers—*C. quindiuense*, *C. parvifrons*, *C. echinulatum*, *C. alpinum*—with their notes of smoothness accented in satin; brilliant white trimmed in silver, copper, or dark gray; and xylophones of parallel-pinnate foliage. Other species with plumose leaves, such as *C. vogelianum*, *C. ventricosum*, and *C. pityrophyllum*, give a softer impression, like queen palms and royal palms with distinctly ringed waxy trunks. Mature crowns range from shuttlecock-shaped to hemispherical and spherical, most species releasing spent leaves cleanly, and two or three species keeping a few dead leaves before they drop.

The San Francisco Botanical Garden in Golden Gate Park is the home of two of the largest Andean wax palms (*C. quindiuense*) growing in North America, as well as of a single mature *C. vogelianum*. One of the two *C. quindiuense* is now 70 feet (21.3 m) tall; the three palm trees were planted as seedlings in the mid-1980s at around the same time that these same species, plus *C. alpinum*, were planted at the Lakeside Palmetum at the Gardens at Lake Merritt in Oakland. The Oakland

Leaves of *Ceroxylon alpinum* (front) and *C. quindiuense* at the Gardens at Lake Merritt (Lakeside Palmetum), Oakland, California

C. vogelianum specimens were the first of the genus to produce flowers and fruit in North America; the rosettes of foliage and massive incipient trunks are a remarkable sight tucked among veteran trident maples (*Acer buergerianum*) near the shore of the lake.

This palm species grows slowly as juveniles and moderately upon trunk formation. They are unusually well suited to coastal California and similar climates; even the species from the lowest altitude, *C. amazonicum*, found most commonly at 3280 feet (1000 m) above sea level in the equatorial Amazon, is viable in protected Bay Area locales. Colombia chose in 1985 to protect *C. quindiuense* as its national tree in a cloud forest wildlife preserve, Valle de Cocora, where other rare and endangered species, such as the yellow-eared parrot, also live. The Andean cloud forests are the origin of many of California's favorite ornamental plants, such as angel's trumpets (*Brugmansia* spp.) and fuchsias.

Its cousins within the genus *Ceroxylon* vary in size, and some smaller species are exquisite palms for home gardens in the Bay Area and coastal California. Since the 1980s, the Botanical Garden has added to its collection with additional specimens of these species as well as others in the genus—*C. alpinum*, *C. amazonicum*, *C. ceriferum*, *C. echinulatum*, *C. parvifrons*, *C. parvum*, and *C. ventricosum*. Many of these I volunteered in the nursery at the garden. The development of the *Ceroxylon* collection set the garden on a path to being granted full accreditation for its high-altitude palm collection (also including such genera as *Chamaedorea*, *Parajubaea*, and *Trachycarpus*) by the North American Plant Collections Consortium, a conservation program.

We try to keep in stock at least a limited supply of seedling wax palms at Flora Grubb Gardens. The smallest growing species that have entered cultivation in

California are *C. parvifrons*, *C. pityrophyllum*, and *C. vogelianum*, which reach heights of 13 to 39 feet (4.0 to 11.9 m); midrange cultivated species include the exquisite *C. alpinum* and *C. echinulatum*, at 16 to 69 feet (4.9 to 21.0 m) in habitat; and the tallest, *C. quindiuense*, the world's record tallest palm tree, reaches 43 to 197 feet (13.1 to 60.0 m) in habitat.

Quintessential tree palms, ceroxylons lend themselves to planting in open groves or mingled among woody shrubs and trees that they will someday surpass, in lines and allées, as singular accents, or as doubles and triples. Plant them for the beauty of their foliage, however, because their establishment phase can last for decades in the largest species. Although quite erect, trunks can often subtly curve and lean. Growers wanting seed production should plant at least five individuals of a species in this dioecious genus to assure pollination of pistillate (female) plants for fruit. It's best to plant the youngest seedlings you can protect and care for in the ground; young plants of most species, even in misty, cool areas, appreciate some shade. Results of transplanting young plants have varied in California; roots of young plants are peculiarly sparse, often consisting of a few short roots with a long dominant root, which, if severed, dooms the plant. Plants subjected to drought stall but don't immediately collapse.

Details for the various *Ceroxylon* species are consolidated here.

Ceroxylon ventricosum at the Sullivan garden in Ventura, California

APPEARANCE *leaves*, 6 ft. (1.8 m) long in smaller species such as *C. vogelianum*, to 9 ft. (2.7 m) long in the midsize species such as *C. alpinum*, to 13 ft. (4 m) in the largest (*C. quindiuense*); *crown span*, 12 ft. (3.7 m) in the smallest, to 27 ft. (8.2 m) in the largest species; *trunk*, 16 ft. (4.9 m) tall for the smallest (*C. parvum*), to 120-plus ft. (36.6 m) tall in *C. quindiense*, the tallest species; 9 in. (23 cm) thick for the thinnest, *C. parvifrons*, to 18 in. (46 cm) thick in *C. ventricosum*

CULTURE *hardiness*, 23°F (−5°C) (*C. parvifrons*) to 32°F (0°C) (*C. amazonicum*); *exposure*, shade to sun with age; *soil*, moist, acid, well-drained; *climate*, cool tropical, mild warm temperate, Mediterranean

TOLERANCE *drought*, low to moderate; *salt*, presumed low

HEAT REQUIREMENT low to moderate

USES AND EFFECTS foliage, focal point, avenue planting, groves, near balconies and windows where trunks can be admired, floral design (leaves, fruits); *effects*, modern, architectural, colorful (silver, copper, glaucous, jade, marble), cloud forest, jungle; *special use*, skyline tree; *avoid* dry, hot conditions

ALTERNATE SPECIES *Jubaea chilensis, Roystonea oleracea, R. regia*

AVAILABILITY rare

Chamaedorea

Mostly from Central America and Mexico, with several species in South America, this large dioecious genus of small to moderate-size feather palms includes some of the most useful palms for garden design. Most species form a crownshaft, but several commonly grown types, such as *C. elegans*, do not. They're excellent container plants, bamboo proxies, hedges, screens, understory, even groundcovers and color accents, and they make nice silhouettes against walls or fences. All tolerate shade, some can handle dense shade, and a few can grow in full sun. Leaves tend to be thin, almost ferny, and bright green, with leafbases on most species forming a closed green sheath around the upper part of the stem that turns to strawlike husks upon senescing and often remaining attached, though they're easily peeled off. Exposed stems on groomed plants tend to be smooth, slender, and green, with conspicuous and thin leaf scars between long internodes; some species have short internodes and others have mottled or gray-green internodes. The pale yellow flowers of many species emit a pleasing, fresh fragrance. Ripening fruits on female plants are usually showy red, orange, or black against a complementary color of the inflorescence branchlets. Most common in cultivation are the bamboo palms, clustering, thin-stemmed plants such as *C. seifrizii*, a popular, adaptable plant for indoors and in gardens especially in Florida. Established specimens of clustering species hit with unusual cold have been known to lose all top growth only to rebound from the roots.

A few single-stem species not illustrated here are available, too, such as the ubiquitous parlor palm, *C. elegans*, a perfect tiny palm tree for indoors or outside in shade in all frost-free climates except deserts. It made a big impression on me as a kindergartner when my mother lovingly nursed one venerable 3-foot specimen given to her by a friend back to health from a pest infestation. Similar to the parlor palm but hardier, *C. oreophila* is a rare, attractive, small species that tolerates temperatures as low as 25°F (−4°C). Similarly cold-hardy, *C. carchensis* (syn. *C. benziei*) is a rare, larger crowned but shorter species that is worth seeking out. *Chamaedorea woodsoniana* and *C. linearis*, both beautiful and rare species amenable to growing in nearly frost-free cool tropical, mild Mediterranean, and warm temperate climates, are among the largest in the genus—each a veritable small tree. More often available is *C. tepejilote*, another small tree (or few-stemmed cluster), preferring warmer conditions.

Chamaedorea costaricana

BAMBOO PALM

Vigorous, fast-growing, and substantial, this bamboo palm from the mountains of Central America has a graceful, luxuriant look, with multiple stems sporting gently arching feather leaves with wide leaflets. It's the best species for cool, mild climates, but it also thrives in more tropical areas. Over time, clumps can become dense and tall. Red-orange fruits form on female plants growing within pollinator distance of males. It's a nice hedge for shade and a neat bamboo alternative if you don't want bamboo's constant leaf litter but appreciate the bony green canes and verdant foliage. It can also form a part of a composed hedge (or even hedgerow), its feathery leaves distinctive amidst more common foliage forms. The habit tends to be upright and bowed; some individuals remain sculptural and open by contrast to the species' characteristic density. Pruning can maintain an open silhouette—a smart look against a contrasting background such as a wall or fence. It looks great in a container, too. Thriving in shade, it can tolerate partial sun when established, especially in humid and cooler areas.

APPEARANCE *leaves*, 3–5 ft. (0.9–1.5 m) long; *clump span*, 3–10 ft. (0.9–3.0 m); *trunk*, 8–20 ft. (2.4–6.1 m) tall and 1–2 in. (3–5 cm) thick

CULTURE *hardiness*, 28°F (−2°C); *exposure*, shade to part sun; *soil*, moist, well-drained; *climate*, cool tropical, mild Mediterranean, frost-free warm temperate, subtropical

TOLERANCE *drought*, low; *salt*, low

HEAT REQUIREMENT low

USES AND EFFECTS hedge, screen, bamboo substitute, focal point in shade, color (fruit and flowers), fragrance (flowers), wall silhouette, containers, floral design (leaves, inflorescences, infructescences, entire stems); *effects*, jungle, hacienda; *special uses*, very cool-summer areas; *avoid* full sun, hot and dry conditions, frosty winters

ALTERNATE SPECIES *Chamaedorea hooperiana* (tropical, subtropical, mild warm temperate, Mediterranean), *C. microspadix*, *C. pochutlensis* (tropical, subtropical, mild warm temperate, Mediterranean), *C. seifrizii* (tropical, subtropical, mild warm temperate, Mediterranean)

AVAILABILITY uncommon

above: *Chamaedorea costaricana* at Ganna Walska Lotusland, Montecito, California

right: *Chamaedorea metallica* in Flora Grubb's garden, Berkeley, California

Chamaedorea metallica

METALLIC PALM

A moderate growing, tiny, single-stem palm from Mexico, the glinting metallic palm looks good as an understory element planted in groups with ferns and shade perennials, slowly lifting its stiff, leathery, warped blue-green paddles atop thin green stems. Curious inflorescences emerge from within the crown. Containers suit it perfectly, too, and it's one of the more reliable interior plants. Tolerating a surprisingly high level of light, it's a marvelous accent in shade, and it even puts up with spells of complete dryness. Most *C. metallica* plants in cultivation have undivided fronds, but some specimens' leaves divide and show separate leaflets on stiff fronds. Fruits (black) rarely form on the female plants outside habitat unless they're hand-pollinated. Older plants with crowns no more than 12 inches (31 cm) across and centimeter-thick trunks to 6 feet (1.8 m) tall are conspicuous, cute, or peculiar, according to taste.

APPEARANCE *leaves*, 10 in. (25 cm) long and 6 in. (15 cm) wide; *crown span*, 15 in. (38 cm); *trunk*, 3–10 ft. (0.9–3.0 m) tall and 0.5 in. (1 cm) thick

CULTURE *hardiness*, 26°F (–3°C); *exposure*, shade to part sun; *soil*, well-drained, adaptable; *climate*, tropical, subtropical, mild Mediterranean, mild warm temperate

TOLERANCE *drought*, high; *salt*, low

HEAT REQUIREMENT moderate

USES AND EFFECTS understory foliage, miniature groves, groundcover, silhouette against walls, containers, color (leaves, fruit, infructescences, flowers), floral design (leaves, inflorescences, infructescences); *effects*, jungle, modern; *special use*, interior; *avoid* full sun, frosty winters

ALTERNATE SPECIES *Chamaedorea ernesti-agusti* (softer, broader, apple-green leaves, adapted to the same climates)

AVAILABILITY common

Chamaedorea microspadix

HARDY BAMBOO PALM

Among the two hardiest species in the genus, this open-growing, sparse clumper with a few apple-green matte leaves per stem looks its best when several seedlings are planted intermingling together to increase the density of the clump. This arrangement also increases the chance of getting two sexes and thus colorful fruit yield on the female. Its stems are thin, often leaning, and its inflorescences are dainty. Growing at a slow to moderate rate, it tolerates a good half day of sun in an atmosphere with at least moderate humidity.

APPEARANCE *leaves*, 15 in. (38 cm) long; *clump span*, 3–10 ft. (0.9–3.0 m); *trunk*, 5–10 ft. (1.5–3.0 m) tall and 0.4 in. (1 cm) thick

CULTURE *hardiness*, 20°F (−7°C); *exposure*, part sun to shade; *soil*, well-drained, adaptable; *climate*, warm temperate, cool tropical, Mediterranean, desert (shade)

TOLERANCE *drought*, moderate; *salt*, low

HEAT REQUIREMENT moderate

USES AND EFFECTS screen, bamboo substitute, color (orange-red fruits), fragrance, wall silhouette, floral design (leaves, inflorescences, infructescences, entire stems); *effects*, woodland, jungle, hacienda; *special use*, calcareous soils; *avoid* dark shade, severe freezes

ALTERNATE SPECIES *Chamaedorea costaricana*, *C. hooperiana*, *C. pochutlensis*, *C. seifrizii*

AVAILABILITY uncommon to common

above: *Chamaedorea microspadix* in a garden designed by Davis Dalbok, Living Green Design, San Francisco

right: *Chamaedorea plumosa* in a garden designed by Davis Dalbok, Living Green Design, San Francisco

242

Chamaedorea plumosa

BABY QUEEN PALM

Among the fastest growing, most adaptable, and best-scaled palms for small gardens, this single-stem native of Chiapas, Mexico, grows at elevations up to 3900 feet (1189 m). It tolerates light frosts, deep shade or nearly full sun, and wind, among other bugaboos of gardening. Its thready, fluffy leaves rise on a 1- to 2-inch-thick (3- to 5-cm) green stem, with a languorous, weeping crown—softer in deep shade, more taut in full sun—that resembles that of a small queen palm (*Syagrus romanzoffiana*). Long inflorescences are a conspicuous accent. It appreciates ample water and fertilizer but, once established, will tolerate dry periods. Shoehorn it into narrow light wells, or plant it out to give vertical definition in exposed spaces. In the windiest and coldest districts, plant it in a protected lee spot; otherwise, it's adaptable to most subtropical, cool tropical, and mild Mediterranean climates.

APPEARANCE *leaves*, 4.25 ft. (1.3 m) long; *crown span*, 8 ft. (2.4 m); *trunk*, 10 ft. (3 m) tall and 1.5–2.5 in. (4–6 cm) thick

CULTURE *hardiness*, 29°F (−2°C); *exposure*, full sun to shade; *soil*, well-drained; *climate*, cool tropical, subtropical, Mediterranean, warm temperate

TOLERANCE *drought*, moderate; *salt*, presumed low

HEAT REQUIREMENT low

USES AND EFFECTS open screen, accent, containers; *effect*, blowsy; *special use*, vertical effects in narrow space; *avoid* frost, root disturbance

ALTERNATE SPECIES *Chamaedorea linearis*, *C. radicalis* (tree form), *C. tepejilote*, *C. woodsoniana*

AVAILABILITY common to uncommon

Chamaedorea radicalis

This slow-growing, single-stem palm with few leaves is perhaps the most cold-hardy of the genus. It grows in elevations up to 3280 feet (1000 m) in northeast Mexico's Sierra Madre Oriental. Two habits occur, sometimes in phases: one, a ground-dwelling plant with trunk buried and creeping, with leaflets on flat, arched fronds relatively broad; the other, a quite vertical, treelike plant with long internodes and flat, finely divided, upswept leaves. Inflorescences emerge vertically on both phases and female plants when fertilized and proffer bright, tomato-colored fruits; these can end up hanging below the crown on tree-form specimens. Palms in the ground-dwelling phase work nicely as container plants

Chamaedorea radicalis in Carole Bowen's garden, Alamo, California

and as understory or bed elements planted in groups, mixed with ferns and groundcovers, even tolerating some sun. The tree form makes a beautiful impact in groups, best with at least five individuals, and even better with dozens, their fruits adding to the show; a singular plant can be a disappointment if not given a focused space such as a container or niche in which to display its delicate features.

APPEARANCE *leaves*, 16 in. (41 cm) tall when trunkless; *crown span*, 5 ft. (1.5 m) when trunkless and 3 ft. (0.9 m) when trunking; *trunk*, 13 ft. (4 m) tall and 1 in. (3 cm) thick

CULTURE *hardiness*, 22°F (−6°C); *exposure*, part sun or shade; *soil*, well-drained, adaptable; *climate*, warm temperate, Mediterranean, cool tropical, mild desert (shade)

TOLERANCE *drought*, moderate; *salt*, presumed low

HEAT REQUIREMENT moderate

USES AND EFFECTS understory, miniature tree groves, open screen, foliage, color (infructescences), floral design (leaves, inflorescences, infructescences); *effects*, jungle, woodland; *special use*, dense groves; *avoid* planting in groups of fewer than three, severe freezes, hot and dry areas, wet soils

ALTERNATE SPECIES *Chamaedorea benziei*, *C. costaricana*

AVAILABILITY uncommon

Chamaedorea stolonifera

Stolons arch out from this clumping species to establish new stems with the thickness of yarn, carrying crowns of small, entire, fishtail-blade leaves. This plant is from Chiapas, Mexico, where it grows in areas below 2625 feet (800 m). It offers a dense display of beautifully formed, rich green leaves that make it a pleasing, deep groundcover or shrub and a fascinating container plant for close inspection, its new stolons eventually levitating over the pot's rim. When Caitlin and I were visiting his Camarillo, California, garden, John Rees, a doyen of the Southern California Chapter of the International Palm Society, gave me a beautiful plant that I cherish. *Chamaedorea brachypoda* is a similar species that prefers tropical climates and spreads by rhizomes.

APPEARANCE *leaves*, 10 in. (25 cm) long; *crown span*, 18 in. (46 cm); *clump span*, 3–10 ft. (0.9–3.0 m); *trunk*, 5 ft. (1.5 m) tall and 0.25 in. (6 mm) thick

CULTURE *hardiness*, 28°F (−2°C); *exposure*, shade; *soil*, well-drained, moist; *climate*, tropical, subtropical, mild Mediterranean, warm temperate

TOLERANCE *drought*, low; *salt*, low

HEAT REQUIREMENT low

USES AND EFFECTS groundcover, subshrub, understory, containers, floral design (leaves, inflorescences, infructescences, entire stems); *effects*, tidy, jungle; *special use*, groundcover; *avoid* sun, frost

ALTERNATE SPECIES *Chamaedorea brachypoda*, *C. ernesti-agusti*, and *C. metallica* (planted en masse)

AVAILABILITY uncommon

Chamaerops humilis

MEDITERRANEAN FAN PALM

The Mediterranean fan palm is the most versatile ornamental palm. This sole member of its genus naturally produces multiple stems from the same rootstock, slowly developing into a shrubby clump. Regular irrigation and fertilizer will increase its growth rate, but established plants can tolerate many months without water. The plant can be pruned into a cluster of small palm trees—the image of a paradise island—left as a moundy hedge, or manicured into a single small palm

above: *Chamaerops humilis* in a San Francisco garden designed by Christopher Reynolds

right: A silver Mediterranean fan palm, *C. humilis* var. *argentea*, in the late Richard Douglas's garden, Walnut Creek, California

tree. The Med fan, as we call it at Flora Grubb Gardens, thrives in a container, in sun or shade, and tolerates seaside and desert conditions alike. Flexible fronds bearing thorns on their inner stalks handle urban conditions and pose no threats to passers-by, but they can defend themselves from mischief. Its tolerance of cold (as low as 12°F, or –11°C) makes it useful in landscapes anywhere below an elevation of 3000 feet (914 m) in California.

Chamaerops humilis is native to seaside locations as well as scrub-covered hills around the western Mediterranean Sea. This shrubby plant is perhaps the most tol-

erant palm of coastal conditions in Northern California and harmonizes well with the native coastal scrub landscape. Over time and with proper pruning, it can attain a small palm-tree shape, even evoking a paradisiacal island with its cluster of leaning trunks. Its ability to endure drought, thanks to its Mediterranean origin, adds to its usefulness and appeal. In one of the most trying oceanside locations for ornamental plants, container-planted trees at San Francisco's Cliff House (which we at Flora Grubb Gardens supplied) are holding their own. It's also tolerant of moderate shade even in our summer-cool fog belt.

The elegant blue-silver variety, *C. humilis* var. *argentea* (silver Mediterranean fan palm, blue Atlas Mountain fan palm), from the Atlas Mountains of Morocco and Algeria, grows slightly smaller and survives slightly colder temperatures than its more common green sibling. It should be equally tolerant of seaside conditions but will lose some of its silvery sheen in the cooler coastal climate. It is also tolerant of desert as well as tropical conditions. This variety also has sharp spines on the petioles inside the crowns but is perfectly comfortable to brush past.

APPEARANCE *leaves*, 3 ft. (0.9 m) long; *clump span*, 30 ft. (9.1 m) tall and wide; *trunk*, 5–25 ft. (1.5–7.6 m) tall and 7 in. (18 cm) thick

CULTURE *hardiness*, 12°F (–11°C), green form, and 5°F (–15°C), blue-silver variety; *exposure*, full sun to shade; *soil*, well-drained; *climate*, Mediterranean, desert, warm temperate, subtropical, tropical

TOLERANCE *drought*, high; *salt*, high

HEAT REQUIREMENT low

USES AND EFFECTS shrub, solitary tree, hedge, multistem tree cluster, security screen, understory, silhouette, containers, floral design (leaves); *effects*, Mediterranean garrigue, chaparral, classical formality, desert, tropical; *special uses*, coastal exposure, calcareous soils; *avoid* saturated soils

ALTERNATE SPECIES *Guihaia argyrata, Rhapidophyllum hystrix, Serenoa repens*

AVAILABILITY common

Chambeyronia

This genus of two unarmed, monoecious crownshaft species from New Caledonia includes a palm cherished in tropical, subtropical, and even some mild temperate and mild Mediterranean climates for the rosy unfolding leaves found on many specimens and the bold, elegant form of its crown.

Chambeyronia macrocarpa

FLAMETHROWER PALM

Some palms make an impact for their resemblance to another species in a bolder, more graphic key. Other palms catch attention with their colorful fruit, flowers, or foliage. *Chambeyronia macrocarpa* does both. New leaves on most chambeyronias emerge a brilliant scarlet, changing within a few days to a darker red and then to green. The leaf and crownshaft resemble an archontophoenix but pumped-up by 50 percent to a grosser plant—bigger leaves; wider, more leathery leaflets; larger spaces between leaflets; and a bigger crownshaft. The trunk often remains dark green with bright leaf-scar rings well below the crownshaft. This slow-growing species is adapted to tropical, subtropical, and warm Mediterranean climates, appreciating high levels of moisture.

Chambeyronia macrocarpa in Paul Humann's garden, Broward County, Florida

APPEARANCE *leaves*, 10 ft. (3 m) long; *crown span*, 18 ft. (5.5 m); *trunk*, 30–50 ft. (9.1–15.2 m) tall and 10 in. (25 cm) thick

CULTURE *hardiness*, 30°F (−1°C); *exposure*, shade to part shade, full sun in moist climates; *soil*, well-drained, moist; *climate*, cool tropical, subtropical, mild Mediterranean

TOLERANCE *drought*, low; *salt*, low

HEAT REQUIREMENT moderate

USES AND EFFECTS focal point, groves, sentinels, allées, floral design (leaves, inflorescences, infructescences); *effects*, tropical, jungle, Jurassic, formal; *special uses*, color, shady locations; *avoid* drought, freezing

ALTERNATE SPECIES *Archontophoenix* spp., *Dictyosperma album*

AVAILABILITY uncommon

Clinostigma

A dozen species compose this genus of breathtakingly beautiful, large to medium-size palm trees with crownshafts. Solitary and monoecious, they are native to the western Pacific, from the Ogasawara (or Bonin) Islands of Japan, to Pohnpei, to Samoa, Fiji, and Vanuatu. They prefer consistently moist and humid conditions with mild, warm temperatures and acid soils. The habitats of *C. harlandii* and *C. exorrhizum* extend to 5000 feet (1524 m) and 4000 feet (1219 m). All species have finely divided, arching adult leaves with leaflets from semipendent to weeping in a fringe. Branched inflorescences below the crown resemble brooms and bear small red or black fruits. The tallest palms in the genus reach 80 feet (24.3 m). And they rise quickly; *C. samoense* and *C. warburgii* grow very fast where adapted, such as in moist areas of Hawai'i, attaining within a decade the grandeur of *Roystonea oleracea* or *Ceroxylon ventricosum* (whose trunks clinostigmas can resemble in a greener key), while bearing huge, weeping fronds to 20 feet (6.1 m) long, borne in a hemispherical arrangement. The smaller Japanese species, *C. savoryanum*, tolerates cooler conditions.

Clinostigma savoryanum

CABBAGE PALM

Occupying moist forests in Japan's subtropical Ogasawara Islands, this slow-growing species is the smallest and most cool weather–tolerant of the genus, growing to a height of 40 feet (12.2 m) in habitat. The pale green crownshaft forms the apex of a slender, green ringed trunk that fades to gray in older parts. Growing in latitudes near 27°N, this species tolerates a season of cool conditions but not frost, adapting to the mildest Mediterranean and frostless, warm temperate climates in addition to their preferred frost-free subtropical and tropical climates.

APPEARANCE *leaves*, 10 ft. (3 m) long; *crown span*, 18 ft. (5.5 m); *trunk*, 40 ft. (12.2 m) tall and 10 in. (25 cm) thick

CULTURE *hardiness*, 33°F (1°C); *exposure*, shade to part shade, sun at maturity in humid areas; *soil*, moist, well-drained, acidic; *climate*, subtropical, tropical, mild Mediterranean, warm temperate with minimal frost

TOLERANCE *drought*, low; *salt*, presumed low

HEAT REQUIREMENT moderate

USES AND EFFECTS focal point, groves, allées, gate sentries, floral design (leaf, leaf sheath, inflorescences, infructescences); *effects*, jungle, formal; *avoid* dry heat, alkaline soil, frost

ALTERNATE SPECIES *Archontophoenix alexandrae, Howea forsteriana, Satakentia liukiuensis*

AVAILABILITY rare

Coccothrinax

This large genus of mostly unarmed, mostly solitary fan palms from the Caribbean (especially Cuba) and its environs, from Florida to Mexico and the Lesser Antilles, offers numerous delicate to robust, small to medium-size subjects for garden design in tropical and subtropical climates—though many will grow in mild-winter deserts and in dry Mediterranean climates with ample year-round warmth and rare frost. They are all small enough to suit small gardens and look best in groups when used in larger, more open spaces. They are not good container plants. Most in this drought-tolerant genus are sun-loving and prefer sharp drainage. Many come from seasonally dry environments. Some species tolerate bouts of cold and occasional freezing temperatures, many tolerate seaside conditions, and most handle limestone, alkaline soils well. Their leaves, whether sculpted and stiff or relaxed, shiny, and lush, are often accented in silver or copper colors. They meet the trunk in very attractive fibrous leaf sheaths that tend to remain attached in youth and on the upper reaches of the trunk. On some species, fans are so deeply divided and plants so diminutive as to converge toward a single-pruned *Rhapis* spp. in resemblance. Covered in basket-weave patterns, smooth and exposed, or clad in soft gorilla fur, the trunks tend to be thin in relation to the crown. Older plants of many species meet the ground in mounds of proliferating roots; these root masses can also occur higher on the trunk. Creamy white flowers emerge on branched inflorescences within the crown, exceeding the leaves in length on some species. Most species produce small, round black or reddish black fruits, often shiny.

Coccothrinax argentata in habitat, Bahia Honda Key, Florida

Among the most popular species are *C. argentea* (not to be confused with *C. argentata*), a moderate sized (to 30 feet, or 9.1 m), graceful tree with silver-back leaves, from Hispaniola; *C. barbadensis* (sometimes called *C. alta*) a fast, rather tall (to 40 feet, or 12.2 m), graceful species with relaxed leaves from Puerto Rico and the Lesser Antilles; *C. borhidiana*, a rare and bizarre, dense-headed little palm resembling a trunking rosette succulent like nolina or yucca (to 15 feet, or 4.6 m);

C. crinita, the old man palm, with soft leaves and a very full, furry leafbase–covered trunk (to 25 feet, or 7.6 m); and *C. miraguama*, a tall (to 30 feet, or 9.1 m) species with rigid leaves and exquisite, wicker basket–weave leafbases.

Coccothrinax argentata

FLORIDA SILVER PALM

This very slow-growing, sun-loving, salt-tolerant species is native to South Florida, from Palm Beach County through the Keys, as well as the Bahamas, although it is not commonly used in landscapes. Its dark green, shiny leaves are backed in silver. On the upper surface, gold tones in the center of each fan radiate outward along the lines of attachment between the segments, disappearing where the segments divide in the outer two-thirds of the fan. This exquisite color effect is par for the course in this beautiful species, and in a genus of endlessly varied foliage appeal. The Keys plants can develop relatively stout trunks to 20 feet (6.1 m) tall, while the mainland plants' trunks stay quite short, often under 3 feet (0.9 m). We saw the population in habitat at Bahia Honda State Park, a place known for its beach but equally worthy for an encounter with its vegetation.

APPEARANCE *leaves*, 5 ft. (1.5 m) long; *crown span*, 8 ft. (2.4 m); *trunk*, 3–20 ft. (0.9–6.1 m) tall and 5 in. (13 cm) thick

CULTURE *hardiness*, 26°F (−3°C); *exposure*, full sun to part shade; *soil*, calcareous, well-drained; *climate*, tropical, subtropical

TOLERANCE *drought*, high; *salt*, high

HEAT REQUIREMENT high

USES AND EFFECTS groves, focal point in small space, foliage; *effects*, Caribbean, Florida

native; *special uses*, seaside, with salt exposure; *avoid* cold, wet soils, acid soils

ALTERNATE SPECIES *Brahea edulis* and *Chamaerops humilis* (colder climates); many *Coccothrinax* spp., *Pritchardia thurstonii*, and *Thrinax radiata* (tropical); *Trachycarpus* spp. (cooler climates away from immediate coastal exposure)

AVAILABILITY uncommon

Cocos nucifera

COCONUT PALM

Cocos nucifera epitomizes the palm tree. To people outside its preferred tropical climates, the coconut palm signifies a beach vacation, for it grows exceptionally well along beaches in resort areas, even surviving spells of saltwater immersion during storms. In the tropical zones, it's an immensely useful, even necessary, tree that supplies food, water, fiber, oil, and craft and shelter materials; without it, many atolls would be uninhabitable. Many of its products are distributed worldwide on an industrial scale and show up on ingredient lists in packaged foods or as agricultural supplies (such as coconut oil and coir). Cultivated wherever temperatures, pathogens, and rainfall or irrigation allow, it survives in warm subtropical areas such as South Florida, only where frost is rare and light. It declines in sustained cool weather (and thus is absent from Mediterranean climates) and suffers significantly from any freezing temperatures.

As with date palms and apple trees, many cultivated varieties exist, including dwarfs, color variants (especially golden), and, above all, an array of selections for fruit size and shape. Its origin appears to be the western Pacific, where ecological interactions and ethnobotanical uses are most profuse, but humans have served as its vector for colonizing all suitable climes, completing its pantropical spread with the help of Portuguese, Dutch, and Spanish ships into the 1600s. When I lived in New York City, a person who grew up in Florida but had become the consummate culture-steeped urbanite asked me why she saw no coconut palms on a recent trip to Los Angeles, surmising that it was Californians' penchant for lawsuits that kept the big nut-dropping menaces from being planted. I answered that it was just the climate, and that if Californians could grow gorgeous coconut palms they surely would.

Cocos nucifera is a moderately fast–growing tall palm with shiny, rich green, evenly divided feather leaves that tend to twist midblade toward the tips, yielding a bannerlike effect. Leathery textured, the leaflets have conspicuous midveins. The leaves swing and bend even in light breezes. Cream-colored inflorescences within boatlike spathes emerge from the center of the crown, and then flowers develop into very large fruits. Nearly spherical nuts are locked into the fat-football shape of the smooth-skinned husk. The entire husked fruit is half buried in sand or soil and regularly wetted for germination. In resort and urban areas, trees are gelded—shorn of fruit and lower leaves for safety—while in agricultural and some private landscapes the crowns form full, open spheres with bountiful clusters of nuts, pale green or gold. Dying leaves turn

Cocos nucifera at the Naples
Botanical Garden, Florida

to gold and brown and then fall neatly from the trunk (though young trees and the rare adult retain leafbases). Portions of the leaf sheath form a fine, burlaplike mat, but the overall appearance of the crown—the meeting of fleshy leafbases with the relatively thin trunk—is tidy. Leafbases do not form a crownshaft.

The trunk sets the coconut palm apart. Although many palm trees lean and curve, especially as they reach for light, the dominant tendency in single-stem palm trees is toward vertical growth. The coconut's trunk, however, is nearly always canted, curving especially from the base, even sinuous and eccentric, sometimes running nearly horizontal before turning again toward the vertical. It is relatively thin in relation to the crown and marked from swollen base to the crown by ringed leafbase scars.

The coconut's charisma and iconicity are so powerful that it thrills palm enthusiasts and even catches notice from people normally afflicted with plant blindness.

APPEARANCE *leaves*, 22 ft. (6.7 m) long; *crown span*, 30 ft. (9.1 m); *trunk*, 20–90 ft. (6.1–27.4 m) tall and 12 in. (30 cm) thick

CULTURE *hardiness*, 32°F (0°C); *exposure*, full sun to part shade; *soil*, well-drained; *climate*, tropical, frost-free subtropical

TOLERANCE *drought*, moderate; *salt*, high

HEAT REQUIREMENT high

USES AND EFFECTS seaside, groves, focal point, sentinels, avenue planting, paradise-island cluster, hedgerow element, silhouette, skyline tree; *effects*, tropical, seaside, casual; *special use*, seaside; *avoid* deep shade, frost, sustained cool weather

ALTERNATE SPECIES *Beccariophoenix* spp., especially *B. alfredii*; *Howea forsteriana*; *Parajubaea* spp.; *Syagrus amara* (for salt-tolerance and resemblance)

AVAILABILITY common

Copernicia

New World fan palms reach a peak of charisma in this diverse Caribbean and South American genus of two dozen or so mostly single-trunk, treelike, mostly slow-growing, sun-loving species. Leaves can be huge, steely, symmetrically divided stiff fans, or strange, densely packed, deeply cut blades seeming to lack petioles and arranged in a mass like a yucca. Leaf blades vary among species between palmate and costapalmate. Teeth are present on the petioles and even on leaf-blade margins. Trunks can be concealed in the dense thatch of attached dead leaves or heavy, smooth, and monolithic. Their sculptural branched inflorescences, densely packed with tiny flowers, are among the most ornamental in the palm family. Fruits tend to be small and black. Most of the species demand heat, tolerate rare and light frosts, and do well on calcareous soils. They endure seasonal droughts in habitat thanks to plentiful soil moisture and thus should receive regular water in cultivation.

Copernicia alba

CARANDAY PALM

The most cold-hardy species in the genus is also among the fastest growing and tallest. It comes from seasonally flooded savanna in northern Argentina and adjacent Bolivia, Brazil, and Paraguay. Its deeply divided, stiff, waxy-gray leaves gather in a dense crown atop a thin trunk covered on its upper stretch in spiraling leafbases; exposed older trunks are gray, blanching in the sun, and can reach nearly 100 feet (30.5 m) in habitat. Attractive branched inflorescences emerge from the crown, adding to its interest. It's adaptable to Mediterranean and subtropical as well as tropical places, enduring temperatures as low as 25°F (–4°C) with no damage. Regular moisture is best, although established plants become drought-tolerant. Its tough, textured mien stands on its own as a focal point, and the plant looks good in groups, too.

APPEARANCE *leaves*, 5 ft. (1.5 m) long; *crown span*, 8 ft. (2.4 m); *trunk*, 30–80 ft. (9.1–24.3 m) tall and 11 in. (28 cm) thick

CULTURE *hardiness*, 25°F (–4°C); *exposure*, full sun; *soil*, heavy clay to well-drained; *climate*, subtropical, tropical, warm temperate, Mediterranean, desert

TOLERANCE *drought*, high; *salt*, moderate

HEAT REQUIREMENT moderate

USES AND EFFECTS focal point, groves, sentinels; *effects*, savanna, desert; *special use*, seasonally inundated sites; *avoid* shade

ALTERNATE SPECIES *Brahea brandegeei, B. calcarea, Chamaerops humilis* var. *argentea* (single-trunk pruned), *Coccothrinax* spp., *Trachycarpus takil, Trithrinax acanthocoma*

AVAILABILITY uncommon to common

Copernicia baileyana

BAILEY PALM

Along with *C. fallaense* and *C. gigas*, this slow-growing species is the grandest of the genus, a member of a club of monumental palm trees, with *Borassus aethiopum*, *Jubaea chilensis*, and *Roystonea regia*. Its crown of large, stiff leaves are slightly cupped upward. A hypnotic effect is produced by the fine, regularly divided fans overlapping against the sky. Dead leaves remain briefly attached under the crown and then drop to reveal the trunk. Beautiful branched flower structures push well beyond the silhouette of the leaves, complementing the leaves' radial symmetry. Small black fruits follow. The smooth, pale trunk forms a bowed column in maturity. This is a palm for grabbing attention or for creating structure in the landscape.

Copernicia baileyana (with
Guihaia grossefibrosa below)
at Fairchild Tropical Botanic
Garden, Miami

APPEARANCE *leaves*, 10 ft. (3 m) long and 5 ft. (1.5 m) wide; *crown span*, 18 ft. (5.5 m); *trunk*, 40 ft. (12.2 m) tall and 2 ft. (0.6 m) thick

CULTURE *hardiness*, 27°F (−3°C); *exposure*, full sun; *soil*, well-drained, tolerates brief inundation; *climate*, tropical, subtropical

TOLERANCE *drought*, moderate; *salt*, moderate

HEAT REQUIREMENT high

USES AND EFFECTS parklike clusters, allées and avenues, focal point, sentinels, foliage; *effects*, architectural, savanna, formal, Jurassic; *special use*, living monolith; *avoid* shade, planting too close together

ALTERNATE SPECIES *Copernicia fallaense* and *C. gigas* (tropical, subtropical), *Jubaea chilensis* (trunk, not crown resemblance), *Pritchardia pacifica* (foliage, not trunk resemblance)

AVAILABILITY rare to uncommon

Corypha

Enormous monocarpic (technically, hapaxanthic), costapalmate, single-stem tree palms, the half-dozen *Corypha* species occur in a roughly triangular area from northern Australia to the Philippines and India. Their appeal is as much in their sheer enormity as in their visual textures. The leaves on young specimens of the two commonly cultivated species are enormous, with a conspicuous costa bending into the blade; a single leaf could shelter a car. Coryphas can fit only into park-size spaces where the means exist for pruning their gigantic leaves and for removing the trees, for after decades of vegetative growth—starting slowly at first, and then continuing at a moderate rate upon forming a trunk—they produce a huge inflorescence surpassing the leaf crown and then die as they ripen fruit. The conical branched reproductive structure itself resembles a tree, surrounded by skirts of the dead leaves. The inflorescence is ranked as the largest in the plant kingdom. At maturity, it all stands high atop a thick gray trunk. (In *C. utan* the stem swells subtly in a corkscrew spiral like a Solomonic column.) The spectacle of the spent infructescence at the pinnacle of the clean, dead trunk, especially after dead leaves have fallen, is a breathtaking monument to the reproductive cycle.

Corypha species prefer sun (or light shade when young) in tropical and warm subtropical climates and can tolerate periods of drought in a moist monsoonal regime, although best results occur with regular water. Occasional light frost nicks the foliage, affecting *C. utan* more severely than *C. umbraculifera*.

above: *Corypha umbraculifera* at Mike Harris's garden, Broward County, Florida

right: *Cyrtostachys renda* at Hale Mohalu, Big Island, Hawai'i

Corypha umbraculifera

TALIPOT PALM

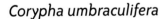

Bright-green, smooth petioles with dark, toothed margins characterize plants of this species found semicultivated from south India through Southeast Asia. Its persistent leafbases, split beneath the petiole, form an irregular lattice pattern on the trunk before peeling off to reveal clear trunk as the tree ages.

The leaves of *C. utan*, the gebang palm, are more deeply divided than those of *C. umbraculifera*. Ebony petioles bear scars inflicted by the spines of lower petioles, a visual analog to the impressions of marginal spines on agave leaves. Leafbases, splitting to form a triangular sinus beneath the petiole, are retained on the trunk of young plants in an appealing spiral pattern. Older plants shed dead leaves spontaneously. *Corypha utan* is even less tolerant of frost than *C. umbraculifera*.

APPEARANCE *leaves*, 25–30 ft. (7.6–9.1 m) long and 20 ft. (6 m) wide; *crown span*, 40 ft. (12.2 m; *trunk*, 60 ft. (18.3 m) tall and 3 ft. (0.9 m) thick

CULTURE *hardiness*, 30°F (−1°C); *exposure*, full sun to part shade; *soil*, well-drained, fertile; *climate*, tropical, warm subtropical

TOLERANCE *drought*, moderate; *salt*, low

HEAT REQUIREMENT high

USES AND EFFECTS focal point, canopy, structure, foliage, massive trios and groves; *effect*, Jurassic; *special use*, massive screen; *avoid* small spaces, areas where removal will be problematic

ALTERNATE SPECIES *Bismarckia nobilis*, *Borassodendron machadonis* (tropical), *Sabal causiarum*, *S. domingensis*, *S. uresana*, *Tahina spectabilis*; no other palm has such huge fan leaves, however

AVAILABILITY common to uncommon

Cyrtostachys

This small genus of pinnate palms from Thailand to New Guinea and the Solomon Islands contains one superstar staple for well-watered tropical gardens—*C. renda*, the sealing-wax palm.

Cyrtostachys renda

SEALING-WAX PALM

No other palm is so beloved for its color. It's a siren for gardeners, including those planting outside its preferred wet tropical zones. From Thailand, Malaysia, Sumatra, and Borneo, this tightly clustering, moderate to tall species grows thin trunks with long green internodes resembling bamboo. Older trunks fade to light gray. The scarlet coloring of the sealing-wax palm's crownshaft extends up the petiole and rachis, contrasting with the deep green leaflets and stems. Stiff leaves are held in a hemispheric arrangement, giving the plant an energetic, leaping effect. Branched inflorescences emerge from sheathing bracts beneath the crownshaft, producing pale green flowers followed by small black fruits. Other less common color forms include maroon, yellow, pale green, and orange. It can grow as a marginal aquatic or with plentiful moisture in well-drained soil, but it dislikes alkaline soil conditions and loathes temperatures below 50°F (10°C). Young plants may prefer some shade, but full sun is ultimately best.

Use this plant in tropical climates for lavish hedges, for bamboo effects, in containers, as a focal point, next to verandas and balconies (to view closely at height), and to line pathways and drives.

APPEARANCE *leaves*, 5 ft. (1.5 m) long; *crown span*, 10 ft. (3 m); *trunk*, 30 ft. (9.1 m) tall and 3 in. (8 cm) thick

CULTURE *hardiness*, 40°F (4°C); *exposure*, full sun to part shade; *soil*, wet, rich; *climate*, tropical

TOLERANCE *drought*, low; *salt*, low

HEAT REQUIREMENT high

USES AND EFFECTS focal point, screen, hedge, containers, dooryard accent; *effects*, color, East Indies; *special uses*, emergent aquatic or water-margin plant; *avoid* cold, drought, alkaline soils

ALTERNATE SPECIES *Areca vestiaria*

AVAILABILITY common

Dictyosperma album

PRINCESS PALM

A tidy, fast-growing, moderate-size, monoecious crownshaft palm from the Mascarene Islands of the southwest Indian Ocean—Mauritius, Réunion, and Rodrigues—the princess palm thrives in tropical and warm subtropical conditions with plentiful moisture and good drainage, although it can endure short periods of drought. Sun-loving, it can grow in light shade, too. Its waxy-gray crownshaft tends to bulge with incipient flowers, which emerge as a conspicuous protuberance in sheathing bracts when the oldest leaf drops. Bracts peel away to reveal the branched rooster-tail inflorescence bearing white to yellow or reddish fragrant flowers, depending on which of the varieties—*D. album* var. *album* or *D. album* var. *conjugatum*—are cultivated, followed by small dark purple or black fruits. The new leaf spear stands needle straight while it rises at the top of the spherical crown of leaves. As the leaf unfolds, conspicuous reins connect leaflet tips for an unusual bound-feather look. They persist for a longer period on *D. album* var. *conjugatum* than on *D. album* var. *album*. Leaflets with conspicuous midribs are evenly arranged and flat to drooping; the leaf blade arches and twists from flat to vertical toward the tip. The palm's ringed gray trunk meets the ground in a distended, elephant-foot base.

This classic, widely available tropical palm tree endures coastal conditions and can grow in slightly acid as well as alkaline calcareous soils. It makes a pleasing addition to small gardens and large parks alike. Its neat appearance and movement make it useful as a focal point. As with most tree palms, it pleases in groves and staggered height clusters, as well as in formal lines and as a street tree.

Dictyosperma album at Patricia
Bullis's garden for Bullis
Bromeliads, Homestead, Florida

APPEARANCE *leaves*, 10 ft. (3 m) long; *crown span*, 16 ft. (4.9 m); *trunk*, 35 ft. (10.7 m) tall and 6 in. (15 cm) thick

CULTURE *hardiness*, 32°F (0°C); *exposure*, full sun to part shade; *soil*, well-drained; *climate*, tropical, subtropical

TOLERANCE *drought*, low; *salt*, high

HEAT REQUIREMENT high

USES AND EFFECTS focal point, street tree, groves; *effect*, tropical; *special use*, regrows quickly from tropical storm damage; *avoid* cold, drought

ALTERNATE SPECIES *Archontophoenix* spp.

AVAILABILITY common

Dypsis

The diversity in this big monoecious genus from Madagascar, the Comoro Islands, and Pemba Island, Tanzania, ranges from tiny, clustering understory palms with subterranean stems (*D. beentjei*) to grand solitary tree palms (*D. robusta*). Pinnate

A *Dypsis* specimen with affinities to *D. onilahensis* and *D. baronii* at the Sullivan garden, Ventura, California

leaves may be plumose, flat, irregularly divided, or entire. Many species have crownshafts, while the leaf sheaths of at least one species (*D. fibrosa*) become fibrous and furry. Some members of the genus can be found to tolerate warm temperate and Mediterranean climate conditions, but most of the species thrive in tropical and subtropical climates. In Southern California's mild coastal climates, many species have proven successful.

Dypsis baronii

This moderate-size clustering species grows at altitudes of up to 4500 feet (1372 m) in Madagascar rainforests and thrives in the mild coastal Mediterranean climate of California as well as in the cool tropical climate of the Big Island, Hawai'i. It does not tolerate much frost or intense heat. It makes an open clump of green, ringed trunks to 20 feet (6.1 m) tall and up to 6 inches (15 cm) thick. Plants often cease to develop new stems after a decade of maturity, and solitary specimens are seen occasionally. Delicate, flat to keeled green feather leaves often accented with reddish petioles emerge from a waxy gray to yellow crownshaft, and branched inflorescences can emerge within the crown or below the crownshaft; the browns, reds, and whites in the many small flowers can seem pinkish from a distance. Round fruits ripen to yellow.

Another elegant, moderate-size clustering palm in the genus from Madagascar inhabits habitats as high as 7874 feet (2400 m) in elevation. *Dypsis onilahensis* can be grown in the same conditions as *D. baronii*, and, although slower-growing, it can serve similar uses. It is also comparable in use to *D. lutescens*, but like *D. baronii* it thrives in cooler conditions. It produces a more open clump and may cease to make additional stems with age. Like all of the *Dypsis* species included here, this palm's contribution of color—glaucous crownshaft, dark petioles—makes it an appealing element in a garden's design. A weeping-leaf form of the species is quite attractive.

APPEARANCE *leaves*, 7 ft. (2.1 m) long; *crown span*, 12 ft. (3.7 m); *clump height*, to 30 ft. (9.1 m); *clump span*, to 10 ft. (3 m); *trunk*, 25 ft. (7.6 m) tall and 6 in. (15 cm) thick

CULTURE *hardiness*, 28°F (−2°C); *exposure*, full sun or part shade; *soil*, rich, well-drained; *climate*, cool tropical, warm temperate, mild Mediterranean

TOLERANCE *drought*, low; *salt*, low

HEAT REQUIREMENT low

USES AND EFFECTS focal point, screen, paradise-island clump, silhouette, dooryard accent; *effects*, tropical, jungle; *special use*, narrow spaces; *avoid* heavy, wet soil and freezing temperatures

ALTERNATE SPECIES *Chamaedorea hooperiana*, *C. radicalis* (trunking form planted in a cluster), *Dypsis ambositrae*, *D. lutescens*, *D. onilahensis*

AVAILABILITY rare to uncommon

Dypsis cabadae

CABADA PALM

A moderate-size to fairly large clustering species from Mayotte, an island near Madagascar, *D. cabadae* makes a very elegant palm copse in tropical and subtropical climates. Between white leaf scars, the trunk's dark green internodes are slivered with a faint waxy coating, an effect intensified in its wintergreen crownshaft. Trunks flare at the base. Arching leaflets attached at an upward angle to the rachis create a keeled effect, especially in full sun, while the rachis tips down in its outer portion. Leaves stay above the horizontal in the crown. Branched inflorescences with little yellow flowers emerge from within the crown, followed by pendent clusters of round red fruits.

Use this serene species in place of bamboo, as a large hedge, along walkways, next to porches and balconies, or as a multistem street tree regularly cleared of unwanted suckers. It prefers uninterrupted moisture and good drainage. Young plants prefer shade but mature well into sun.

Dypsis cabadae at Punta Roquena, Florida Keys

APPEARANCE *leaves*, 10 ft. (3 m) long; *crown span*, 15 ft. (4.6 m); *clump height*, to 30 ft. (9.1 m); *clump span*, to 10 ft. (3 m); *trunk*, 25 ft. (7.6 m) tall and 6 in. (15 cm) thick

CULTURE *hardiness*, 30°F (−1°C); *exposure*, full sun or part shade; *soil*, rich, well-drained; *climate*, tropical, subtropical

TOLERANCE *drought*, low; *salt*, low

HEAT REQUIREMENT high

USES AND EFFECTS focal point, open screen, bamboo alternative, silhouette, dooryard accent; *effects*, tropical, jungle, formal; *special use*, narrow spaces; *avoid* frost, sustained cool weather

ALTERNATE SPECIES *Dypsis ambositrae, D. baronii, D. lutescens, D. onilahensis, D. pembana, Hedyscepe canterburyana* (planted in a grove)

AVAILABILITY common to uncommon

Dypsis decaryi

TRIANGLE PALM

Exceptional for its three-ranked crown of keeled, feather leaves, the triangle palm is a single-stem tree native to a narrow band of seasonally dry woodland in

southern Madagascar. Although it thrives with regular moisture, it can tolerate drought once established, even in mild Mediterranean climates. It sustains foliage damage in light frost but can tolerate rare dips below freezing. Overlapped leafbases do not form a crownshaft, but they replicate the triangular pattern of the three-ranked crown in a sculpted mass where they meet the thick trunk. Black tomentum on the leafbases rubs off with age to show the gray-green leaf color. Leaves are held well above the horizontal, the outer portions curving downward, the lowest leaflets retaining a hanging rein. On mature plants, the leafbases tend to abscise to reveal the trunk surface. Large branched inflorescences emerge from between the flaps of the leafbases in the crown, producing round green, marble-size fruits.

Use its unusual geometry with care, giving the crown sufficient space in the landscape to show it off and arranging groups thoughtfully. Its upward sweep of fronds makes it a good street tree candidate where adapted.

Also adapted to mild-winter desert climates, *D. decaryi* appreciates full sun and regular moisture with good drainage for best performance in hot areas. It grows at a moderate rate.

Dypsis decaryi at Jeff Seyfried's garden, Big Island, Hawai'i

APPEARANCE *leaves*, 10 ft. (3 m) long; *crown span*, 16 ft. (4.9 m); *trunk*, 20 ft. (6.1 m) tall and 20 in. (51 cm) thick

CULTURE *hardiness*, 29°F (−2°C); *exposure*, sun; *soil*, well-drained; *climate*, subtropical, tropical, desert, mild Mediterranean

TOLERANCE *drought*, high; *salt*, low

HEAT REQUIREMENT moderate

USES AND EFFECTS focal point, trios and groves, avenue planting, containers; *effects*, arid tropical, desert, architectural; *special uses*, judiciously placed triples, interior; *avoid* cold, heavy soil and root disturbance

ALTERNATE SPECIES *Butia* spp.

AVAILABILITY common

Dypsis decipiens

MANAMBE PALM

A very slow-growing but cold-hardy and ornamental tree palm, this clustering moderate-size species from 4000 to 6000 feet (1210 to 1830 m) in central Madagascar can form one to six trunks. With its fusiform ringed trunk, prominent whitish gray crownshaft, and vinyl-textured arching plumose leaves, it makes a powerful impact in maturity, resembling a mix of the spindle palm, *Hyophorbe verschaffeltii*, and a young royal palm, *Roystonea regia*. The trunks on veteran trees taper on their upper extents. The crownshaft can be slightly bulging, and bract-enclosed inflorescences form below it, opening to bear pale yellow flowers and then small round fruits, yellow at maturity. Some young plants show red tints on petioles and leafbases. Although drought-tolerant and sun-loving, it prefers excellent drainage and some summer water. It thrives in a Mediterranean or subtropical climate, enduring mild freezing temperatures, but also grows well in the sharp drainage, copious rainfall, and mild tropical temperatures of the Big Island's Puna District; it appears that warm night temperatures are not to its liking.

Dypsis decipiens is a compelling focal point, a good street tree, a companion to succulents and other drought-tolerant plants, and an excellent tree in open groves. Photographs of the plant in its boulder-strewn habitat should inspire designers to pair it with similarly dramatic monoliths, walls, and rocks.

Dypsis decipiens at the Sullivan garden, Ventura, California

APPEARANCE *leaves*, 8 ft. (2.4 m) long; *crown span*, 14 ft. (4.3 m); *trunk*, 6–39 ft. (1.8–12 m) tall and 2 ft. (0.6 m) thick

CULTURE *hardiness*, 26°F (−3°C); *exposure*, sun; *soil*, well-drained; *climate*, mild warm temperate, cool tropical, Mediterranean

TOLERANCE *drought*, high; *salt*, presumed low

HEAT REQUIREMENT low

USES AND EFFECTS focal point, groves, street tree; *effects*, savanna, arid tropical, Jurassic picturesque; *special use*, amidst succulents; *avoid* heavy, wet soil and sustained hot, humid nighttime weather

ALTERNATE SPECIES *Dypsis* spp., *Hyophorbe verschaffeltii*

Dypsis leptocheilos at the Big Island, Hawai'i, in the garden of Tom Piergrossi and Andy Maycem

Dypsis leptocheilos

TEDDY BEAR PALM

Reddish brown fuzz on the leafbases of this charismatic tropical palm from Madagascar inspired its common name. Lacking a true crownshaft, it's a self-cleaning, single-stem tree with a smooth, pale, ringed trunk that contrasts with the leafbases. Inflorescences are produced from within the crown, hanging below it in fruit. Regularly pinnate flat leaves make up a broad, open crown supported on a relatively slender stem. The result is a tree of quite graceful proportions. It thrives in tropical and even subtropical conditions and grows in mild coastal Southern California gardens, too, where it can recover from a light frost. Bright light conditions suit it best. It grows at a moderate rate.

A similar species, *D. lastelliana*, the redneck palm, is more uncommon in cultivation and more exacting in its requirements for tropical conditions and rich soil, with darker reddish brown fuzz on its tighter leafbases and more weeping leaflets.

APPEARANCE *leaves*, 13 ft. (4 m) long; *crown span*, 22 ft. (6.7 m); *trunk*, 33 ft. (10 m) high and 10 in. (25 cm) thick

CULTURE *hardiness*, 28°F (−2°C); *exposure*, part shade to sun; *soil*, well-drained; *climate*, tropical, subtropical, mild Mediterranean

TOLERANCE *drought*, low; *salt*, low

HEAT REQUIREMENT moderate

USES AND EFFECTS groves, focal point, canopy; *effect*, color; *special use*, canopy; *avoid* cold, heavy soil

ALTERNATE SPECIES *Dypsis lastelliana, Satakentia liukiuensis*

AVAILABILITY uncommon

Dypsis lutescens

ARECA PALM

Rare in its coastal forest habitat in Madagascar, this clustering, moderate-size crownshaft species is one of the most commonly cultivated palms in tropical and subtropical landscapes. It's used often as a hedge, for screening, and as an accent plant—especially groomed. It's a useful plant for confined courtyard spaces and as a bounding element for gathering spots. The gold of its petiole, rachis, and senescing leaves, seen clearly on sun-grown specimens, contributes color to landscapes it inhabits. Frost damages this heat-loving, fast-growing, and water-loving species, but it is grown in warm, mild Mediterranean climates such as Los Angeles's to satisfactory effect. It is ubiquitous in South Florida and Hawai'i, and in commercial landscapes throughout the tropical world. It is adaptable to a variety of soils.

Young nursery-grown specimens often contain multiple seedlings. Together these create a very dense clump, which may be managed by thinning stems to reveal structure and its appealing smooth trunks, topped with gray crownshafts. Single seedlings produce a more open cluster of green-to-yellow–surfaced stems with narrow gray leaf scars. Thin, shiny green leaflets are arranged regularly along the golden rachis, which recurves downward toward the end. Shaded leaves tend to be flatter, while leaflets in the sun angle up and curve out, producing a V-shaped cross section to the leaf blade; they dance about in the breeze. Neatly branched inflorescences with yellowish flowers push out from between the leaves in the crownshaft, hang down, and bear yellow-orange olive-shaped fruits.

Dypsis lutescens at Hale Mohalu, Big Island, Hawai'i

APPEARANCE *leaves*, 7 ft. (2.1 m) long; *crown span*, 12 ft. (3.7 m); *clump height*, to 32 ft. (9.8 m); *clump span*, to 20 ft. (6.1 m); *trunk*, 25 ft. (7.6 m) tall and 3 in. (8 cm) thick

CULTURE *hardiness*, 29°F (−2°C); *exposure*, full sun or shade; *soil*, well-drained; *climate*, tropical, subtropical, mild Mediterranean

TOLERANCE *drought*, moderate; *salt*, moderate

HEAT REQUIREMENT moderate to high

USES AND EFFECTS hedge, screen, paradise clump, color, containers; *effects*, tropical, resort; *special use*, hedging; *avoid* planting too densely, frost

ALTERNATE SPECIES *Chamaedorea hooperiana*, *Dypsis cabadae*

AVAILABILITY common

266

Guihaia

Three clumping dioecious palmate species from southern China and northern Vietnam form clusters on limestone cliffs and mountains. Two tolerate cold in cultivation, the third being known only from habitat.

Guihaia argyrata at La Casa de las Palmas, Hilo, Hawai'i

Guihaia argyrata

GUI HAI PALM, CHINESE NEEDLE PALM

A beautiful, quite slow-growing, and very frost-tolerant palm, *G. argyrata* forms low clumps with several growing points that produce circular, dark green, deeply divided fans with a leathery texture. The folds of leaf segments are reduplicate—roof-shaped in cross section—with a prominent midvein on top. Undersides of the leaves are buff colored with a silvery cast. Fibrous leaf sheaths carry prominent spines near the top of the short stems. These aspects, along with its growth habit resembling that of the genus *Rhapidophyllum*, the needle palm, inspire the name Chinese needle palm. Despite its limestone habitat origin, the plant tolerates various well-drained soils; sun or shade; and warm temperate, Mediterranean, subtropical, and tropical climates. Desert zones may not be to its liking.

Use this hard-to-find species as a foliage element in mixed plantings, in a container, or as a low hedge. Or place this cliff-dweller in an elevated position to afford an upward view to the luminous abaxial surfaces of its leaves.

APPEARANCE *leaves*, 4 ft. (1.2 m) long; *clump span*, 6 ft. (1.8 m); *clump height*, 6 ft. (1.8 m); *trunk*, 2 ft. (0.6 m) tall and 2 in. (5 cm) thick

CULTURE *hardiness*, 18°F (−8°C); *exposure*, full sun to part shade; *soil*, calcareous to neutral, well-drained; *climate*, warm temperate, subtropical, tropical, Mediterranean

TOLERANCE *drought*, moderate; *salt*, presumed low

HEAT REQUIREMENT moderate

USES AND EFFECTS shrub, foliage, understory, containers, hedge; *effect*, radial geometry; *special uses*, atop walls and slopes, on limestone substrates; *avoid* poorly drained soils

ALTERNATE SPECIES *Brahea moorei* (multiplanted), *Chamaerops humilis* var. *argentea*, *Rhapidophyllum hystrix*

AVAILABILITY rare

Hedyscepe canterburyana

UMBRELLA PALM, BIG MOUNTAIN PALM

One of the most colorful, clean-looking, and graceful palms we can grow in coastal California and other mild Mediterranean and frost-free temperate climates, this solitary, unarmed, monoecious native of elevations between 1000 and 2400 feet (305 and 732 m) on Australia's tiny Lord Howe Island in the South Pacific slowly develops a powdery blue-green trunk and crownshaft, apple-green foliage, and deep red fruits the size of a robin's eggs on branched inflorescences below the crown. Best in cool, humid regions, *H. canterburyana* is an uncommonly available species that prefers a bright, semishaded position in well-drained soil, and regular water. Its slow growth and modest proportions make it perfect for small gardens, reaching 10 feet (3 m) in thirty years, with a crown spanning 8 feet (2.4 m). It tolerates light frosts but should be planted only in the most frost-protected zones, because its slow growth allows frost-damaged foliage to persist. Minimize root disturbance upon planting. It is not especially tolerant of direct coastal exposure.

Hedyscepe canterburyana at the Gardens at Lake Merritt (Lakeside Palmetum), Oakland, California

APPEARANCE *leaves*, 4 ft. (1.2 m) long; *crown span*, 8 ft. (2.4 m); *trunk*, 20 ft. (6.1 m) tall and 8 in. (20 cm) thick, flared at the base

CULTURE *hardiness*, 28°F (−2°C); *exposure*, shade or part sun; *soil*, well-drained, moist; *climate*, mild warm temperate, cool tropical, mild Mediterranean

TOLERANCE *drought*, low; *salt*, low

HEAT REQUIREMENT low

USES AND EFFECTS groves, foliage, subcanopy tree, focal point, especially in small spaces; *effect*, formality; *special use*, windy locations; *avoid* dry, hot sun; drought; poor drainage; lengthy containerization; root disturbance

ALTERNATE SPECIES *Adonidia merrillii*, *Rhopalostylis baueri*

AVAILABILITY uncommon

Howea

Howea is a genus of two unarmed, monoecious, moderate-size feather palms from Lord Howe Island in the Tasman Sea, east of Port Macquarie in New South Wales, Australia, for which the genus is named. The smaller species, *H. belmoreana*, the curly palm, occupies low-altitude volcanic substrates; the other, *H. forsteriana*, the kentia palm, occupies lowland areas with calcareous soils. Both prefer mild subtropical and Mediterranean climates. They have spicate inflorescences that develop in the crown and are useful for floral design. Their leafbases do not form crownshafts and cling briefly to the stem before cleanly abscising; often a dead leaf or two hangs beneath the crown.

Two other palms are endemic to the tiny Lord Howe Island, both monotypic genera: *Hedyscepe* and *Lepidorrhachis*.

Howea forsteriana at Palihouse Santa Monica, designed by Surfacedesign, Santa Monica, California

Howea forsteriana

KENTIA PALM

A choice moderate-size palm adapted to windy seasides and still, shady dells alike is the kentia palm, *H. forsteriana*, from Australia's Lord Howe Island, where its natural habitat extends from thick forest to the beach. It's a tree with weeping, rustling green fronds; a green-ringed trunk fading to gray on sun-exposed and older portions; and a tendency to lean gently and flare at the base like a coconut palm. In addition to warm temperate and mild Mediterranean climates, this species can grow in warm subtropical and mild tropical climates—best there in shade. It tolerates only light frost: in California's Bay Area, I recommend it for the mildest urban and bayside locations but not for anywhere frost forms regularly on car windshields; its use is much more widespread in coastal Southern California. The slow-growing species tends to look better if grown in shade in its early years, especially away from marine influence.

Also useful in more protected exposures in mild subtropical, Mediterranean, and cool tropical climates is the other species in the genus, *H. belmoreana*. It has a more slender appearance, single-spike inflorescences, and a smaller crown of recurved and keeled leaves.

APPEARANCE *leaves*, 7–12 ft. (2.1–3.7 m) long; *crown span*, 10–18 ft. (3.0–5.5 m); *trunk*, 40 ft. (12.2 m) tall and 6–8 in. (15–20 cm) thick, often flaring at the base

CULTURE *hardiness*, 27°F (–3°C); *exposure*, shade or part shade, full sun at maturity; *soil*, well-drained, tolerant of alkalinity; *climate*, cool tropical, subtropical, mild Mediterranean, warm temperate with minimal frost

TOLERANCE *drought*, low to moderate; *salt*, moderate to high

HEAT REQUIREMENT low

USES AND EFFECTS focal point, leaning clusters and trios, groves, screens, containers, foliage, interiors, floral design (leaves, inflorescences, infructescences); *effects*, formal, mournful romanticism, verticality in confined areas and beneath tree canopy, jungle, movement, Victoriana, Antipodean exoticism; *special uses*, coastal settings, low light; *avoid* hot, dry conditions

ALTERNATE SPECIES *Archontophoenix cunninghamiana* (larger, with flatter leaves and a crownshaft), *Ceroxylon echinulatum*, *Clinostigma* spp., *Cocos nucifera*, *Veitchia joannis*, *V. winin*

AVAILABILITY common

Hyophorbe lagenicaulis at the Miami Beach Botanical Garden, designed by Raymond Jungles

Hyophorbe

A small genus of unarmed, moderate-size, sun-loving, single-trunk crownshaft palms from the Mascarene Islands in the Indian Ocean—Mauritius, Réunion, and Rodrigues—includes two species that are widely cultivated in the tropical and warm subtropical world. They attract attention for their impressively distended trunks and sculptural crowns of few leaves. A third species, *H. indica*, with an evenly cylindrical trunk, is gaining popularity in tropical and warm subtropical gardens as well. All prefer regular moisture in well-drained soil and are rare or endangered in habitat; one species, *H. amaricaulis*, is considered the rarest palm in the world, with a single, sterile, specimen growing in a botanical garden on Mauritius.

270

Hyophorbe lagenicaulis

BOTTLE PALM

The bottle palm is named for the heavy lower trunk, often cinched at the soil line, which tapers quickly to a narrower cylindrical neck below the glaucous green crownshaft and sparse crown of dark green, recurving, keeled feather leaves. Young plants' trunks are nearly globular, often with split leaf sheaths remaining attached before they adopt a neatly abscising habit in maturity and revealing regular leaf-scar rings; these fade with age, the trunk acquiring a gray, monolithic appearance. Beneath the crown form numerous inflorescences shaped in bud like steer horns. When the enclosing bracts fall, a disproportionately large, complex branched structure bearing the flowers opens, followed by small round fruits, brown when ripe. The open inflorescences and spent infructescences resemble tumbleweeds glued beneath the crownshaft.

The impression the palm makes is gnomelike and picturesque, with a weighty, fleshy character. It's inevitably a focal point, but it's also an excellent subject for close group planting. In addition to the tree's diminutive scale, its idiosyncratically leaning and swelling trunk defies the regularity most designers expect from palms. Do not rely on it for structuring a large space unless a parade of chess pieces suits the mood; its singular presence in tight quarters, however, can be thrilling. This palm grows at a moderate rate.

APPEARANCE *leaves*, 3–6 ft. (0.9–1.8 m) long; *crown span*, 8 ft. (2.4 m); *trunk*, 20 ft. (6.1 m) tall and 2 ft. (0.6 m) thick, tapering to 8 in. (20 cm)

CULTURE *hardiness*, 35°F (2°C); *exposure*, sun; *soil*, well-drained, tolerant of alkalinity; *climate*, tropical, warm subtropical

TOLERANCE *drought*, moderate; *salt*, moderate to high

HEAT REQUIREMENT high

USES AND EFFECTS focal point, small groups, containers, floral design (leaves, inflorescences, infructescences); *effects*, picturesque, sculptural, grotesque; *special uses*, coastal settings, lawn accent, among succulents; *avoid* frost

ALTERNATE SPECIES *Dypsis decipiens*

AVAILABILITY common

Hyophorbe verschaffeltii

SPINDLE PALM

The spindle palm's trunk is fusiform, swelling along the middle, and it grows taller than the bottle palm. It carries itself with greater formality. Like *H. lageni-caulis*, its leaves form a V-shape in cross section, but the leaflets' insertion to the rachis at more varied angles offers a more plumose effect. The crownshaft is waxy gray-green. Hornlike budded inflorescences are similar to those of *H. lagenicaulis*,

Hyophorbe verschaffeltii at Paul Humann's garden, Broward County, Florida

but in this species they are more pendulous and hang like a ponytail in bloom, producing smaller, darker, more oblong fruits. Young plants often have reddish or golden pigments on their petioles and rachises. The spindle palm grows at a moderate rate.

APPEARANCE *leaves*, 5–8 ft. (1.5–2.4 m) long; *crown span*, 10 ft. (3 m); *trunk*, 25 ft. (7.6 m) tall and 11–18 in. (28–46 cm) thick

CULTURE *hardiness*, 30°F (–1°C); *exposure*, sun; *soil*, well-drained, tolerant of alkalinity; *climate*, tropical, warm subtropical

TOLERANCE *drought*, moderate; *salt*, moderate

HEAT REQUIREMENT high

USES AND EFFECTS focal point, small groups, groves, street trees, containers, sentries, floral design (leaves, inflorescences, infructescences); *effects*, formal, sculptural, colorful; *special uses*, coastal settings, lawn accents, among succulents; *avoid* frost

ALTERNATE SPECIES *Dypsis decipiens*

AVAILABILITY common

272

Jubaea chilensis

CHILEAN WINE PALM, *PALMA CHILENA*

The majestic Chilean wine palm inhabits coastal mountains in its native central Chile habitat, where summer-dry Mediterranean climate conditions, with cooling coastal influence, are very similar to those in California. The trunk—the thickest of all palms—can measure up to 4 feet (1.2 m) in diameter, tapering with age to a narrower cylindrical stem, like a huge wine bottle. The crown of pinnate leaves appears stiff, surprisingly narrow and upright in most young trunked specimens, expanding into a broader globe of flexile leaves, particularly as the trunk begins tapering. For such a grand tree—and unlike the comparable-size Canary Island date palm (*Phoenix canariensis*)—it fits surprisingly well into narrow planting plots; by the time the crown of this slow-growing palm has expanded to its full breadth, it's tall enough for clearance.

Jubaea chilensis at the de Young Museum, San Francisco, in a landscape designed by Walter Hood

The leaves on many mature jubaeas fall in conspicuously spiraling ranks, from the newest spear down to the lowest dying leaves, adding the air of a pinwheel to the massive crown. Each leaf attaches to the trunk in a triangular leafbase that leaves behind a subtle diamond-shape scar; young plants retain leafbases. Jubaeas do not form a crownshaft. Tough, heavy vinyl–texture leaves resist wind, and established plants tolerate summer drought. It surpasses the similar scale Canary Island date palm in tolerance of cold and equals the Canary in its wind tolerance. Young plants are narrower and slower growing, but they catch up to the Canary as trunks develop. Although they take advantage of moderate year-round moisture in well-drained soils, jubaeas do not tolerate very warm, humid night temperatures, and they achieve their greatest beauty in Mediterranean climates. They can also be grown in temperate climates with ocean-moderated winters, such as in southwest England and western France.

APPEARANCE *leaves*, 12 ft. (3.7 m) long; *crown span*, 20–25 ft. (6.1–7.6 m); *trunk*, 60 ft. (18.3 m) tall and 3–4 ft. (0.9–1.2 m) thick

CULTURE *hardiness*, 14°F (−10°C); *exposure*, sun; *soil*, any but saturated; *climate*, Mediterranean, warm temperate, mild subtropical, desert

TOLERANCE *drought*, high; *salt*, moderate

HEAT REQUIREMENT low

USES AND EFFECTS monumental focal point, small groups, avenue planting, groves, among Mediterranean scrubs and succulents, sentries, floral design (inflorescences, bracts, infructescences); *effects*, formal, Jurassic, Mediterranean; *special uses*, monument, edible seeds; *avoid* hot, humid summers and nights

ALTERNATE SPECIES *Copernicia baileyana*, *C. fallaense* (trunk resemblance, not crown), *Parajubaea torallyi* var. *torallyi*, *Phoenix canariensis*

AVAILABILITY uncommon

×*Jubautia splendens*

An often fertile hybrid between two cold-hardy, drought-tolerant species, this rare, robust, monoecious solitary palm tree grows more quickly than either parent. One progenitor, the moderate-size *Butia odorata*, is particularly versatile, thriving in wet-summer climates, sun or shade, and seaside locations as well as inland and in summer-dry areas; the other, *Jubaea chilensis*, is a signature Mediterranean climate monarch among palms, sun-loving and grand. The plant's size can vary from nearly that of the behemoth Chilean parent *Jubaea* to a middle size between it and the Brazilian *Butia* parent. The crown tends toward the *Butia* form, but often with a clearer, more open leaf architecture that makes for a nice container subject. Hybrid palm seedlings more closely resemble the seed-bearing parent; thus, if the mother is *B. odorata* (×*Jubautia splendens* 'Dick Douglas'), the hybrid seedling tends to show a slightly greater resemblance to the butia, and seedlings from *J. chilensis* mothers (×*Jubautia splendens* 'Don Nelson') resemble that species slightly more than the butia pollen parent. Leafbases do not form a crownshaft. Use it in place of *Jubaea* species where summers are too hot and wet, in park-size settings, along avenues, as a specimen tree, in varied-height trios, as gate sentries—even in large containers, where it can be sustained for many years.

APPEARANCE *leaves*, 13 ft. (4 m) long; *crown span*, 18 ft. (5.5 m); *trunk*, 50 ft. (15.2 m) tall and 2–3 ft. (0.6–0.9 m) thick

CULTURE *hardiness*, 15°F (−9°C); *exposure*, sun; *soil*, any but saturated; *climate*, Mediterranean, warm temperate, subtropical, high desert

TOLERANCE *drought*, high; *salt*, high

HEAT REQUIREMENT low

USES AND EFFECTS focal point, avenue planting, containers, small groups, sentries, floral design (leaves, inflorescences, bracts, infructescences); *effects*, Jurassic, Mediterranean, tropical; *special use*, seaside; *avoid* excessively wet conditions

ALTERNATE SPECIES *Butia odorata* (crown resemblance)

AVAILABILITY rare

above: ×*Jubautia splendens* 'Dick Douglas' at the late Dick Douglas's garden, Walnut Creek, California

right: *Kerriodoxa elegans* at Hale Mohalu, Big Island, Hawai'i

Kerriodoxa elegans

Occupying a monotypic, dioecious genus, this low-growing, shade-loving, thirsty foliage palm from Phuket, Thailand, produces very large, flat, circular fans from a short trunk. *Kerriodoxa elegans* slowly becomes a short tree with a broader than tall crown. Green on the upper surface, the leaves' undersides are silvery white, while the sharp-edged but toothless leaf stalks are ebony. The leaf blades are divided one-third to one-half the distance from segment tips to the point of petiole attachment. Short inflorescences with white flowers emerge within the leaves. Best protected from wind, this plant works well in groupings in an understory planting, especially on a hill or above a retaining wall, to emphasize the contrasting leaf surfaces. It tolerates light frost but requires ample regular water, making it suitable for tropical and subtropical landscapes and for irrigated gardens in the warmest maritime-influenced Mediterranean and warm temperate gardens.

APPEARANCE *leaves*, 8 ft. (2.4 m) long; *crown span*, 12 ft. (3.7 m); *trunk*, rarely to 15 ft. (4.6 m) tall and 5–8 in. (13–20 cm) thick

CULTURE *hardiness*, 30°F (−1°C); *exposure*, sun; *soil*, moist, well-drained, tolerates calcareous substrates; *climate*, tropical, subtropical, mildest Mediterranean, warm temperate

TOLERANCE *drought*, low; *salt*, low

HEAT REQUIREMENT high

USES AND EFFECTS understory, grouped focal point, large scale in small spaces, containers, floral design (leaves, inflorescence, infructescence); *effects*, Jurassic, tropical; *special uses*, hillsides, atop walls; *avoid* wind, sun, drought

ALTERNATE SPECIES *Brahea calcarea*; young, shaded *Livistona chinensis* and *L. saribus*; young *Pritchardia* spp.; young *Saribus rotundifolius* (in container, tropical, warmest subtropical); all become taller tree palms with age, however

AVAILABILITY uncommon

Latania

LATAN PALMS

This small genus of moderate to large, unarmed, solitary tree palms from Mauritius, Réunion, and Rodrigues islands in the southwest Indian Ocean is one of the most poised and charismatic in the family. Deeply cut, heavy-texture costapalmate leaves, silvery gray in maturity, form open, orbicular crowns with jagged silhouettes atop thin, clean trunks, their bases pleasingly flared where they meet the ground. Leaves carry woolly indumentum on stout, unarmed petioles. Leafbases lack fibers and split neatly beneath the petiole, forming a triangular sinus. Inflorescences are sculptural and appealing as cut floral material. Latan palms can tolerate a modicum of drought as well as coastal conditions with some salt exposure. All demand frost-free tropical or subtropical conditions with sustained warmth and bright light. Supply regular moisture in the landscape for best performance. The three species—*L. loddigesii*, *L. lontaroides*, and *L. verschaffeltii*—may produce hybrid offspring when cultivated together.

Latania loddigesii

BLUE LATAN PALM

An exceptionally beautiful palm regularly available for tropical and warm subtropical landscapes, *L. loddigesii* survives in habitat on islets around its native Mauritius, the main island, from which it's been extirpated. It grows at a slow or moderate rate, preferring full sun and regular moisture. Use it as singular focal point, in small groves, or as a street or allée tree, and take advantage of its serenely colorful character and elegance.

Latania loddigesii at Pat Tierney's garden, Key West, Florida

APPEARANCE *leaves*, 8 ft. (2.4 m) long; *crown span*, 15 ft. (4.6 m); *trunk*, 35 ft. (10.7 m) tall and 10 in. (25 cm) thick, flared at the base

CULTURE *hardiness*, 35°F (2°C); *exposure*, full sun or part shade; *soil*, well-drained, tolerates calcareous substrates; *climate*, tropical, frostless subtropical

TOLERANCE *drought*, moderate; *salt*, high

HEAT REQUIREMENT high

USES AND EFFECTS focal point, duos and trios, groves, large scale in small spaces, street tree, allées, sentries, floral design (leaves, inflorescences, infructescences); *effects*, tropical, color; *special use*, large scale in a small space; *avoid* frost

ALTERNATE SPECIES *Bismarckia nobilis, Brahea clara, Pritchardia hillebrandii*

AVAILABILITY common

Lepidorrhachis mooreana

LITTLE MOUNTAIN PALM

The perfect coastal fog-belt palm, this extraordinarily rare, small, single-trunk pinnate species grows in a one-half-square-kilometer area atop a windy, mist-draped mountain on Australia's tiny Lord Howe Island in the Tasman Sea. With a green, ringed trunk, and lacking a complete crownshaft, it's a steadily growing treelet that prefers "full fog" exposure. In shade it will grow more slowly. Adapted to wind, but not to direct coastal exposure, it's useful for its diminutive size (to 6 feet, or 1.8 m, tall); clean, upswept appearance; and adaptation to a low-heat, high-humidity climate—qualities that make it an exceptional plant for San Francisco urban gardens and coastal California, especially in cool, foggy districts.

APPEARANCE *leaves*, 8 ft. (2.4 m) long; *crown span*, 12 ft. (3.7 m); *trunk*, 15 ft. (4.6 m) tall and 5–8 in. (13–20 cm) thick

CULTURE *hardiness*, 28°F (−2°C); *exposure*, full sun or part shade; *soil*, moist, well-drained; *climate*, cool tropical, cool temperate, Mediterranean with minimal frost

TOLERANCE *drought*, low; *salt*, low

HEAT REQUIREMENT low

USES AND EFFECTS understory, small groups, mini tree, containers, floral design (leaves); *effects*, cloud forest, woodland; *special uses*, chilly, windy, foggy locations; *avoid* heat, drought

ALTERNATE SPECIES *Chamaedorea carchensis* (cool tropical, subtropical, mild warm temperate, Mediterranean), *Hedyscepe canterburyana*

AVAILABILITY rare

Licuala

Licuala is a very large genus of ornamental, monoecious, moisture-loving costapalmate palms from South and Southeast Asia, the Malesia region, and Australia. They are characterized by mostly circular, appealingly pleated leaf blades that are irregularly (sometimes regularly) divided or entire, with outer margins that look like they've been clipped by pinking shears. Often armed, *Licuala* species range from tiny understory palms and trunkless foliage plants to clustering shrubs and singular, tall trees. Attractive inflorescences are often long, wiry, and branched, developing into infructescences with colorful red or black fruits. They tend to require tropical conditions, although a few species are adaptable to subtropical and even very mild Mediterranean and warm temperate landscapes with irrigation. Recently, the largely Vietnamese and Chinese genus *Lanonia* has been separated from *Licuala*; a number of species in this new genus, such as *Lanonia dasyantha*, may prove cold-hardy enough for subtropical, Mediterranean, and warm temperate climates.

Licuala peltata var. sumawongii

From Thailand, this moderate- to slow-growing, single-trunk tree shares with the widely available *L. grandis* a leaf blade with segments entirely joined along their margins; the blade of this species, however, is much larger, less undulate, shinier, and more elegant. The crown is much larger and very open because of its long petioles. It's an excellent large-scale element for a small space, a good container plant, an attention-grabbing accent amidst finer foliage, and a lovely moderate-scale tree in a wind-protected location, solitary or grouped. It offers greater tolerance of cool weather, including that of very mild Mediterranean climates such as coastal Southern California. Give it good drainage, regular moisture, and shade when it's young.

Licuala peltata var. *peltata*, more widespread in habitat but less popular in cultivation, occurs in a swath from northeast India to peninsular Malaysia and features irregularly split leaves, also very ornamental, and otherwise a similar plant to *L. peltata* var. *sumawongii*.

Licuala peltata var. *sumawongii* at the Naples Botanical Garden, Florida

APPEARANCE *leaves*, 10 ft. (3 m) long; *crown span*, 18 ft. (5.5 m); *trunk*, 20 ft. (6.1 m) tall and 4 in. (10 cm) thick

CULTURE *hardiness*, 28°F (−2°C); *exposure*, shade or part sun; *soil*, moist, well-drained, tolerates some alkalinity; *climate*, tropical, subtropical, mild Mediterranean

TOLERANCE *drought*, low; *salt*, low

HEAT REQUIREMENT moderate to high

USES AND EFFECTS focal point, small groups, floral design (leaves, inflorescences, infructescences); *effects*, tropical Southeast Asia; *special use*, large scale in small spaces; *avoid* wind

ALTERNATE SPECIES *Licuala grandis* and *L. orbicularis* (tropical), *Pritchardia* spp.

AVAILABILITY uncommon

Licuala ramsayi

A single-trunk, moderate-size, slow-growing tree with flat, divided leaves forming an open crown, this species occurs in rainforest habitat in Queensland, Australia. Fibrous leafbases cling to the trunk on younger palms, abscising with age to reveal a slender trunk. White flowers are borne on long inflorescences, yielding to hanging orange-red fruits. Happiest in partial shade, this tropical palm tolerates subtropical and very mild Mediterranean and warm temperate climates, but it cannot withstand drought.

Licuala ramsayi at La Casa de las Palmas, Hilo, Hawai'i

APPEARANCE *leaves*, 10 ft. (3 m) long; *crown span*, 18 ft. (5.5 m); *trunk*, 40 ft. (12.2 m) tall and 8 in. (20 cm) thick

CULTURE *hardiness*, 32°F (0°C); *exposure*, shade or part sun; *soil*, moist; *climate*, tropical, subtropical, mild warm temperate, Mediterranean

TOLERANCE *drought*, low; *salt*, low

HEAT REQUIREMENT high

USES AND EFFECTS focal point, small groups, groves, floral design (leaves, inflorescences, infructescences); *effect*, radial geometry; *special use*, sky silhouette; *avoid* wind

ALTERNATE SPECIES other *Licuala* spp. (tropical)

AVAILABILITY uncommon

Livistona australis at The Huntington Botanical Gardens shows typical spiraling trunk swelling and a weeping crown with a clutch of dead leaves.

Livistona

This genus of small to large, mostly monoecious single-trunk palm trees with armed costapalmate leaves ranges from Japan to India, Yemen and the Horn of Africa, Malaysia, Indonesia, the Philippines, New Guinea, and Australia. The commonly cultivated Australian species tend to be undemanding in their fertility requirements, at least in California landscapes. *Saribus rotundifolius*, formerly *Livistona rotundifolia*, is a fast-growing, very attractive tropical species with mahogany brown trunks, shiny round leaves, and sigmoid leafbase fiber patterns. Notable species not detailed here include *L. saribus*, a spectacular foliage palm slow to gain height, hardy to 26°F (−3°C); *L. mariae* and *L. carinensis*, desert-adapted tree palms, the former hardier to cold, 23°F (−5°C), than the latter, 30°F (−1°C), and with attractive reddish purple juvenile foliage, and the latter taller, to 70 feet (21.3 m) versus 40 feet (12.2 m).

Livistona australis

AUSTRALIAN FAN PALM, AUSTRALIAN CABBAGE PALM

The underused Australian fan palm inhabits wet forests on the eastern extreme of Victoria and the east coast of New South Wales, where it can be seen growing nearly up to the beach; it rises into the hills as its habitat stretches north in Queensland. Plant this lush, steadily growing, cold-hardy species in shade or sun. Its broad, weeping crown and comparatively thin, gently leaning trunk make it a graceful plant for park, avenue, and street tree planting, and for use under high tree canopy. In small residential gardens, this moderate- to fast-growing palm makes a big impact with a small footprint. Warm temperate, subtropical, and well-watered Mediterranean climate landscapes suit its needs, and it performs adequately in heat-starved and coastal areas.

Deeply divided, dark green, glinting leaves are stiffer and flatter in youth, particularly in shade. Quickly the segments become weeping and the petioles elongate as the plant matures to bear an open, spherical crown that susurrates in the wind. Plumey branched inflorescences briefly illuminate the crown's volumes with pale, off-white flowers, followed by small, black, marble-size fruits. Bloom cycles are reflected in the crown's alternating waves of longer and shorter leaves. Young plants' trunks retain dead leafbases. Older ones only briefly hold dead leaves; they peel off to reveal a cinnamon-brown trunk textured with shallow vertical fissures and rings of leafbase scars. Early leafbase stubs often remain at the flared base of the otherwise clean trunk.

APPEARANCE *leaves*, 8 ft. (2.4 m) long; *crown span*, 15 ft. (4.6 m); *trunk*, 50 ft. (15.2 m) tall and 10 in. (25 cm) thick, flared at the base

CULTURE *hardiness*, 18°F (−8°C); *exposure*, shade or full sun; *soil*, adaptable, tolerates wet soil; *climate*, warm temperate, subtropical, cool tropical, Mediterranean

TOLERANCE *drought*, moderate; *salt*, moderate to high

HEAT REQUIREMENT low

USES AND EFFECTS canopy tree, sentries, allées, small group, groves, lawns, vertical element under tree canopy, floral design (leaves); *effect*, fountain; *special use*, canopy in narrow spaces; *avoid* excessive root disturbance

ALTERNATE SPECIES *Livistona decora*, *Washingtonia robusta*

AVAILABILITY uncommon

Livistona chinensis

CHINESE FAN PALM

One of the most common ornamental palms in subtropical, warm temperate, and tropical areas, the moisture-preferring Chinese fan palm's habitat is scattered from Hainan and Guongdong in China to Japan's Ryukyu Islands, Kyushu, and Shikoku. It's rather frost-hardy and durable, a steady grower in warm-summer areas, fairly fast in tropical areas, and glacially slow in cool-summer coastal California. This latter case makes it useful as a foliage plant, for its glossy, shallowly divided juvenile fans are very appealing in shaded areas, the rosettes remaining trunkless for decades. Sun-grown, young plants take on a yellow-green hue, vibrant in some color combinations, sallow in others.

Segment tips hang down on maturing trees, especially in full sun, giving rise to another moniker, the Chinese fountain palm. Trunks readily lean toward light. Long, branching flower stalks in the crown eventually produce globose fruits, often a dark turquoise color.

Similar but larger, *L. boninensis*, from Japan's Ogasawara (or Bonin) Islands, has proven more cold-hardy than *L. chinensis* in Edith Bergstrom's garden in Atherton, California.

above: *Livistona chinensis* planted as foliage understory at the Gardens at Lake Merritt (Lakeside Palmetum), Oakland, California

right: *Livistona decora* at Carole Bowen's garden, Alamo, California

APPEARANCE *leaves*, 7 ft. (2.1 m) long; *crown span*, 12 ft. (3.7 m); *trunk*, 40 ft. (12.2 m) tall and 12 in. (31 cm) thick, flared at the base

CULTURE *hardiness*, 20°F (−7°C); *exposure*, shade or full sun; *soil*, adaptable, tolerates wet soil; *climate*, subtropical, tropical, warm temperate, Mediterranean

TOLERANCE *drought*, moderate; *salt*, moderate

HEAT REQUIREMENT moderate

USES AND EFFECTS foliage and understory (an enduring use in cooler areas), sentries, street tree, allées, small groups, groves, in lawns, vertical element under tree canopy, containers, floral design (leaves, infructescences); *effects*, fountain, Asian motif; *special uses*, foliage, interior; *avoid* excessive root disturbance

ALTERNATE SPECIES *Brahea calcarea*, *Livistona australis*, *L. boninensis* (same climates but slightly more cold-hardy), *L. saribus* (tropical, subtropical, mild warm temperate, mild Mediterranean)

AVAILABILITY common

Livistona decora

RIBBON PALM

Shiny ribbons hang in the crown of this tall, fast-growing, cold-hardy palm tree, now fairly common on the market in California and quite popular in Florida. I call it the weeping willow of palms. There's nothing else like it. As a very young plant, its pointy, deeply divided leaves, often reddish purple upon unfolding, give no clue as to the shimmering, languid beauty it soon will become. The leaf divides nearly to the base of the fan, allowing the segments to curve out and then straight down like tinsel. With its thin trunk and broad crown, this sturdy species appears quite delicate. Breezes accentuate the effect. It appreciates regular moisture and can be quite fast growing.

APPEARANCE *leaves*, 8 ft. (2.4 m) long; *crown span*, 16 ft. (4.9 m); *trunk*, 50 ft. (15.2 m) tall and 10 in. (25 cm) thick, flared at the base

CULTURE *hardiness*, 20°F (−7°C); *exposure*, sun; *soil*, adaptable, tolerates wet soil; *climate*, subtropical, tropical, warm temperate, Mediterranean

TOLERANCE *drought*, moderate; *salt*, low

HEAT REQUIREMENT moderate

USES AND EFFECTS sentries, street tree, allées, small groups, groves, in lawns, canopy; *effects*, fountain, luster, oasis, night lighting; *special uses*, movement and sound; *avoid* excessive root disturbance

ALTERNATE SPECIES *Livistona australis*, *Syagrus romanzoffiana*

AVAILABILITY common

Livistona fulva at the Gardens at Lake Merritt (Lakeside Palmetum), Oakland, California

Livistona fulva

BLACKDOWN TABLELAND PALM

Livistona fulva carries a crown of shiny, leathery leaves with stiff segment tips—the latter a distinctive characteristic. With an alluring coppery cast to the undersides of new leaves, the modest-size palm makes a poised impression—and it's my favorite of the livistonas. Slow-growing and never too large, it's a welcome foliage plant-cum-palm tree for smaller spaces, planted in groves or rows, and as a focal point. Plant atop a wall or upslope to afford a view to the coppery leaf glow. As with many fan palms, dead leafbases remain attached for years until the plant reaches maturity and begins to shed them spontaneously.

APPEARANCE *leaves*, 10 ft. (3 m) long; *crown span*, 16 ft. (4.9 m); *trunk*, 20 ft. (6.1 m) tall and 12 in. (31 cm) thick

CULTURE *hardiness*, 26°F (−3°C); *exposure*, sun or part shade; *soil*, adaptable, tolerates wet soil; *climate*, subtropical, tropical, warm temperate, Mediterranean

TOLERANCE *drought*, moderate; *salt*, low

HEAT REQUIREMENT low

USES AND EFFECTS sentries, street tree, small groups, groves, silhouette, in lawns, floral design (leaves); *effects*, sculptural, night lighting; *special uses*, color, view from below; *avoid* excessive root disturbance

ALTERNATE SPECIES *Brahea calcarea, B. edulis*

AVAILABILITY rare

Livistona nitida

CARNARVON FAN PALM

A cold-hardy, large, and beautiful rare fan palm from the inland Carnarvon Gorge area of Queensland, Australia, this moderate- to fast-growing species is adaptable to inland as well as coastal climates. The well-proportioned, elegant crown with a weeping fringe grows atop a tall, ramrod-straight, robust trunk that retains leafbases for years until the plant begins spontaneously abscising them. It resembles a thicker *L. australis* with less deeply divided leaves and earns mention as well for its tolerance of cold. Plant in full or half sun in well-drained soil, water moderately, and fertilize regularly for speedy growth; the palm reaches 10 to 15 feet (3.0 to 4.6 m) in fifteen years. It will provide great satisfaction in cool zones as well as warmer areas. *Livistona nitida* has also proven tolerant of coastal conditions in southwest Ireland, in a climate as heat-deprived as any palm grower might encounter—and close to the antipode of its origin.

APPEARANCE *leaves*, 8 ft. (2.4 m) long; *crown span*, 15 ft. (4.6 m); *trunk*, 70 ft. (21.3 m) tall and 12 in. (31 cm) thick

CULTURE *hardiness*, 18°F (−8°C); *exposure*, sun or part shade; *soil*, adaptable; *climate*, subtropical, desert, tropical, warm temperate, Mediterranean

TOLERANCE *drought*, moderate; *salt*, moderate

HEAT REQUIREMENT low

USES AND EFFECTS large sentries, street tree, small groups, groves, allées, floral design (leaves); *effects*, height, night lighting; *special uses*, colder zones, heat-starved locations; *avoid* excessive root disturbance

ALTERNATE SPECIES *Livistona australis, Washingtonia robusta*

AVAILABILITY rare

Marojejya

In a genus of only two species (*M. darianii* and *M. insignis*), this big, rare, unarmed tropical feather palm from Madagascar with exceptional form warrants a peek and a mention. Leafbases do not form a crownshaft.

Marojejya darianii

FEATHER PALM

Large, entire to irregularly divided, upright feather leaves with no discernible petiole funnel water and leaf litter to the base of this slow- to moderate-growing, water-loving species. Its habitat is limited to a wet valley bottom in northeast Madagascar. Its stunning appearance warrants including *M. darianii* as a giant foliage element in wet-tropical or moist, frost-free subtropical gardens that can afford it some shade. Growers say that even in a downpour, the canopy creates a dry haven close to the tree. It tolerates near freezing temperatures and less-than-sweltering summers, perhaps because of its 1300-foot (396 m) habitat altitude. The palm becomes arborescent over time, changing but not reducing its majestic impact, even as leaves become more divided. Dark pink fingered inflorescences emerge from among the leaves, which remain attached to the trunk for a period after dying.

APPEARANCE *leaves*, 12 ft. (3.7 m) long; *crown span*, 15 ft. (4.6 m); *trunk*, 10 ft. (3 m) tall and 12 in. (31 cm) thick

CULTURE *hardiness*, 32°F (0°C); *exposure*, shade or part sun; *soil*, wet, acidic; *climate*, tropical, warm subtropical

TOLERANCE *drought*, low; *salt*, low

HEAT REQUIREMENT moderate

USES AND EFFECTS foliage, understory, floral design (leaves, inflorescences); *effects*, Jurassic, tropical; *special uses*, shade, tropical understory; *avoid* drought, wind

ALTERNATE SPECIES *Rhopalostylis* spp. (upright crown, slow trunk growth, but regularly divided leaves); *Verschaffeltia splendida* (upright, undivided leaves, but with quick vertical growth)

AVAILABILITY rare

Parajubaea

This genus of unarmed, single-trunk monoecious palms from high altitudes in the Andes appears to tolerate bayside winds and—surprisingly—some light salt exposure, in particular the Bolivian *P. torallyi* var. *torallyi*; we have been observing this palm the past few years at Emery Cove Yacht Harbor on San Francisco Bay, facing the windy Golden Gate. Like many California palm enthusiasts, we at Flora Grubb Gardens call these Andean coconuts because they superficially resemble their cousin the coconut palm, and they produce small, edible, coconutlike seeds. Leafbases adhere to the trunk until the tree is well into maturity, at which point they slough off, leaving naked, somewhat smooth trunks; a few dead leaves remain attached below the crown. Leafbases do not form a crownshaft. These plants are all rather speedy growers in our cool-summer climate, and they perform much better here than the common queen palm, to which they're also related. They're lovely subjects for park planting, in groves, with low shrubs and succulents, and as street trees. Single trees work best in smaller spaces. All prefer full sun.

Parajubaea sunkha, the zunca palm, from altitudes as high as 7200 feet (2195 m) in the Bolivian Andes, is the smallest of the genus. Although it thrives without heat, it appears to have greater tolerance of heat and drought than the other two species in the genus, and it may also have greater cold tolerance. It is rare in the trade but worthy of much greater use, particularly in Mediterranean and warm temperate climates.

A palm enthusiast who gardens with seaside exposure in Hobart, Tasmania, reports success with all the taxa in the genus—*P. cocoides*, *P. sunkha*, as well as *P. torallyi* var. *torallyi* and *P. torallyi* var. *microcarpa*.

Parajubaea cocoides

QUITO PALM, *COCO CUMBI*

This graceful and rare coconut look-alike graces the colonial streets of Quito and other Andean cities of Ecuador and Colombia. No other palm except *Beccariophoenix alfredii* looks more like a coconut while tolerating cool temperatures. The moderate-size to tall tree produces a crown of flat, arching, satin-backed, dark green and shiny leaves that swing dramatically in the wind atop a straight trunk clad in leafbases well into maturity. Older trees' relatively slender trunks are smooth and slightly flared at the base. Narrow, branched inflorescences produce creamy flowers in the crown followed by coconutlike green-brown fruits on infructescences that arch out and down. Almost extinct in the wild, it's one of the fastest growing palms for San Francisco and similar fresh climates, requiring cool summers to thrive. It tolerates light frosts. Plant as young as possible in its permanent, full-sun location—it will not tolerate root disturbance—provide ample water and fertilizer, and within fifteen years it will be a 15-foot (4.6-m) tree producing one-tenth–scale edible coconuts. It is happy in the foggiest locales as

below left: *Parajubaea cocoides* at the Gardens at Lake Merritt (Lakeside Palmetum), Oakland, California

below: *Butia odorata* × *Parajubaea cocoides* at Bergstrom Gardens, Atherton, California

well as in mild areas with humid air. Once established, it will survive occasional drought but needs regular water to thrive.

A hybrid of the versatile, durable *Butia odorata* and the cloud-forest–adapted *P. cocoides* grows very quickly into a large, graceful, cold-hardy, drought-tolerant tree. Dimensions and uses are similar to those of *P. torallyi* var. *torallyi*. It is very rare.

APPEARANCE *leaves*, 12 ft. (3.7 m) long; *crown span*, 20 ft. (6.1 m); *trunk*, 50 ft. (15.2 m) tall and 12 in. (31 cm) thick, with subtle basal flare

CULTURE *hardiness*, 23°F (−5°C); *exposure*, sun; *soil*, well-drained; *climate*, cool tropical, warm temperate, mild Mediterranean

TOLERANCE *drought*, moderate; *salt*, moderate

HEAT REQUIREMENT low

USES AND EFFECTS street tree, groves, allées, floral design (leaves, bracts, infructescences); *effects*, cloud forest, tropical, Spanish colonial, color; *special uses*, movement and sound, edible seeds; *avoid* dry, hot conditions; warm nights; transplanting

ALTERNATE SPECIES *Beccariophoenix alfredii, Cocos nucifera, Parajubaea sunkha, P. torallyi*

AVAILABILITY rare

Parajubaea torallyi var. *torallyi*

PASOPAYA PALM, BOLIVIAN COCONUT

A rare, fast-growing, large tree from high in the Bolivian Andes (reputedly up to 10,500 feet, or 3200 m), this promising palm species looks like a husky, straight-trunk coconut palm in need of a shave (at least when young). Give it full sun, good drainage, and moderate water, and then stand back to watch it develop into a graceful and substantial palm with a hefty, fiber-clad trunk and finely divided pinnate leaves with pale satiny undersides. It has minimal requirements for fertilizer but responds well to its application. Once established, it will tolerate drought and significant frost and produces edible miniature coconuts inside a thick, corneous shell at maturity. It grows well in California's coastside and coastal-valley microclimates, from the San Francisco Bay Area to San Diego, and succeeds in mild areas of the Central Valley. It tolerates moderate frosts. Plant as young as possible and avoid disturbing its roots. This species has shown tolerance of coastal conditions in Hobart, Tasmania, and along San Francisco Bay.

APPEARANCE *leaves*, 18 ft. (5.5 m) long; *crown span*, 25 ft. (7.6 m); *trunk*, 60 ft. (18.3 m) tall and 2 ft. (0.6 m) thick

CULTURE *hardiness*, 22°F (−6°C); *exposure*, sun; *soil*, well-drained; *climate*, cool, dry subtropical and tropical, warm temperate, Mediterranean

TOLERANCE *drought*, moderate to high; *salt*, moderate

HEAT REQUIREMENT low

USES AND EFFECTS street tree, groves, allées, landmark tree, floral design (bracts, infructescences); *effects*, wild and woolly; *special uses*, movement and sound, edible seeds; *avoid* warm and wet conditions together, transplanting

ALTERNATE SPECIES *Beccariophoenix alfredii, Cocos nucifera, Jubaea chilensis, Parajubaea cocoides, P. sunkha, Phoenix canariensis*

AVAILABILITY uncommon

Phoenix

The dioecious date palms come from a scattered range starting in the Canary Islands at the west and ending in China and Taiwan at the east. Characterized by a set of spiny, often fierce, modified leaflets on the pinnate leaves close to the center of the crown, the genus includes tree palms as well as trunkless, shrubby foliage plants, and is divided between clustering and single-stem members. Besides the dagger- and needlelike modified basal leaflets, another telltale sign that you've encountered a *Phoenix* species is that its leaflets are folded upward, making a V-shape in cross section. The leaflets on most species are angled in two or more slightly divergent planes along the rachis, rendering a slightly plumose or corrugated effect to the leaf blade.

The cliff date palm, *P. rupicola*, with leaflets in one plane rendering a flat leaf, is a notable exception. Leafbases do not form a crownshaft. Those with groomed trunks exhibit a pattern of regular, often diamond-shaped or spiraling stubby leaf scars; ungroomed plants with retained fiber-edged leafbases have a wild vitality. Many species are quite cold-hardy and drought-tolerant.

Phoenix canariensis

CANARY ISLAND DATE PALM

The very large, single-trunk palm is a staple of Mediterranean climate landscapes; it grows on San Francisco's Dolores Street, promenades along the Mediterranean Sea, and shows up in shots of movies and television, marking the sybaritic side of Los Angeles. Native to the Canary Islands, Spain's volcanic archipelago off the Atlantic coast of Morocco, it thrives in summer-dry climates, tolerating significant winter cold, coastal exposure, and drought in cultivation. Slow to moderate growing but healthy in foggy, heat-starved areas, it will also grow in the heat and summer rain of subtropical and warm temperate climates. The stately, diamond-patterned trunk topped with a "pineapple" boss of cut leafbases beneath the huge, even crown of rich green leaves on a well-groomed "canary" forms a singular entity.

Phoenix canariensis at the California Academy of Sciences, San Francisco

This palm creates its own context, establishing a patterned, canopied realm when planted in groves, setting a pace in avenue plantings. A single mature tree in a moderate-size to large urban garden can make the space, providing a benevolent column and canopy, often festooned with epiphytes; on the other hand, it can easily overwhelm modest or small spaces, especially as a young plant in rosette phase. Nonetheless, its durability, ease of propagation (feral and intentional), and low cost destine it to overwhelm many unwitting gardeners' landscapes. Young specimens perform beautifully as long-term container plants when positioned to minimize exposure to the leaf spines near the crown's center, the wounds of which are notoriously long-lasting and prone to infection.

Because of the risk of fatal fusarium wilt on Canary Island date palms in California, it's best to use the similar-size Chilean palm, *Jubaea chilensis*, wherever possible, instead; tall specimens of the latter are expensive and rare, however. *Parajubaea torallyi* var. *torallyi*, as yet rarely available, reaches the same size as Canaries and Chilean palms in Mediterranean and cooler subtropical climates, but faster. *Phoenix dactylifera* is another substitute if the goal is to plant at full size.

APPEARANCE *leaves*, 18 ft. (5.5 m) long; *crown span*, 30 ft. (9.1 m); *trunk*, 80 ft. (24.3 m) tall and 3 ft. (0.9 m) thick

CULTURE *hardiness*, 20°F (−7°C); *exposure*, sun or shade; *soil*, well-drained but adaptable; *climate*, Mediterranean, warm temperate, subtropical

TOLERANCE *drought*, moderate to high; *salt*, high

HEAT REQUIREMENT low

USES AND EFFECTS sentries, groves, bosquets, allées, focal point, containers, floral design (leaves, inflorescences, infructescences); *effects*, Mediterranean, architectural, formal, ranch, night lighting; *special use*, place-making tree; *avoid* wet, saturated soils

ALTERNATE SPECIES *Jubaea chilensis, Phoenix dactylifera, P. sylvestris* (tropical, subtropical, desert, Mediterranean, warm temperate)

AVAILABILITY common

Phoenix dactylifera

DATE PALM

Plentiful trunked date palm trees for landscapes originate in the fruit orchards of the California and Arizona deserts, and of course from their original Middle Eastern and North African homes, where thousands of varieties of one of our first cultivated fruit trees have been developed over millennia. The species is naturally clustering, but farmers in the United States usually keep orchard-grown trees free of suckers, replanting those clones for future fruit production. In the landscape, blue-green, open crowns of stiffly arching, spine-tipped leaves burst from the summit of thin, knobby trunks (groomed or diamond-cut), or huskier trunks (with fibrous leafbases attached). The cultivars 'Zahidi' and 'Medjool' seem to tolerate humid summers better than 'Deglet Noor'. Slightly more cold-hardy than Canary Island date palms, true date palms look best where summer warmth enables the crown to renew the waxy blue-gray cast on the leaves. True date palms, though slender and glaucous, can replace Canary Island date palms where fusarium wilt is a risk when tall specimens are needed. Plants managed for multiple leaning stems often with a basal fringe of foliage can be very attractive large focal points. Take care to position younger plants to account for the sharpness of the leaflet tips. Unlike leaves of agaves, yuccas, or cactuses, date palms' daggered leaves can flail around in the wind. This species grows at a moderate speed.

APPEARANCE *leaves*, 15 ft. (4.6 m) long; *crown span*, 20 ft. (6.1 m); *clump span*, 50 ft. (15.2 m); *trunk*, 80 ft. (24.3 m) tall and 20 in. (51 cm) thick

CULTURE *hardiness*, 15°F (−9°C); *exposure*, sun; *soil*, well-drained but adaptable; *climate*, desert, Mediterranean, warm temperate, subtropical, tropical

TOLERANCE *drought*, moderate to high; *salt*, high

HEAT REQUIREMENT moderate

USES AND EFFECTS sentries, bosquets, groves, allées, focal point, natural or groomed cluster, security barrier, floral design (leaves, inflorescences, infructescences); *effects*, oasis, architectural, formal, ranch, night lighting; *special uses*, edible fruit in hot desert and areas with long, hot, dry seasons; *avoid* contact with spines; wet, saturated soils

ALTERNATE SPECIES, *Phoenix canariensis*, *P. reclinata*, *P. sylvestris* (tropical, subtropical, desert, Mediterranean, warm temperate)

AVAILABILITY common

Phoenix reclinata

SENEGAL DATE PALM

Perhaps no other widely grown palm embodies the clustering habit as ostentatiously as this wide-ranging and adaptable African species. Slender, sinuous, arborescent stems grow up and away from each other while younger growth fringes the base. Ungroomed thickets conjure a jungle atmosphere with a wall of foliage and peek-a-boo stems. Pruning and grooming can articulate a specimen to make it worthy of the spotlight. Modest-size crowns of languid, nearly plumose, green to yellowish leaves carry creamy flowers and deep orange fruit clusters within them. Spiny near the leaf base, the palm's leaflet tips are sharp all along the plume. With

a native range spanning Sub-Saharan Africa from Senegal in the west to Ethiopia, Madagascar, and South Africa in the east and south, and climbing from sea level to 9000 feet (2743 m), the plant tolerates moderate frosts and cool weather (especially if propagated from seed from its most southerly and highest altitude habitats), yet it burgeons in tropical heat and performs best in sun. It often grows near water; moisture suits it, but it tolerates dry spells begrudgingly. In the driest desert heat, plants may seem scorched and haggard. It's a good, salt-tolerant seashore plant. Use it as a focal point above all, or as part of a hedgerow, a screen, or a copse. Prune it to one trunk or a few to manage it as a street tree where space allows (those pokey leaves). It's a plant that demands care and commands attention. This species grows at a moderate speed.

above: *Phoenix reclinata* (bottom) with a *P. reclinata* hybrid (top) at Ganna Walska Lotusland, Montecito, California

left: *Phoenix dactylifera* 'Medjool' with diamond-cut leafbases in a Sonoma County, California, garden designed by Exteriors Landscape Architecture

APPEARANCE *leaves*, 8–15 ft. (2.4–4.6 m) long; *crown span*, 12–18 ft. (3.7–5.5 m); *clump span*, 50 ft. (15.2 m); *trunk*, 30 ft. (9.1 m) tall and 4–8 in. (10–20 cm) thick

CULTURE *hardiness*, 25°F (−4°C); *exposure*, sun or part shade; *soil*, well-drained but adaptable; *climate*, tropical, subtropical, warm Mediterranean, warm temperate, mild desert

TOLERANCE *drought*, moderate; *salt*, high

HEAT REQUIREMENT moderate

USES AND EFFECTS focal point, natural or groomed cluster, sentries, avenue planting, silhouette, security barrier, single-trunk–pruned tree, floral design (leaves, inflorescences, infructescences); *effects*, oasis, jungle, night lighting; *special use*, seaside; *avoid* freezing, dry conditions

ALTERNATE SPECIES *Phoenix dactylifera* (natural clustering form and groomed), *P. roebelenii* (planted in clusters or in its rare, wild, clustering form), *P. rupicola* (planted in clusters)

AVAILABILITY common

Phoenix roebelenii

PYGMY DATE PALM

The pygmy date palm is the perfect small palm tree. Fully grown plants (to 10 feet, or 3 m, in thirty years) look to be plucked at one-to-one scale from a Bierstadt painting, with shiny, feathery leaves; little clusters of flowers and dates; and relaxed, leaning trunks with a diameter of 3 to 4 inches (8 to 10 cm). They are slow growing and thus useful for many years as little foliage plants to accompany ferns and perennials, staying happy in containers, too, in sun or shade. Plants in the fog belt are not as reliable as those on the warmer east side of San Francisco and elsewhere in the mild Bay Area. Frost below 27°F (–3°C) will damage leaves, but plants rebound from 24°F (–4°C) with the onset of warm weather. Regular water is key to keeping this type of palm happy, though it's not as thirsty as a tree fern. It is at its best in subtropical and tropical areas.

Phoenix roebelenii at Richard Gervais's garden, San Francisco

APPEARANCE *leaves*, 3–6 ft. (0.9–1.8 m) long; *crown span*, 6–10 ft. (1.8–3.0 m); *trunk*, 12 ft. (3.7 m) tall and 3 in. (8 cm) thick

CULTURE *hardiness*, 25°F (–4°C); *exposure*, shade or full sun; *soil*, well-drained but adaptable; *climate*, tropical, subtropical, mild warm temperate, Mediterranean

TOLERANCE *drought*, low to moderate; *salt*, low

HEAT REQUIREMENT moderate

USES AND EFFECTS focal point, small-space tree, foliage accent, understory, duos and trios, groves, screens, informal hedges, containers, interiors, floral design (leaves, inflorescences, infructescences); *effects*, jungle, oasis, miniature, Asian motif, shift of scale; *special use*, containers; *avoid* freezing, dry conditions

ALTERNATE SPECIES, *Phoenix rupicola, Ravenea hildebrandtii* (tropical, subtropical, mild warm temperate, Mediterranean), *Syagrus* spp. (formerly *Lytocaryum*; subtropical, tropical, mild warm temperate, Mediterranean)

AVAILABILITY common

Phoenix rupicola

CLIFF DATE PALM

The most graceful of the genus, this moderate-size palm tree grows slowly and prefers ample water, good drainage, and fertile soil. Looking best in tropical and subtropical zones, it can also grow in Mediterranean and warm temperate climates as long as nutrition is sufficient—lower leaves tend to yellow through winter. Its

Phoenix rupicola at Sherry
Merciari's garden, Oakland,
California

arching leaves are flat and shiny, contributing a good part to its beauty. The trunk, when it forms, is relatively slender. Carrot-orange clusters of small fruits form on female plants.

APPEARANCE *leaves*, 8 ft. (2.4 m) long; *crown span*, 15 ft. (4.6 m); *trunk*, 18 ft. (5.5 m) tall and 10 in. (25 cm) thick

CULTURE *hardiness*, 24°F (−4°C); *exposure*, full sun or part shade; *soil*, well-drained; *climate*, tropical, subtropical, mild warm temperate, Mediterranean

TOLERANCE *drought*, low; *salt*, low

HEAT REQUIREMENT moderate

USES AND EFFECTS focal point, foliage accent, duos and trios, groves, screens, containers, floral design (leaves, inflorescences, infructescences); *effects*, jungle, formal, color (fruit); *special use*, containers; *avoid* freezing or dry conditions, wet or saturated soils

ALTERNATE SPECIES single-trunk–pruned *Phoenix reclinata*, *P. roebelenii* (larger specimens)

AVAILABILITY uncommon

Pinanga

This very large genus of unarmed, monoecious crownshaft palms comprises numerous appealing species for moist tropical gardens. Gorgeous inflorescences and colorful infructescences distinguish most of the species. One, *P. coronata*, has shown tolerance of mild Mediterranean and cool subtropical conditions.

Pinanga coronata

IVORY CANE PALM

A palm combining gracious form and texture, subtle and vivid color, this slow-growing Indonesian native thrives in moist, mild tropical climates, subtropical zones, and even very mild irrigated Mediterranean and warm temperate gardens. It's a medium-size clustering palm with grouped leaflets that produce a striated texture and meet in opposite symmetrical pairs on the rachis. The leaves' varied greens form a mottled, dappled pattern. New leaves open a deep rosy brown. Ringed trunks have long internodes between leafbase scars and resemble bamboo canes in their smooth green vitality. The inflorescence bears dense chains of triangular white flower buds on its pendent, yellowtail tuna–tinted branches. As black fruits form, the branches turn red. Use *P. coronata* as a tidy bamboo substitute, a glamorous container plant, or a tufted hedge in shade.

APPEARANCE *leaves*, 5 ft. (1.5 m) long; *crown span*, 6 ft. (1.8 m); *clump span*, 10 ft. (3 m); *trunk*, 15 ft. (4.6 m) tall and 2 in. (5 cm) thick

CULTURE *hardiness*, 29°F (–2°C); *exposure*, shade; *soil*, well-drained; *climate*, tropical, subtropical, mild warm temperate and Mediterranean

TOLERANCE *drought*, low; *salt*, low

HEAT REQUIREMENT moderate

USES AND EFFECTS focal point, screens, hedge, understory, courtyard accent, containers, floral design (leaves, inflorescences, infructescences); *effects*, jungle, formal, color (flowers, fruit); *special use*, containers; *avoid* anything less than moist conditions, hot sun

ALTERNATE SPECIES *Areca vestiaria, Chamaedorea costaricana, Dypsis cabadae*

AVAILABILITY uncommon

Plectocomia

The vining rattan palms are largely kept out of ornamental gardens because they are ferociously spiny and quite unruly, climbing rapidly into and over trees and shrubs, often branching and suckering and rooting along recumbent stems. However, their spine patterns, feathery leaves, and reptilian fruits have a curious appeal. *Plectocomia* is one of several genera of vining palms, along with species of *Calamus, Daemonorops, Desmoncus*, and others. Leafbases form a sort of crownshaft.

Pinanga coronata at Hale Mohalu, Big Island, Hawai'i

Plectocomia himalayana

This clustering species from the Himalayas thrives in the cool climate of the San Francisco Botanical Garden, where it has invaded the canopy of a veteran *Magnolia doltsopa*, branching and clambering to neighboring trees. A second plant cropped to the ground has resprouted from its roots and begun a new canopy invasion. Beautiful spines on the leafbases and elongated feather leaves with spined tips make young plants especially interesting. Use this moderate- to fast-growing vine to intimidate or impress the neighbors and to challenge the energetic gardener. Same for all the climbing rattans, most of which prefer tropical and subtropical conditions; however, a number of *Calamus* species from Australia tolerate warm temperate and Mediterranean climates.

APPEARANCE *leaves*, 5 ft. (1.5 m) long; *crown span*, 8 ft. (2.4 m); *clump span*, 4 ft. (1.2 m) at base to 50 ft. (15.2 m) across tips of diverging stems; *trunk*, 65 ft. (19.8 m) long and 4 in. (10 cm) thick

CULTURE *hardiness*, 26°F (−3°C); *exposure*, shade or full sun; *soil*, well-drained, moist; *climate*, cool tropical, subtropical, mild warm temperate, Mediterranean

TOLERANCE *drought*, low; *salt*, low

HEAT REQUIREMENT low

USES AND EFFECTS vine, security barrier, understory, containers as juveniles, floral design (leafbases, leaves, infructescences, entire stems); *effect*, jungle; *special use*, containers; *avoid* angering the neighbors, immiserating the gardener—place with forethought

ALTERNATE SPECIES *Calamus caryotoides* and *C. muelleri* (tropical, subtropical, mild warm temperate, Mediterranean; tolerate cool weather and light frost)

AVAILABILITY rare

Pritchardia

This beautiful genus of unarmed, monoecious, short to tall, solitary, costapalmate tree palms epitomizes tropical Pacific island landscapes, being native to Hawai‘i, Tonga, Fiji, French Polynesia, and the Cook Islands. The deeply folded, often shallowly divided, heavy-textured fans of the cultivated species compel attention wherever they grow. Trunks on mature trees are clear of leafbases, smooth or ringed or striated with vertical fissures, and in many species will taper from a thickened base and lean toward brighter light when planted closely together. Use these tidy fan palms in groves, clusters, and evenly spaced rows; as singular focal points in open spaces; and as a tree substitute in small gardens. Young plants and slow-growing species serve as voluptuous foliage elements.

Pritchardia hillebrandii

LOULU

Pritchardia is the sole palm genus native to the Hawaiian Islands, with more than two dozen species distributed from tiny Nihoa in the northwestern Hawaiian Islands to the Big Island. They can be grown in mild tropical and subtropical climates, and all the Hawaiian species are worth trying in frost-free Mediterranean and warm temperate climates. The most frequently used native Hawaiian species, *P. hillebrandii*, is a modest-size, moderately fast–growing tree, with a globular crown of stiff gray-green or green leaves on a warm-gray trunk. Young plants and those in shade have flatter leaves; the blades of mature plants are undulate. The

Pritchardia hillebrandii, the Moloka'i *loulu* palm, at Hale Mohalu, Big Island, Hawai'i

leaf stalks often have a wooly material on the lowest portion closest to the trunk. Golden flowers form on branched inflorescences within the crown; small, marble-size fruits ripen to brownish. Native to the windy north coast of Moloka'i, the *loulu* tolerates coastal conditions well and forms the dominant canopy in its sole remaining habitat: the summit of a large sea stack. It's a spectacular image well worth searching for online and captured in photos in Don Hodel's book on the genus, *Loulu: The Hawaiian Palm*.

Most of the Hawaiian species are endangered or rare in remnant native habitats. Two of these, *P. maideniana* (perhaps the scruffiest of the genus) and *P. remota* (among the fastest growing and most wind- and drought-tolerant), come from near sea level and are used occasionally in Hawaiian and Southern California gardens. But more species come from moist mountain slopes. Among the montane species occasionally available in the trade, *P. minor*, a small species on Kaua'i, and *P. beccariana*, a grand tree on the Big Island, both from as high as 4000 feet (1219 m), can be grown in cool coastal California gardens protected from frost. Several botanical gardens in Hawai'i, including Wahiawa Botanical Garden and Waimea Valley on O'ahu, and the National Tropical Botanical Garden's McBryde Garden on Kaua'i, have excellent collections of native species.

APPEARANCE *leaves*, 5 ft. (1.5 m) long; *crown span*, 10 ft. (3 m); *trunk*, 20 ft. (6.1 m) tall and 8 in. (20 cm) thick

CULTURE *hardiness*, 29°F (−2°C); *exposure*, sun or shade; *soil*, well-drained, moist; *climate*, tropical, warm subtropical, mild warm temperate, Mediterranean

TOLERANCE *drought*, moderate; *salt*, high

HEAT REQUIREMENT low

USES AND EFFECTS groves, duos and trios, sentries, street trees, foliage accents, floral design (leaves, inflorescences, infructescences); *effects*, elegant, Hawaiian; *special uses*, seaside, containers; *avoid* frost; cold, wet soil

ALTERNATE SPECIES *Brahea edulis, Latania loddigesii*

AVAILABILITY uncommon

Pritchardia pacifica

FIJI FAN PALM

Tropical and warm subtropical gardens can take advantage of two sun-loving, fast-growing species, *P. pacifica* and *P. thurstonii*, the latter documented from seaside habitat on limestone islands in Tonga and Fiji. In addition to growing in limestone-derived substrate, both species are amenable to growing in other moist, well-drained soil types. *Pritchardia thurstonii* tolerates salt spray better than *P. pacifica*, and neither tolerates frost or sustained cool temperatures.

Pritchardia pacifica, a moderately tall, fast-growing species, carries a full, spherical crown of stiff, flat to undulating leaves, their blades shallowly divided, on a smooth, relatively slender, bleached gray trunk. The leaf blades end in a fine fringe of stiff leaflets, rendering the silhouette elusive, almost ethereal at the edges of the dark green fans. Inflorescences with rich yellow flowers develop inside the crown of leaves, remaining there or hanging down as they bear shiny black-brown fruit less than half an inch (1 cm) in diameter. It's one of the most handsome palms and the most commonly used *Pritchardia* species in Hawaiian landscapes, where it can be seen upon arrival at most island airports. Intolerant of frost or sustained cool weather and vulnerable to lethal yellowing disease, *P. pacifica* is grown in the Florida Keys but rarely farther north.

Pritchardia pacifica (left) and *P. thurstonii* at Jeff Seyfried's garden, Big Island, Hawai'i

APPEARANCE *leaves*, 6 ft. (1.8 m) long; *crown span*, 12 ft. (3.7 m); *trunk*, 40 ft. (12.2 m) tall and 10 in. (25 cm) thick

CULTURE *hardiness*, 32°F (0°C); *exposure*, sun or shade; *soil*, well-drained; *climate*, tropical, warm subtropical

TOLERANCE *drought*, moderate; *salt*, high

HEAT REQUIREMENT high

USES AND EFFECTS duos and trios, groves, sentries, street trees, silhouettes; *effects*, elegant, South Seas; *special use*, seaside; *avoid* frost

ALTERNATE SPECIES *Brahea edulis, Copernicia baileyana, Latania loddigesii*

AVAILABILITY common

Pritchardia thurstonii

LAU FAN PALM

The distinctive features of *P. thurstonii* are its club-shaped inflorescences, with long stalks that arch well beyond the leaves to carry the branches of flowers and quarter-inch (6-mm) fruits, and a smaller stature than *P. pacifica*. The proportionally shorter petioles on its leaves create a cute crown of flatter leaves, the crown's orb appearing slightly scrunched in the vertical axis (oblate). This, combined with the conspicuous flower stalks, slender trunk, and modest height, make for a winsome palm tree. It is a moderately fast grower.

APPEARANCE *leaves*, 5 ft. (1.5 m) long; *crown span*, 10 ft. (3 m); *trunk*, 25 ft. (7.6 m) tall and 8 in. (20 cm) thick

CULTURE *hardiness*, 33°F (1°C); *exposure*, sun; *soil*, adaptable, tolerates calcareous soils; *climate*, tropical, warm subtropical

TOLERANCE *drought*, moderate; *salt*, high

HEAT REQUIREMENT high

USES AND EFFECTS groves, duos and trios, sentries, street trees, silhouettes, focal point, vertical elements in small spaces; *effects*, elegant, winsome, South Seas; *special use*, seaside; *avoid* frost, shade

ALTERNATE SPECIES *Brahea calcarea*, *Coccothrinax* spp., *Latania loddigesii*

AVAILABILITY uncommon to common

Pseudophoenix

This small genus ranges from the Yucatán Peninsula of Mexico and Belize, to Cuba, Hispaniola, Puerto Rico, and Dominica, and to the Bahamas and the Florida Keys. It comprises solitary, colorful, moderate-size, slow-growing, plumose crownshaft palms. They are unarmed and monoecious, and they perform best in sun with good drainage and regular moisture.

Pseudophoenix sargentii

BUCCANEER PALM, CHERRY PALM

The buccaneer palm is a salt-tolerant, slow-growing, sun-loving, and somewhat drought-tolerant small tree from calcareous soils near the sea. Its remaining Florida habitat is Elliott Key in Biscayne National Park, where it was nearly wiped out by Hurricane Andrew in 1992; it has been extirpated from its other Florida Keys habitats (Long Key, Sands Key) by overcollecting for landscapes, and it can suffer in Florida gardens from a slowly progressing fungal disease. It also grows in the Yucatán (especially along the resort coast near Cancun and Playa del Carmen) and Belize, Cuba, the Bahamas, Hispaniola, and Dominica. Navassa

Island (administered by the United States but claimed by nearby Haiti) is home to a single tree, from which seedlings have proven to be much faster growing than seedlings from other sources. The crown of few dark, gray-green, vinyl-textured plumose leaves, hemispherical in maturity, meets the trunk in a short, bulging, gray-green to yellow-green crownshaft. The crown often looks gawky and asymmetrical, like a scribbled cartoon palm, and the effect of mature plants can be charmingly gnomish. Young plants grow in a distichous fashion before forming a trunk—leaves fall to two sides of the growing point into a fanlike arrangement. The moderately thick trunk is irregularly cylindrical, sometimes tapering and bulging, with dark rings of leaf scars between pale gray-green, waxy internodes; in age, the trunk surface loses chlorophyll and fades to gray. Branched inflorescences form between the leaves, producing yellowish green flowers, becoming pendant with the weight of small green fruit ripening to dark cherry red.

Adaptable to well-drained, nonacid soils and tolerant of rare, light frosts, the heat-loving buccaneer palm can be coaxed to grow in mild desert climates and warm Mediterranean climates as well as in subtropical and tropical zones. It's a natural for a courtyard or patio planting, in seaside gardens, and in group plantings. Factor in the contributions of its glaucous trunk and crownshaft and steely green foliage.

Pseudophoenix sargentii at the Bait Shack garden designed by Nicholas D'Ascanio for D'Asign Source in the Florida Keys

APPEARANCE *leaves*, 7 ft. (2.1 m) long; *crown span*, 10 ft. (3 m); *trunk*, 25 ft. (7.6 m) tall and 8 in. (20 cm) thick

CULTURE *hardiness*, 26°F (−3°C); *exposure*, sun; *soil*, well-drained, tolerates calcareous soils; *climate*, tropical, subtropical, mild desert, warm Mediterranean

TOLERANCE *drought*, high; *salt*, high

HEAT REQUIREMENT high

USES AND EFFECTS groves, duos and trios, silhouettes, focal point, vertical elements in small spaces; *effects*, picturesque, Florida and Caribbean native, color (fruit, trunk, foliage); *special use*, seaside; *avoid* wet, cold soils

ALTERNATE SPECIES *Dypsis decipiens*, *Hyophorbe* spp.

AVAILABILITY uncommon

Pseudophoenix vinifera

The dramatic bulging trunk and graceful spherical crown of this moderate-size, slow-growing species from Hispaniola commend it for warm subtropical and tropical landscapes. It tolerates seasonal dryness in habitat, but regular moisture will serve it best in landscape cultivation. Leaves are soft, deep green, long and arching, extending from a tapered, glaucous crownshaft on glaucous petioles. Greenish yellow flowers form on a loosely branching inflorescence among the leaves, giving

Pseudophoenix vinifera (left) at
Villa Paradiso, Franco D'Ascanio's
garden in the Florida Keys

way to showy, small scarlet fruits. The strongly bottle-shaped, ringed trunk sets it
apart from the royal palm (*Roystonea regia*), which it might otherwise resemble, at
half scale. It can be used for some of the same effects in a smaller residential-size
garden, in an allée planting, as a focal point, or in staggered-height groves.

APPEARANCE *leaves*, 9 ft. (2.7 m) long; *crown
span*, 15 ft. (4.6 m); *trunk*, 35 ft. (10.7 m) tall and
1–2 ft. (31–61 cm) thick

CULTURE *hardiness*, 30°F (–1°C); *exposure*, sun;
soil, well-drained, tolerates calcareous soils;
climate, tropical, warm subtropical

TOLERANCE *drought*, high; *salt*, high

HEAT REQUIREMENT high

USES AND EFFECTS focal point, groves, duos
and trios, silhouettes, sculptural elements in
small spaces; *effects*, picturesque, sculptural,
Caribbean native; *special use*, seaside; *avoid*
frost, wet and cold soils

ALTERNATE SPECIES *Dypsis decipiens*,
Hyophorbe lagenicaulis

AVAILABILITY uncommon

Ptychosperma

Concentrated in New Guinea, Melanesia, and Australia, these small to medium-size, slender, pinnate, crownshaft palms make desirable additions to tropical and subtropical landscape designs, preferring regular moisture and intolerant of frosty temperatures. They are monoecious. The species included here adapt to sun or bright shade. At least one proves tolerant of very mild Mediterranean climates. Ripped-looking (praemorse) tips on leaflets, like deckle-edge paper strips, give them a distinct silhouette. Branched inflorescences open beneath the crownshaft.

Ptychosperma elegans

SOLITAIRE PALM

Elegant, indeed, the Australian *P. elegans* is an admirable, modest-size, single-trunk palm for the narrowest of spaces, shaded or sunny, in subtropical and tropical climates, and even in warm and mild Mediterranean zones. I've seen its utility as a small palm tree planted densely, like bamboo, in a street median on Key Biscayne, Florida; tucked into tight, multistory atriums open to the sky; and dotting lawns like pinwheels. The open, upswept tuft of dark green leaves tops a thin, ringed stem. The leaves are keeled in sun, flatter in shade. Internodes remain green on the uppermost portion of the trunk, becoming pale gray with time. The conspicuous, sometimes bulging, crownshaft has a waxy bluish bloom and charcoal-like strokes up toward the petioles. Branched, twiggy inflorescences bear white (staminate) or green (pistillate) flowers from green buds and then orange-red, gooseberry-size fruits.

The fast-growing plant's dimensions and presentation change markedly depending on age and sun exposure. Younger, shaded plants look more stately, and older, sun-grown plants have a winsome charm. It can resemble *Areca catechu*, the betel-nut palm.

above: *Ptychosperma elegans* at Punta Roquena, Florida Keys

right: *Ptychosperma macarthurii* at Punta Roquena, Florida Keys

APPEARANCE *leaves*, 3–8 ft. (0.9–2.4 m) long; *crown span*, 6–14 ft. (1.8–4.3 m); *trunk*, 30 ft. (9.1 m) tall and 4 in. (10 cm) thick

CULTURE *hardiness*, 29°F (–2°C); *exposure*, sun or part shade; *soil*, well-drained, tolerates calcareous soils; *climate*, tropical, subtropical

TOLERANCE *drought*, moderate; *salt*, moderate

HEAT REQUIREMENT moderate to high

USES AND EFFECTS vertical elements in small spaces, groves, duos and trios, silhouettes, street and avenue trees; *effects*, tropical, formal, architectural; *special use*, courtyards; *avoid frost*

ALTERNATE SPECIES *Areca catechu, Chamaedorea radicalis, C. plumosa*

AVAILABILITY common

Ptychosperma macarthurii

MACARTHUR PALM

This moderate-size, fast-growing palm from New Guinea and Australia shares the neatness of its cousin *P. elegans* but with a scaled-down leaf, greener crownshaft, and thinner trunk in an open clustering habit. It thus forms a good freestanding element in a smaller garden, or it can be assembled into a hedge. Inflorescences are branched, spidery, and open, bearing whitish green flowers followed by bright red fruits. It has an old-fashioned air in Florida, where it's been supplanted by the larger, single-trunk *P. elegans* planted in clusters—an imperfect substitute. An alternate plant for denser hedging thanks to its more upright stems, persistent suckering, and wider leaflets is *P. schefferi*; more colorful, its flowers form on an orange inflorescence and develop into burgundy-to-black fruits.

APPEARANCE *leaves*, 3–6 ft. (0.9–1.8 m) long; *crown span*, 8 ft. (2.4 m); *clump span*, 20 ft. (6.1 m); *trunk*, 25 ft. (7.6 m) tall and 2 in. (5 cm) thick

CULTURE *hardiness*, 32°F (0°C); *exposure*, sun or part shade; *soil*, adaptable, moist; *climate*, tropical, warm subtropical

TOLERANCE *drought*, low; *salt*, moderate

HEAT REQUIREMENT high

USES AND EFFECTS focal point, screening, bamboo hedge alternative, vertical element in small spaces, silhouettes, groves, avenue clusters, floral design (leaves, inflorescences, infructescences); *effects*, tropical, formal; *special use*, courtyards; *avoid* frost, drought

ALTERNATE SPECIES large *Chamaedorea* spp., *Ptychosperma schefferi* (tropical, warm subtropical)

AVAILABILITY common

Ravenea

A dioecious genus characteristic of Madagascar and the Comoro Islands, the diverse, pinnate-leaf *Ravenea* contains shamelessly cute mini tree palms (*R. hildebrandtii*) and robust canopy giants (*R. robustior*), one of the few truly aquatic palms (*R. musicalis*), and a root-succulent inhabitant of semiarid regions (*R. xerophila*). Allied to the cool-growing genus *Ceroxylon*, *Ravenea* species palms often exhibit a tolerance for cooler climates, and a few species range across a wide altitudinal range—as high as 6560 feet (2000 m)—in habitat. They lack crownshafts but many tend to shed dead leaves spontaneously from the crown and thus stay tidy. Flowers emerge within the crown, and budded inflorescences can be quite ornamental. Although the riparian *R. rivularis* is sold in nearly every big box store and florist shop, most other *Ravenea* species are quite rare in the trade.

Ravenea glauca

SIHARA PALM

With a fine foliage texture and glaucous cast, this neat, small to moderate-size tree palm is useful for small spaces and group planting. It's the perfect small palm tree. Its scale lands it between a pygmy date palm (*Phoenix roebelenii*) and a kentia palm (*Howea forsteriana*), and its texture and cold-hardiness bear comparison to both as well. It tolerates full sun or partial shade, regular moisture or periods of drought, and prefers well-drained soil. This palm is a slow to moderately fast grower.

APPEARANCE *leaves*, 6 ft. (1.8 m) long; *crown span*, 10 ft. (3 m); *trunk*, 20 ft. (6.1 m) tall and 4 in. (10 cm) thick above a flared base

CULTURE *hardiness*, 28°F (−2°C); *exposure*, sun or part shade; *soil*, well-drained; *climate*, mild subtropical, tropical, mild warm temperate, Mediterranean

TOLERANCE *drought*, low to moderate; *salt*, low

HEAT REQUIREMENT moderate

USES AND EFFECTS *groves*, patio and courtyard planting, silhouettes, vertical elements in small spaces; *effects*, tropical, formal, graceful; *special use*, shift scale; *avoid* frost

ALTERNATE SPECIES *Phoenix roebelenii* (larger specimens), *P. rupicola*, *Syagrus* spp. (subtropical, tropical, mild warm temperate, Mediterranean)

AVAILABILITY rare

above: *Ravenea glauca* at La Casa de las Palmas, Big Island, Hawai'i

right: *Ravenea rivularis* at Mike Harris's garden, Broward County, Florida

Ravenea rivularis

MAJESTY PALM

A fast-growing, moderate-size to large palm tree that's used far beyond the zones where it thrives, the majesty palm well-grown has a stout, whitish gray trunk with a luxuriant spherical crown of flat leaves that twist halfway toward the tips. The crown resembles that of a coconut palm. Native to riverbanks, it tends to turn yellow in drier soils, seeming in need of nutrition. Indoor plants perish a few years—or weeks—after being purchased from vendors as cheap stand-ins for kentia palms (*Howea forsteriana*).

APPEARANCE *leaves*, 8 ft. (2.4 m) long; *crown span*, 14 ft. (4.3 m); *trunk*, 50 ft. (15.2 m) tall and 14–20 in. (36–51 cm) thick

CULTURE *hardiness*, 27°F (−3°C); *exposure*, sun or part shade; *soil*, rich, moist, even saturated; *climate*, tropical, mild subtropical, mild desert, mild warm temperate, Mediterranean

TOLERANCE *drought*, low to moderate; *salt*, low

HEAT REQUIREMENT moderate

USES AND EFFECTS focal point, groves, silhouettes, avenue planting; *effects*, tropical, formal; *special use*, wet areas; *avoid* dry or infertile soil

ALTERNATE SPECIES *Beccariophoenix alfredii*, *Cocos nucifera*, *Jubaea chilensis*

AVAILABILITY common

Rhapidophyllum hystrix

NEEDLE PALM

The hardiest palm species is a clustering shrub with deeply divided palmate leaves and indistinct, stubby trunks from moist forests in Alabama, Florida, Georgia, Mississippi, and South Carolina. Plants tolerate the climates of Washington, DC,

New York City, and the Ohio Valley, but they require summer warmth to bounce back from deep-freeze winters. A mild, cool-summer climate slows them down without taxing their beauty. Their elegant fan leaves resemble those of the genus *Rhapis*, rendered at three or four times the size. Leafbases bear long, piercing needles that conceal dense inflorescences and fruit clusters. Tolerant of sun or shade and preferring ample water, this slow-growing palm makes a mound of shiny, dark green foliage with a slight silvery glint to the undersides.

APPEARANCE *leaves*, 5 ft. (1.5 m) long; *crown span*, 8 ft. (2.4 m); *clump span*, 15 ft. (4.6 m) or more; *trunk*, 5 ft. (1.5 m) tall and 4 in. (10 cm) thick

CULTURE *hardiness*, −5°F (−21°C); *exposure*, shade or sun; *soil*, adaptable; *climate*, subtropical, warm temperate, Mediterranean, tropical

TOLERANCE *drought*, moderate; *salt*, low

HEAT REQUIREMENT low

USES AND EFFECTS understory and accent foliage, informal hedge, containers, foundation planting, floral design (leaves); *effects*, tropical, woodland; *special uses*, wet areas, cold-winter climates; *avoid* dry conditions

ALTERNATE SPECIES *Brahea moorei*, *Chamaerops humilis*, *Guihaia argyrata*, *Serenoa repens*

AVAILABILITY uncommon

Rhapis

This genus of delicate-looking, slow-growing, small, clustering fan palms from Southeast Asia is found throughout the world as an interior plant and as a staple hedge plant and bamboo alternative in tropical and subtropical climates. Its closest allied genus is *Trachycarpus*, and I fantasize about someday seeing intergeneric hybrids. The growth habit resembles a small, clumping bamboo, but the plants produce almost no litter (though they require grooming), making them appealing alternatives to bamboo. All of them have palmate leaves divided nearly to the center of the fan and quite thin stems covered in adherent leafbases that split into attractive netting. Remove leafbases to reveal the smooth green surface for a variant look. The most cold-hardy species (to 14°F, or –10°C, in California), fairly new to the trade, is the most refined and beautiful *R. multifida*; a larger scale version that appears in mild California and Japanese gardens, *R. humilis*, can look like a grove of small trees. All perform well in shade, tolerating a great deal of sun in warm, humid climates. None of them tolerates drought; good drainage is helpful, and although many occur on limestone in habitat, they are tolerant of a range of soil pH. Diverse cultivars of *R. humilis* and *R. excelsa* are grown in Japan as container plants in a rarified manner akin to bonsai.

Rhapis excelsa

LADY PALM

By far the most common species of the genus in cultivation, the lady palm, with its broad, blunt-tip segments, makes an excellent hedge, container plant, accent, and interior plant. Prune stems for a more open look. Common in hot, humid climates, it's also useful in Mediterranean and warm temperate zones, albeit quite slow growing in areas of cool summer nights.

APPEARANCE *leaves*, 2 ft. (61 cm) long; *crown span*, 3 ft. (0.9 m); *clump span*, 15 ft. (4.6 m) or more; *trunk*, 10 ft. (3 m) tall and 1 in. (3 cm) thick

CULTURE *hardiness*, 22°F (−6°C); *exposure*, shade or part sun (in humid climates); *soil*, adaptable, tolerates calcareous soils; *climate*, tropical, subtropical, warm temperate, Mediterranean, desert

TOLERANCE *drought*, moderate; *salt*, moderate

HEAT REQUIREMENT moderate

USES AND EFFECTS understory and accent foliage, informal hedge, containers, bamboo alternative, foundation planting, floral design (leaves, entire stems); *effects*, Asian, tropical; *special use*, bonsai; *avoid* hot sun, dry conditions

ALTERNATE SPECIES *Acoelorrhaphe wrightii*, *Chamaedorea* spp. (bamboo effects with feather leaves), *Rhapis humilis, R. multifida*

AVAILABILITY common

Rhopalostylis

Two species of moderate-size crownshaft palm trees from moist forests of New Zealand and Australia's Norfolk Island thrive in cooler climates but tolerate only mild winters. The upright crowns of both resemble feather dusters.

Rhopalostylis baueri

NORFOLK ISLAND PALM

I find this palm tree, along with its slower growing, smaller cousin, *Hedyscepe canterburyana*, one of the most beautiful plants for irrigated, mostly frost-free gardens in coastal Central and Southern California. It can thrive in mild subtropical and marine-influenced Mediterranean climates. Native to Norfolk Island in the South Pacific, it also occurs on New Zealand's Raoul Island in the Kermadec Island chain. The palm's cylindrical trunk, shiny green with bright leaf-scar rings, ages to gray. It supports a short cylindrical or bulging crownshaft below a crown of straight, pinnate leaves that arch winsomely at their tips. Broad leaflets angled

Rhopalostylis baueri at the Santa Barbara County Courthouse, California

slightly upward and over from the rachis make a shallow trough of the upper face of the leaf. White flowers are borne on a branched inflorescence beneath the crownshaft once the enclosing bracts are pushed aside. Small, round red fruits add a touch of color to the fascinating structure. The upswept, vivid green, articulated crown; self-cleaning habit; and proportionate trunk combine to make a very pretty palm tree.

Regular moisture and well-drained, fertile soil are to its liking. It's a steady, not fast, grower that tolerates higher light levels when young and less wind at any age than its cousin, *R. sapida*.

It's useful as a single specimen or grouped into a casual cluster and would make a striking allée along a path. Thanks to its upswept crown, it fits into tight spaces. Unhappy with drought, it mixes nicely with tree ferns, astelias, and the evergreen shrubs of its homeland, but it cannot be a street tree in a climate with continental heat or sustained drought. Never have I seen it planted with the Norfolk Island pine, *Araucaria heterophylla*, a natural and aesthetically promising combination.

APPEARANCE *leaves*, 10–12 ft. (3.0–3.7 m) long; *crown span*, 15 ft. (4.6 m); *trunk*, 35 ft. (10.7 m) tall and 8 in. (20 cm) thick

CULTURE *hardiness*, 28°F (−2°C); *exposure*, shade or sun (in cooler climates); *soil*, adaptable; *climate*, mild subtropical, mild warm temperate, Mediterranean, desert

TOLERANCE *drought*, low; *salt*, moderate

HEAT REQUIREMENT low

USES AND EFFECTS focal point, vertical element beneath high canopy, groves, vertical element in narrow spaces, floral design (leafbases, inflorescences, infructescences); *effects*, Antipodean, tropical; *special uses*, cool, shady, windy locations; *avoid* hot sun, dry conditions, warm nights

ALTERNATE SPECIES *Archontophoenix cunninghamiana, Areca catechu, Rhopalostylis sapida*

AVAILABILITY uncommon

Rhopalostylis sapida

NĪKAU, SHAVING-BRUSH PALM

New Zealand's native palm is the *nīkau*, *R. sapida*. If you know anything about common garden plants in San Francisco, you know that New Zealand is the origin of many of our best, because our two climates are quite similar. The *nīkau* likes cool, humid weather, and in its native habitat it occupies forests near the sea, even sometimes growing where exposed directly to ocean winds. To succeed in these conditions it must have sufficient moisture and be given the shady protection of shrubs or trees (or buildings) as a young plant. But it's such a stunning plant that it's worth coddling. The *nīkau* is stouter and stiffer than *R. baueri*, with a more geometrical look. Its flowers are lavender, and fruits are red and smaller than those of *R. baueri* and are held on a shorter, branched flower stalk.

Rhopalostylis sapida grows farther from the Equator than any other palm, at the 44th parallel south in the Chatham Islands, about 500 miles (805 km) east of New Zealand's South Island. That latitude in the Northern Hemisphere runs by Eugene, Oregon; Portland, Maine; Toronto, Canada; and Genoa, Italy. On the California coast, specimens have succeeded at least as far north as the Mendocino Coast Botanical Gardens (and certainly as far south as San Diego's Balboa Park). There are reports of specimens surviving in the "banana belt" of the southern Oregon coast, which would be a good place in which to experiment with *nīkau* palms.

This moderately fast–growing palm likes some shade when young, but once it forms a trunk, it thrives in full sun in the fog belt. Even moisture and mild fertilizing will keep it growing steadily; it is not drought-tolerant and will not endure freezing temperatures below about 24°F (–4°C). Inland, where ocean fog rarely penetrates, dry heat and winter frost limit its usefulness, but it is worth planting where nights are cool under protective evergreen tree canopy. It is reputed to tolerate clay soils better than most palms.

Rhopalostylis sapida at the San Francisco Botanical Garden, California

APPEARANCE *leaves*, 10–12 ft. (3.0–3.7 m) long; *crown span*, 15 ft. (4.6 m); *trunk*, 35 ft. (10.7 m) tall and 8 in. (20 cm) thick

CULTURE *hardiness*, 24°F (–4°C); *exposure*, shade or sun (in cooler climates); *soil*, adaptable, including heavy, wet soils; *climate*, mild subtropical, mild warm temperate, Mediterranean

TOLERANCE *drought*, low; *salt*, moderate

HEAT REQUIREMENT low

USES AND EFFECTS focal point, vertical element in narrow spaces or beneath high canopy, groves, floral design (leafbases, inflorescences, infructescences); *effects*, Antipodean, architectural; *special uses*, cool, shady, windy locations; *avoid* hot sun, dry conditions, warm nights

ALTERNATE SPECIES *Areca catechu*, *Ptychosperma elegans*, *Rhopalostylis baueri*

AVAILABILITY uncommon

Roystonea

The tall, fast-growing royal palms reign over their native Caribbean islands and shores, from Florida to Venezuela, and are now planted in tropical and subtropical landscapes around the world. Their rich green, plumose leaves form a long, gleaming crownshaft atop a tall, smooth, often concrete-pale single trunk varying from moderately thick to monumental. Inflorescences emerge below the crownshaft as a jutting, baseball bat–shaped structure whose enclosing bracts peel and break to reveal a large, pale cream, branched perch for thousands of flowers, followed by tiny red fruits.

Roystonea oleracea

CARIBBEAN ROYAL PALM

The Caribbean royal palm, native to the Lesser Antilles, Colombia, and Venezuela, reaches the greater height of the two commonly cultivated species (the other being the Cuban royal, *R. regia*). Its trunk is more slender and even in thickness than the Cuban, and its plumose leaves, forming a hemispherical crown that barely descends below the horizontal, look flatter than the leaves of the Cuban. This fast-growing palm thrives in moist, tropical regions and can be maintained in warm subtropical areas and the mildest Mediterranean climates as well. Crossing allées of this palm at the Rio de Janeiro Botanical Garden (imported from Sir Seewoosagur Ramgoolam Botanical Garden in Pamplemousses, Mauritius, in the early 1800s) are one of the world's great botanical spectacles.

APPEARANCE *leaves*, 15 ft. (4.6 m) long; *crown span*, 25 ft. (7.6 m); *trunk*, 100 ft. (30.5 m) tall and 2 ft. (61 cm) thick

CULTURE *hardiness*, 30°F (−1°C); *exposure*, sun or part shade; *soil*, adaptable, including calcareous soils and seasonally wet sites; *climate*, tropical, warm subtropical

TOLERANCE *drought*, low; *salt*, moderate

HEAT REQUIREMENT moderate

USES AND EFFECTS avenue planting, focal point, vertical element in narrow spaces, groves, floral design (leafbases, inflorescences); *effects*, tropical, monumental; *special uses*, avenue planting, wet sites; *avoid* dry conditions

ALTERNATE SPECIES *Ceroxylon quindiuense, C. ventricosum, Clinostigma* spp., *Jubaea chilensis*

AVAILABILITY common to uncommon

Roystonea regia

ROYAL PALM

With a massive, often bulging trunk, the Cuban royal palm (also native to Florida, Mexico, Belize, Honduras, the Cayman Islands, and the Bahamas) lifts a spherical crown of heavily plumose, subtly arching leaves. The crown's rich green contrasts with a smooth, pale, often white-gray trunk with clear rings at the top that fade quickly, rendering the effect of a monolithic column that invites avenue planting (such as the double allée along Royal Palm Way at Palm Beach, Florida) and staggered height groves alike. The trunk is a mesmerizing, dynamic sculpture. Young plants produce a thin emergent trunk that swells to reach adult diameter; many adults taper at the top of the bottle-shaped trunk, and a subtle swelling often begins a few feet above the tree's footing. The trunks of plants in Hawai'i often have irregularly swollen trunks, while those in Florida form a more consistent pattern from the base toward the crown; I've wondered whether the seasonality of rainfall (winter peak in leeward Hawai'i, summer peak in Florida) might affect trunk development. I have not noticed this contrast in *R. oleracea*.

Roystonea regia at Paul Humann's garden, Broward County, Florida

APPEARANCE *leaves*, 11 ft. (3.4 m) long; *crown span*, 19 ft. (5.8 m); *trunk*, 100 ft. (30.5 m) tall and 2 ft. (61 cm) thick

CULTURE *hardiness*, 27°F (−3°C); *exposure*, sun or part shade; *soil*, adaptable, including calcareous soils and seasonally wet sites; *climate*, tropical, warm subtropical, mild desert, warmest temperate, mild Mediterranean

TOLERANCE *drought*, low; *salt*, high

HEAT REQUIREMENT moderate

USES AND EFFECTS avenue planting, focal point, vertical element in narrow spaces, groves, floral design (leafbases, inflorescences); *effects*, tropical, monumental; *special uses*, avenue planting, wet sites; *avoid* dry conditions

ALTERNATE SPECIES *Ceroxylon quindiuense, C. ventricosum, Clinostigma* spp., *Jubaea chilensis, Syagrus romanzoffiana, Wodyetia bifurcata*

AVAILABILITY common

Sabal

Species in this genus of small, moderate-size, and large single-stem palms with conspicuously costapalmate leaves characterize the Caribbean and its shores, Mexico, and the southeast United States and Texas. Some *Sabal* species are among the most cold-hardy and salt-tolerant of palms. Though they tend to prefer hot summer weather, even species from tropical climates usually show some tolerance of cool weather and can often survive freezing temperatures. Many thrive in the mild desert, too. Leafbases—called boots—retained in youth are split at the base, resulting in a pleasing geometry of lattice on the trunk that can also serve as a temporary host for epiphytes such as ferns, orchids, and bromeliads. Older plants shed leafbases to reveal their fibrous surface, ranging from warm gray to white-gray in color.

The three species discussed here represent three groupings by scale. *Sabal minor* is the main trunkless variety, but *S. etonia* is also cultivated; *S. palmetto* is a medium-size palm tree along with rarer *S. bermudana* (reputed to require less summer heat to thrive), *S. gretherae*, *S. maritima*, *S. mexicana*, *S. pumos*, and *S. rosei*. *Sabal uresana* is a rarely cultivated gray-leaved species whose large-scale role can also be played by *S.* 'Riverside', *S. causiarum*, and *S. domingensis*. The beautiful tropical species *S. mauritiiformis* and *S. yapa* offer the delicacy of deeply divided leaves and slender trunks; both tolerate mild Mediterranean and subtropical climates with minimal frost.

Sabal minor

DWARF PALMETTO

One of the two most cold-hardy palms and the northernmost species of palm found in eastern North America, the slow-growing dwarf palmetto dwells on the ground, lacking an aboveground trunk in most cases. It's an excellent plant for sun or shade. Its army-green, slightly glaucous, upright, barely costapalmate leaves often split down the middle with age and flop out, adding a casual (or messy) air unless pruned off. Wet soils can be to its liking, yet it tolerates moderate moisture and passing drought when established. Flower spikes emerge upright from the plant budded in a lovely telescope of bracts (visible above); these bracts turn to straw-colored husks once the short inflorescence branches emerge. Creamy flowers develop into little shiny black fruits, the infructescence arching over with their weight. It's native from central Texas and southeast Oklahoma to eastern North Carolina and South Central Florida and can be cultivated in sunny, protected spots

at least as far north as Washington, DC, and in warm-summer areas of the Pacific Northwest that remain above 10°F (−12°C) in winter. Only *Rhapidophyllum hystrix*, the needle palm, rivals it for cold-hardiness, partly because the needle palm is naturally clumping and thus can reemerge after severe winters from multiple growing points, while the dwarf palmetto has a single bud. Dwarf palmetto can also be cultivated in tropical and desert climates (where it prefers shade).

Sabal minor at Mary Alice Woodrum's garden in North Augusta, South Carolina

APPEARANCE *leaves*, 4–5 ft. (1.2–1.5 m) long; *crown span*, 3–9 ft. (0.9–2.7 m); *trunk*, usually subterranean, or 10 ft. (3 m) tall and 12 in. (30 cm) thick

CULTURE *hardiness*, −5°F (−21°C); *exposure*, shade or sun; *soil*, adaptable, including seasonally wet sites; *climate*, subtropical, temperate, tropical, Mediterranean, desert

TOLERANCE *drought*, moderate; *salt*, high

HEAT REQUIREMENT moderate

USES AND EFFECTS foliage, understory, hedge, floral design (leaves, inflorescences); *effects*, woodland, swamp, tropical, sculptural; *special use*, wet sites; *avoid* singular or specimen planting

ALTERNATE SPECIES *Brahea moorei*, *Sabal etonia* (subtropical, tropical, warm temperate, Mediterranean, desert), *Serenoa repens*

AVAILABILITY common to uncommon

Sabal palmetto

PALMETTO, CABBAGE PALMETTO

The state tree of both South Carolina and Florida, the palmetto is also native along the coast from North Carolina to Mississippi and the Florida Panhandle, and throughout Florida, the Bahamas, and Cuba. It's a moderate-size, moderate- to fast-growing palm tree (rarely taller than 45 feet, or 13.8 m) with a somewhat amorphous crown of deeply cut, deeply costapalmate leaves and plentiful inflorescences often pushing out from the crown. Plants will lean and curve, but more often they are straight. Unusually salt-tolerant, palmettos are staples of coastal plantings in Florida and the Southeast United States, tolerating sandy, mucky (if not alkaline), or loamy soils and occasional freshwater or brackish inundation. They are easily transplanted—albeit at the cost of completely regrowing the crown. Often growing in the company of pines and oaks, the species, although native to sharp-drained limestone substrates in South Florida, does not thrive in the limestone clay of central Texas. It's one of the most cold-hardy palm trees for areas of hot, humid summers. It also thrives in tropical regions and can be successful with irrigation in Mediterranean climates. Although an uncharismatic species, the most breathtaking native palm habitat I've seen in the United States is hundreds of thousands of palmettos growing in a wet savanna off the Tamiami Trail near Naples, Florida, the predominant tree over a horizon of grass.

Sabal palmetto at Charleston, South Carolina

APPEARANCE *leaves*, 6–8 ft. (1.8–2.4 m) long; *crown span*, 10–15 ft. (3.0–4.6 m); *trunk*, 50 ft. (15.2 m) tall and 8–14 in. (20–36 cm) thick

CULTURE *hardiness*, 10°F (−12°C); *exposure*, shade or sun; *soil*, adaptable, including seasonally wet sites; *climate*, subtropical, tropical, warm temperate, Mediterranean, desert

TOLERANCE *drought*, moderate; *salt*, high

HEAT REQUIREMENT moderate

USES AND EFFECTS street tree, groves, avenue planting, vertical element in narrow spaces, floral design (leaves, inflorescences, infructescences); *effects*, woodland, tropical, beachy; *special use*, wet sites; *avoid* deep shade

ALTERNATE SPECIES *Brahea edulis* (Mediterranean, warm temperate), *Sabal pumos, S. rosei*

AVAILABILITY common

Sabal uresana

SONORAN PALMETTO

A broad crown with large leaves ranging from silver to gray and green is the conspicuous appeal of this slow-growing, stately species from desert scrub environments in northwest Mexico. The specimen at Edith Bergstrom's gardens is so large that it feels like a live gazebo. *Sabal uresana* is an excellent, heavy-trunked plant for desert gardens with irrigation, but it also tolerates subtropical, Mediterranean, and tropical environments. Established plants also tolerate drought, especially in cooler areas, and even repeated winter freezes in 2007 left it unscathed in Bergstrom Gardens. Other species reaching the scale of *S. uresana* (but with consistently green leaves) include *S.* 'Riverside', a cultivar circulating in California (possibly a selection of *S. mexicana*); *S. domingensis*, from the hills of Hispaniola and Cuba; and *S. causiarum*, from low altitudes in Puerto Rico, Hispaniola, and the British Virgin Islands. All of the comparable species tolerate cold and frost to varying degrees and offer a wondrous encounter with large fan leaves during their long rosette phase.

Sabal uresana at Bergstrom Gardens, Atherton, California

APPEARANCE *leaves*, 8–12 ft. (2.4–3.7 m) long; *crown span*, 14–20 ft. (4.3–6.1 m); *trunk*, 45 ft. (13.8 m) tall and 18 in. (46 cm) thick

CULTURE *hardiness*, 16°F (−9°C); *exposure*, sun; *soil*, well-drained; *climate*, subtropical, tropical, warm temperate, Mediterranean, desert

TOLERANCE *drought*, high; *salt*, moderate

HEAT REQUIREMENT moderate

USES AND EFFECTS focal point, groves, avenue planting, canopy palm, floral design (inflorescences, infructescences); *effects*, oasis, tropical, Jurassic; *special uses*, desert environments; *avoid* shade, small spaces

ALTERNATE SPECIES *Brahea clara*, *Sabal causiarum* and *S. domingensis* (tropical, subtropical, desert, warm temperate, Mediterranean), *S.* 'Riverside' (subtropical, tropical, warm temperate, Mediterranean, desert)

AVAILABILITY uncommon

Satakentia liukiuensis

SATAKE PALM

Warm purple- and rosy-brown tones mark the shiny crownshaft of this elegant, unarmed, moderate-size solitary palm tree from Ryukyu Islands of Japan. Its arching feather leaves often twist from horizontal to vertical toward their outer tips. This feature and the palm's occasionally leaning trunk create from a distance a resemblance to the coconut palm, *Cocos nucifera*. In its moist habitat, the Satake palm's 12-inch–thick (31-cm) trunk produces a boss of roots at the base. Although it can be coaxed to grow in the mildest Mediterranean climate of coastal Southern California, the moisture-loving, frost-disliking, monotypic species is at its best and most popular in subtropical South Florida and will thrive in tropical climates such as in Hawai'i as well. Like so many crownshaft palms, its rosy-brown budded inflorescence makes a hornlike protuberance below the leaves. Bracts fall, bursting into a broom of flower-bearing branchlets that eventually sport half-inch (1-cm) black fruits. Young plants grow well in shade but respond best to sun after trunking.

Satakentia liukiuensis at the Naples Botanical Garden, Florida

APPEARANCE *leaves*, 8 ft. (2.4 m) long; *crown span*, 14 ft. (4.3 m); *trunk*, 50 ft. (15.2 m) tall and 12 in. (31 cm) thick

CULTURE *hardiness*, 28°F (−2°C); *exposure*, shade or sun; *soil*, well-drained, moist; *climate*, tropical, warm subtropical

TOLERANCE *drought*, low; *salt*, high

HEAT REQUIREMENT high

USES AND EFFECTS focal point, groves, bosquets, street tree, canopy palm, floral design (leaves, leafbases, inflorescences, infructescences); *effects*, tropical, formal; *special use*, color; *avoid* drought, sustained chill

ALTERNATE SPECIES *Archontophoenix purpurea*

AVAILABILITY uncommon

Serenoa repens

SAW PALMETTO

The aesthetic signature of the saw palmetto is its evasion of the obvious regularity and symmetry that characterize most palms. Tossed together in an undulating mass, its leaves don't instantly read as fans, and the result of its irregular branching is an eccentric arrangement of crowns. This low, clustering fan palm is native to the Florida peninsula and the coastal plain from southeast Louisiana to southeast South Carolina. Indifferent to soil types, it forms understory thickets in pine woods and patches on coastal dunes and is adapted to fire, salt air, and periods of drought. A slow-growing plant in Mediterranean climates, it will tolerate temperatures well below freezing but thrives in hot, humid conditions. It can be difficult to transplant in California. Branching stems remain buried or develop occasionally above ground, sometimes curving up but mostly reclining, and are not a reliable feature on this shrubby foliage palm. Leaves, commonly pale to medium green,

above: *Serenoa repens* at The Huntington Botanical Gardens, San Marino, California

right: *Syagrus romanzoffiana* at Carole Bowen's garden, Alamo, California

can also be gray or silver—the latter form a popular cultivar. Leaf blades are deeply cut and undulate; petioles bear recurving teeth. Stems retain fibrous leafbases. Branched clusters of evening-fragrant white flowers are produced in the crown in spring and yield centimeter-size black berries, the source for a widely used herbal remedy, in fall. It's a lovely low element for a foundation planting, an informal hedge, or a shrub and perennial border, and it makes an excellent underplanting for trees. Use it for its salt-tolerance in coastal areas, too.

APPEARANCE *leaves*, 4 ft. (1.2 m) long; *crown span*, 6 ft. (1.8 m); *clump span*, 6–30 ft. (1.8–9.1 m); *trunk*, usually subterranean, sometimes creeping above ground, to 20 ft. (6.1 m) long and 6 in. (15 cm) thick

CULTURE *hardiness*, 10°F (−12°C); *exposure*, shade or sun; *soil*, adaptable; *climate*, subtropical, tropical, warm temperate, desert, Mediterranean

TOLERANCE *drought*, high; *salt*, high

HEAT REQUIREMENT high

USES AND EFFECTS understory, foliage, hedge, floral design (leafbases, inflorescences); *effects*, woodland, sculptural; *special use*, seaside; *avoid* transplant shock

ALTERNATE SPECIES *Brahea decumbens* (subtropical, warm temperate, Mediterranean, desert), *Chamaerops humilis* var. *argentea*

AVAILABILITY common

Syagrus

In a large and diverse genus of feather palms from South America (mostly Brazil) and the Lesser Antilles, one species, *S. romanzoffiana*, is a very widely grown moderate to large tree in subtropical, tropical, Mediterranean, and warm temperate climates. In tropical regions, it often loses out in the selection contest to more widely loved species. Leafbases do not form a crownshaft. Other species range from small, trunkless plants that blend into their grassland habitat, such as *S. graminifolia*, to a charismatic clustering species, *S. ruschiana*, that acquires with age the look of a tight grove of delicate coconut palms. The overtop palm from the West Indies, *S. amara*, is a tall, fast-growing species with dark green, languid, slightly plumose leaves and is useful in coastal gardens in the tropics and warmer subtropics. *Syagrus sancona*, the South American foxtail palm, resembles a lusher, much taller queen palm with a more delicate trunk and can be grown in tropical climates as well as frostless subtropical zones. An appealing hybrid between *S. romanzoffiana* and *S. schizophylla*, *Syagrus ×montgomeryana*, smaller and with a more architectural crown than its *S. romanzoffiana* parent, is registered by the name Coconut Queen by Jungle Jack Nursery in Vista, California, a pioneering producer of this plant.

Syagrus romanzoffiana

QUEEN PALM

The queen palm is a good choice for a fast-growing, narrow, medium-size palm tree where moisture and fertilizer can be provided to get it established. Well grown, they pretty quickly make a subtly ventricose, dark gray ringed trunk and bear unarmed, apple-green, plumose leaves with whitish petioles and elongated triangular leaf-bases that stick to younger trees and peel spontaneously off older trees' trunks. In exposed, chilly-summer sites, they can look terrible. In most other areas, they will thrive and quickly reach maturity but can be killed by freezes below 20°F (−7°C). This palm is at its best where winter temperatures rarely touch 25°F (−4°C) and summer highs consistently surpass 70°F (21°C). Better choices for cool-summer areas or low-fertility soils are the *Parajubaea* species, none of which demands as much fertilizer or water as the queen palm, although none has its plumose leaf.

APPEARANCE *leaves*, 8–12 ft. (2.4–3.7 m) long; *crown span*, 14–22 ft. (4.3–6.7 m); *trunk*, 70 ft. (21.3 m) tall and 16 in. (41 cm) thick

CULTURE *hardiness*, 22°F (−6°C); *exposure*, sun or shade; *soil*, rich, non-alkaline, but adaptable; *climate*, subtropical, tropical, warm temperate, Mediterranean

TOLERANCE *drought*, moderate; *salt*, moderate

HEAT REQUIREMENT low

USES AND EFFECTS street tree, vertical element in small spaces, canopy, groves, containers, floral design (bracts); *effects*, languid, mournful, tropical; *special use*, street tree; *avoid* chilly winds, alkaline soils

ALTERNATE SPECIES *Livistona decora* (for its weeping fan leaves), *Parajubaea* spp., *Roystonea regia*, *Syagrus sancona* (tropical, subtropical, mild warm temperate, Mediterranean, mild desert), *Wodyetia bifurcata*

AVAILABILITY common

Lytocaryum (now included in *Syagrus*)

Four single-trunk species, all from Brazil's subtropical and tropical southern reaches, compose this group of attractive small feather palms that often resemble tiny versions of the coconut palm, *Cocos nucifera*. Botanists have settled them into the *Syagrus* genus, but I think it is important to discuss them together under their former name because of their small size.

These slow-growing palms are useful as understory foliage, trees under higher canopy, focal points in small spaces, and silhouettes. They do not form crown-shafts. Conspicuous, marble-size seeds, like miniature coconuts, develop inside husks that split open upon maturity. Long, branched inflorescences grow from among the leaves. The most popular species, *S. weddelliana*, is commonly grown indoors, especially in Europe, for its fine, shiny feather leaves and its slow development into a charming miniature palm tree. In the landscape, it prefers mild, shaded, subtropical and tropical conditions but can be coaxed to grow in mild warm temperate and Mediterranean gardens, where it tolerates occasional freezing temperatures to 27°F (–3°C). *Syagrus insignis* is the largest species (to 30 feet, or 9.1 m, tall in habitat), very rare in cultivation, but with promise for cooler climates as it comes from seasonally dry mountain forests near Rio de Janeiro at altitudes of 3280–5905 feet (1000–1800 m). *Syagrus hoehnei*, also very rare, lands between the two in size and likely will tolerate a range of climates, thanks to its origin at altitudes of 2625–3200 feet (800–975 m) in the subtropical state of Paraná, south of São Paulo; it is reputed to tolerate occasional drops to 25°F (–4°C).

APPEARANCE *leaves*, 3 ft. (0.9 m) (*S. weddelliana*) to 5 ft. (1.5 m) (*S. insigne*) long; *crown span*, 4 ft. (1.2 m) (*S. weddelliana*) to 8 ft. (2.4 m) (*S. insigne*); *trunk*, 6 ft. (1.8 m) (*S. weddelliana*) to 20 ft. (6.1 m) (*S. insignis*) tall and 2–4 in. (5–10 cm) thick

CULTURE *hardiness*, 25°F (–4°C); *exposure*, shade or part sun; *soil*, well-drained, moist; *climate*, subtropical, tropical, warm temperate, Mediterranean

TOLERANCE *drought*, moderate to low; *salt*, low

HEAT REQUIREMENT moderate to low

USES AND EFFECTS understory, containers, patio tree, focal point in small spaces, groves, floral design (leaves, inflorescences, infructescences); *effects*, miniature, graceful, jungle; *special use*, interiors (*S. weddelliana*); *avoid* hot sun

ALTERNATE SPECIES *Chamaedorea oreophila* (cool tropical, subtropical, warm temperate, Mediterranean), *Phoenix roebelenii*

AVAILABILITY rare to common

Tahina spectabilis

New to science in 2006, this enormous single-trunk, unarmed fan palm from northwest Madagascar is named for Tahina, the daughter of Xavier Metz, who brought it to worldwide attention. The monotypic palm's huge, elegantly folded costapalmate leaves stay stiff to their tips. Waxy gray undersides cast light into the domed canopy. In early growth, long before trunk development, the leaves—particularly the petioles—fan out in a single plane. The nearly 2-foot–thick (61-cm) trunk retains a few dead older leaves before they drop to reveal clean trunk. Purely vegetative growth continues for decades before culminating in the development of a single, pyramidal terminal inflorescence 12–15 feet (3.7–4.6 m) high, enclosed in whitish bracts. A profusion of chartreuse flowers emerge to attract insect and bird pollinators and produce small, green fruits. The palm dies upon flowering and fruiting.

Only one hundred or so plants are found in the wild, in seasonally inundated deep soils at the base of limestone outcroppings, and local residents have organized to sell a limited quantity of seeds when individual trees reach maturity and meet their demise. The habitat's seasonally dry, tropical climate along with early cultivation experiences show the plant thriving in tropical and subtropical climates and imply established plants' tolerance of some drought and temporarily waterlogged, as well as alkaline, soils. I've seen young plants thriving both in the volcanic soil in rainy districts of the Big Island, Hawai'i, and in the alkaline substrate of winter-dry South Florida. Gardeners in the mildest areas of California have found it tolerant of some cool weather, though its future in Mediterranean climates is likely limited. It will be useful for extraordinary foliage effects in broad, parklike landscapes. Don't use it in less-than-expansive gardens or as a tree for the centuries.

APPEARANCE *leaves*, 20 ft. (6.1 m) long; *crown span*, 35 ft. (10.7 m); *trunk*, 60 ft. (18.3 m) tall and 20 in. (51 cm) thick

CULTURE *hardiness*, 30°F (−1°C); *exposure*, sun or part shade; *soil*, moist; *climate*, tropical, warm subtropical, warm Mediterranean

TOLERANCE *drought*, moderate to low; *salt*, presumed low

HEAT REQUIREMENT high

USES AND EFFECTS focal point, landmark tree; *effect*, Jurassic; *special use*, landmark; *avoid* constrained spaces, maintenance budgets

ALTERNATE SPECIES *Corypha* spp.

AVAILABILITY rare

left: *Tahina spectabilis* at Mike Harris's garden, Broward County, Florida

right: *Thrinax radiata* at Punta Roquena, Florida Keys

Thrinax

A small genus of small to modest-size, single-trunk, unarmed, palmate-leaf palm trees resemble and are related to plants in the *Coccothrinax* and *Leucothrinax* genera (the latter hardy to the mid-20s F, or about –4°C). Two species endemic to Jamaica, *T. excelsa* and *T. parviflora*, adapted to tropical and subtropical climates, are slightly larger than *T. radiata*.

Thrinax radiata

THATCH PALM

What *Adonidia merrillii* is to tropical feather palms, *T. radiata* is to fan palms. This common species from coastlines around the northern Caribbean, the Bahamas, and the Florida Keys shares the flouncy charm and modest, approachable scale of the feather palm from the Philippines, along with its adaptation to limestone soils. The thatch palm is the emblematic palm of Tulum, the coastal Mayan site and resort in the Mexican Yucatán, where it clutches its roots to rocky limestone bluffs and raises its shiny crown of undulating, 360-degree fans against the sparkle—and occasional hurricane—of the sea. Young plants in a bit of shade produce elegant, slightly cupped fans that lack the golden tones in the centers of sun-grown leaves. Leaves are green on both sides, a clear distinction from *Leucothrinax morrisii* and *Coccothrinax argentata*, which also grow wild in the Florida Keys. We saw a multitude of these elegant young thatch palms at many heights growing in the dappled shade at Crane Point Museum and Nature Center, at Marathon in the Florida Keys. Leafbases split beneath the petiole where they meet the slender trunk. Dead leaves fall quickly from the crown, and leafbases slough off to reveal the smooth, unringed trunk. Flowers on a wandlike inflorescence protruding from the crown mature to tiny, distinctive ivory-colored fruits.

Use slow-growing thatch palms in tropical and subtropical landscapes for their salt-tolerance, versatility, durability, and neat charm. Although humid heat is their preference, they encounter cool weather in habitat and can be grown in warm climates where frosts are rare and light. In habitat, rain can be seasonal and sporadic and heat can be intense, making them somewhat drought-tolerant. As a street tree, they're an accent, not a statement, though denser bouquet plantings make a bigger impact. Make sure they have sharp drainage.

APPEARANCE *leaves*, 4–6 ft. (1.2–1.8 m) long; *crown span*, 6–8 ft. (1.8–2.4 m); *trunk*, 30 ft. (9.1 m) tall and 4 in. (10 cm) thick

CULTURE *hardiness*, 27°F (−3°C); *exposure*, sun or part shade; *soil*, well-drained, tolerant of calcareous soils; *climate*, tropical, warm subtropical, warm Mediterranean

TOLERANCE *drought*, high; *salt*, high

HEAT REQUIREMENT high

USES AND EFFECTS coastal accent tree, focal point in small spaces, groves and clusters, understory in part shade, en masse for screening, containers, interiors, floral design (leaves, inflorescences, infructescences); *effects*, Caribbean, Yucatecan, tropical, coastal; *special use*, seaside; *avoid* heavy, wet soil

ALTERNATE SPECIES *Coccothrinax* spp., *Trachycarpus* spp.

AVAILABILITY common

Trachycarpus

Eight solitary, dioecious palmate palm species, all but one becoming trees, grow along the Himalayan uplift from Uttarakhand in north-central India, through the mountains of Southeast Asia to central China. Habitat elevations within the genus range from 3280 to 7874 feet (1000 to 2400 m), a hint to their usefulness in less-tropical climates, including those with cool summers and long, chilly, wet winters. Petioles on most bear insignificant small teeth. In addition to the commonly grown *T. fortunei* and *T. fortunei* 'Wagnerianus', the genus offers untapped potential for attractive, moderate-size palms adapted to cool climates and tolerant of freeze events. They are all adaptable to sun or shade, though some burning may occur in very hot, dry situations; although *T. fortunei* is grown in Las Vegas, the genus is not for lower deserts (or for the persistent heat of South Florida and other such sweltering places). This most commonly cultivated species is the least attractive—and the most adaptable. All these moderate-size species look good in groves, as container plants, and in small spaces. Except in the smallest of lanes, street plantings work best when trachycarpus palms are clustered, several to a tree well. Allée and median plantings demand high density and careful consideration of scale.

Trachycarpus fortunei

CHINESE WINDMILL PALM

The Chinese windmill palm, a larger crowned version of the waggie, *T. fortunei* 'Wagnerianus', can tolerate drought, wind, and some neglect, but at the expense of looking trashy and parched. An inverted halo of persistent, half-yellowed leaves occurs on many stressed specimens. The best-looking Chinese windmills (or Chusan palms) receive plentiful moisture, some shade when young, and fertilizer that includes magnesium; they can grow rather fast with such generous treatment. Inflorescences emerge from sheathing bracts in spring to reveal branched, cauliflower-like bud clusters; then they open into a show of pale yellow in the crown, turning black and untidy on male plants or bearing pea-size blue-black fruits on female trees. As demonstrated on the beaches of Vancouver, British Columbia, the palms' salt tolerance is moderately high. They also benefit enormously from group planting. Give them an updated look by pruning off the gorilla-hairy leafbases to reveal their smooth, ringed trunks, the upper parts of which will green up after exposure, especially where shaded. Or leave them natural and tuck epiphytes such as bromeliads, orchids, and ferns among the fibrous leafbases. Hot-summer climates are to its liking as long as winters cool down. North Florida is home to many (especially in clay soils), though South Florida's persistent heat and gritty soils are hostile to them. The most tropical location I've seen the species growing is Hilo, Hawai'i, where average nighttime low temperatures stay below 70°F (21°C) for eleven months of the year and highs rarely break 86°F (30°C).

Trachycarpus fortunei at Mary Alice Woodrum's garden, North Augusta, South Carolina

APPEARANCE *leaves*, 4–5 ft. (1.2–1.5 m) long; *crown span*, 6–8 ft. (1.8–2.4 m); *trunk*, 45 ft. (13.8 m) tall and 6 in. (15 cm) thick

CULTURE *hardiness*, 10°F (−12°C); *exposure*, sun or shade; *soil*, adaptable, tolerant of calcareous soils; *climate*, warm temperate, Mediterranean, cool tropical, subtropical

TOLERANCE *drought*, moderate; *salt*, moderate

HEAT REQUIREMENT low

USES AND EFFECTS vertical element in small spaces, groves and clusters, street tree, understory in part shade, en masse for screening, containers, floral design (leaves, leafbases, inflorescences, infructescences); *effects*, woodland, East Asian; *special use*, epiphyte host; *avoid* year-round hot climates, windy spots

ALTERNATE SPECIES *Coccothrinax* spp., *Trachycarpus* spp., *Trithrinax acanthocoma*

AVAILABILITY common

Trachycarpus fortunei 'Wagnerianus'

WAGGIE PALM

The moderate- to fast-growing waggie palm makes a modest-size palm tree in good time. Its trim, dark green fan leaves look adorable in a container for two decades or more, but grown in the ground with regular irrigation and fertilizer, this species can expand upward rather fast (to 10 feet, or 3 m) in ten to fifteen years. Its crown stays pretty narrow, 5–7 feet (1.5–2.1 m) across in full sun, wider in shade. Flowers and fruits are the same as those of *T. fortunei*. The 4- to 5-inch–thick (10- to 13-cm) trunk is covered in furry leafbases, giving it greater girth and an animal vibe, sculptural and huggable at the same time. Give it regular, moderate irrigation in well-drained soil for best appearance; plants will tolerate

Trachycarpus fortunei 'Wagnerianus' at the late Richard Douglas's garden, Walnut Creek, California

drought, however, by slowing down and staying diminutive longer. Regular fertilizing and watering through dry spells will reduce the golden-halo effect on aging lower leaves. It's equally happy in fog-belt gardens and hot, inland valleys, even thriving in mountain gardens below 4000 feet (1219 m) in elevation in California. It thrives in milder parts of the Pacific Northwest, in areas where temperatures rarely reach 10°F (−12°C).

APPEARANCE *leaves*, 4 ft. (1.2 m) long; *crown span*, 6 ft. (1.8 m); *trunk*, 45 ft. (13.8 m) tall and 6 in. (15 cm) thick

CULTURE *hardiness*, 10°F (−12°C); *exposure*, sun or shade; *soil*, adaptable, tolerant of calcareous soils; *climate*, warm temperate, Mediterranean, cool tropical, subtropical

TOLERANCE *drought*, moderate; *salt*, moderate

HEAT REQUIREMENT low

USES AND EFFECTS vertical element or focal point in small spaces, groves and clusters, bonsai, street tree, understory in part shade, en masse for screening, containers, floral design (leaves, leafbases, inflorescences, infructescences); *effects*, woodland, East Asian; *special use*, bonsai; *avoid* hot climates, use as focal point in large spaces

ALTERNATE SPECIES *Chamaerops humilis* (single-trunk form), *Coccothrinax* spp., other *Trachycarpus* spp.

AVAILABILITY uncommon

Trachycarpus latisectus at
Bergstrom Gardens, Atherton,
California

Trachycarpus latisectus

WINDAMERE PALM

The Windamere palm was named by Tobias Span-
ner and Martin Gibbons in the 1990s; they found
the palm growing in Darjeeling, India, in the garden
at the Windamere Hotel. It possesses a vivid green
crown of slightly undulate fan leaves. The segments
of the glossy fan (often covering a 360-degree radius)
cling together in twos and threes at their tips. Lowest dying leaves change quickly from green to yellow
to straw, evading the sickly yellow reverse halo that
can occur on the persistent lower leaves of *T. fortunei*.
Together, these features make for an effect of lush
vitality. Petioles, uniquely unarmed, are edged with
soft white fuzz. Its thin trunk is covered in youth with
the flat, mesh fiber of old leafbases, often a reddish
brown color; these peel off readily on older parts of
the trunk. Extremely rare in habitat, this palm occupies steep slopes at the lower altitudes of the genus,
and although it responds to plentiful water in cultivation, it is not exceptionally thirsty in cool-summer climates, comparable to a Japanese maple. In the warm,
inland San Diego County yards of Flora Grubb Gardens' wholesale division, East West Trees, this species grows at a moderate speed, outpacing its cousin
T. martianus, and looks its best in partial sun. Temperatures below 25°F (−4°C) will damage leaves, and
lower temperatures can kill the plant.

APPEARANCE *leaves*, 4 ft. (1.2 m) long; *crown
span*, 6 ft. (1.8 m); *trunk*, 40 ft. (12.2 m) tall and
6 in. (15 cm) thick

CULTURE *hardiness*, 22°F (−6°C); *exposure*,
sun or part shade; *soil*, well-drained, moist,
non-alkaline; *climate*, cool tropical, warm
temperate, Mediterranean, subtropical

TOLERANCE *drought*, low; *salt*, presumed low

HEAT REQUIREMENT low

USES AND EFFECTS foliage accent, vertical
element in small spaces, groves and clusters,
sentinels, containers, floral design (leaves,
leafbases, inflorescences, infructescences);
effects, tropical, lush; *special use*, small tree
substitute; *avoid* drought

ALTERNATE SPECIES *Brahea calcarea*,
Coccothrinax spp., *Livistona fulva*, other
Trachycarpus spp.

AVAILABILITY rare

Trachycarpus martianus

HIMALAYAN WINDMILL PALM

The most elegant and graceful of the *Trachycarpus* genus, this uncommon species comes from two major populations—one in central Nepal at elevations as high as 8000 feet (2438 m), the other in the Khasia Hills of northeast India at elevations as low as 3280 feet (1000 m). They are known in the nursery trade under their cultivar names, 'Nepal' and 'Khasia Hills', accordingly. Part of the tree's elegance is its leaves' radial regularity and fine segmentation. An ellipse of connected segments appears in the leaf blade and echoes the outer silhouette formed by the divided segment tips. Another elegant feature is the palm's long petioles, tufted with fuzz. Its open crown and thin, leaning trunk create graceful proportions in this moderate-size tree. Like its close relative, *T. latisectus*, leafbase fibers resemble burlap pulled tightly to the trunk. A few dead leaves hang plumb from the crown (often creating an acute angle to the trunk's lean), but petioles eventually break near their connection to the leafbase and, later, leafbases abscise readily from the trunk, revealing persistent rings.

The Khasia Hills cliff-dwelling plant from the very wet, lower elevation habitat (one of the wettest places on Earth), needs regular water and good drainage in cultivation; the Nepal-origin plants are reputed to tolerate more drought and cold, but this species and its close relative *T. latisectus* are among the least cold-hardy of the genus. Temperatures below 25°F (−4°C) will damage leaves, and lower temperatures can kill plants of Khasia Hills origin.

APPEARANCE *leaves*, 6 ft. (1.8 m) long; *crown span*, 8 ft. (2.4 m); *trunk*, 40 ft. (12.2 m) tall and 6 in. (15 cm) thick

CULTURE *hardiness*, 22°F (−6°C); *exposure*, sun or part shade; *soil*, well-drained, moist, non-alkaline; *climate*, cool tropical, warm temperate, Mediterranean, subtropical

TOLERANCE *drought*, low; *salt*, presumed low

HEAT REQUIREMENT low

USES AND EFFECTS foliage accent, vertical element in small spaces, sentinels, groves and clusters, containers, floral design (leaves, leafbases, inflorescences, infructescences); *effects*, woodland, tropical, color, lush, elegant, sculptural; *special uses*, leaning effects; *avoid* drought

ALTERNATE SPECIES *Coccothrinax* spp., *Trachycarpus* spp.

AVAILABILITY rare

above: *Trachycarpus martianus* at Bergstrom Gardens, Atherton, California

right: *Trachycarpus oreophilus* at Bergstrom Gardens, Atherton, California

Trachycarpus oreophilus

THAI MOUNTAIN FAN PALM

This lovely rare palm, from mountain habitat as high as 7135 feet (2175 m) from northwest Thailand to northeast India, falls into a group with a very similar and rare species, *T. takil*. The latter comes from altitudes as high as 7875 feet (2400 m) in the lower Himalayas of Uttarakhand, India, where it grows in a temperate forest alongside fir trees, oaks, rhododendrons, and birches. Both improve upon the common *T. fortunei* with equally stiff and flat, but more regularly divided, leaf blades that have more conspicuously waxy undersides and that hold up better to wind. Both species have leafbase fibers that are neater and less hairy than those of *T. fortunei* and that more readily peel from the trunk. Leaves of *T. oreophilus* have brighter, more reflective undersides than those of *T. takil*. In the San Francisco Botanical Garden, *T. takil* is the fastest growing of palms, robust and vigorous, while young *T. oreophilus* palms grow steadily there in both sun and shade. *Trachycarpus takil* has shown great tolerance for salty winds near Berkeley, California, retaining good color and form in a chilly site some 65 feet (about 20 m) from San Francisco Bay. In habitat, *T. oreophilus* experiences rare snowfalls, and it is worthy of testing wherever *T. fortunei* can be grown, and beyond.

APPEARANCE *leaves*, 5 ft. (1.5 m) long; *crown span*, 8 ft. (2.4 m); *trunk*, 40 ft. (12.2 m) tall and 8 in. (20 cm) thick

CULTURE *hardiness*, 15°F (−9°C); *exposure*, sun or part shade; *soil*, adaptable, tolerant of calcareous soils; *climate*, cool tropical, warm temperate, Mediterranean

TOLERANCE *drought*, moderate; *salt*, moderate to low

HEAT REQUIREMENT low

USES AND EFFECTS foliage accent, vertical element in small spaces, groves and clusters, sentinels, containers, floral design (leaves, leafbases, inflorescences, infructescences); *effects*, woodland, elegant, sculptural; *special uses*, seaside (*T. takil*) and windy locations; *avoid* poor drainage

ALTERNATE SPECIES *Coccothrinax* spp., other *Trachycarpus* spp., *Trithrinax acanthocoma*

AVAILABILITY rare

Trachycarpus princeps

STONE GATE PALM

Perhaps the most beautiful cold-hardy fan palm tree, the very rare Stone Gate palm comes from the cliffs and slopes of one canyon of the Salween River in Yunnan, China, at altitudes from 5085 to 6070 feet (1550 to 1850 m). The waxy cast of its leaves gives them a bluish, frosted impression on the upper surfaces and a reflective, almost white look on the undersides. Their leaves have the elegant radial symmetry of *T. martianus* while displaying the precocious charm of *T. fortunei* 'Wagnerianus'. One of the shorter trees in the genus, its maximum known height in habitat is 26 feet (8 m). It requires good drainage and appears to tolerate some drought.

APPEARANCE *leaves*, 6 ft. (1.8 m) long; *crown span*, 8 ft. (2.4 m); *trunk*, 30 ft. (9.1 m) tall and 8 in. (20 cm) thick

CULTURE *hardiness*, 15°F (−9°C); *exposure*, sun or part shade; *soil*, well-drained, tolerant of calcareous soils; *climate*, cool tropical, warm temperate, Mediterranean, subtropical

TOLERANCE *drought*, moderate; *salt*, presumed low

HEAT REQUIREMENT low

USES AND EFFECTS foliage accent, focal point in small spaces, groves and clusters, sentinels, floral design (leaves, leafbases, inflorescences, infructescences); *effects*, woodland, color, elegant, sculptural; *special uses*, planted atop walls or upslope to view glaucous leaf undersides; *avoid* poor drainage

ALTERNATE SPECIES *Chamaerops humilis* var. *argentea* (single-trunk specimen), *Coccothrinax* spp., other *Trachycarpus* spp., *Trithrinax acanthocoma*

AVAILABILITY rare

Trithrinax

Southern Brazil, Paraguay, eastern Bolivia, and northern Argentina are home to this small genus of hardy, slow-growing, moderate-size palmate palms, best culti-vated in subtropical, warm temperate, and Mediterranean climates. Two species are clustering, shrubby to treelike; two are solitary trees. Their armature rivals that of cactus and agaves. Leaf segment tips end in stiff, sharp points. Adher-ent leafbases form a beautiful matrix of long, wicker-stiff needles on the trunk. Only petioles and older trunks shorn of leafbases present unarmed surfaces. All the species are drought-tolerant and endure temperatures at least as low as 20°F (–7°C).

Trithrinax acanthocoma at Ganna Walska Lotusland, Montecito, California

Trithrinax acanthocoma

BRAZILIAN NEEDLE PALM

The single-trunk Brazilian needle palm's broad fan leaves are flat and stiff, dark green, with a matrix of silver scales on the undersides. The crown is bold and dramatic. Showy yellow to white inflo-rescences are produced in spring and summer, followed by attractive, marble-size, shiny, ivory fruits. The basket weave of spines on the leafbases, which remain attached to the trunk, and the spiny tips of each segment of the leaf blade provide natural security, an obstacle. This slow grower is a good palm to place where intru-sions are unwelcome, and it's not a good candidate for planting beside walkways or doorways. Leafbases can be removed to disarm the trunk, reveal its surface, and alter the proportions of the tree.

APPEARANCE *leaves*, 5 ft. (1.5 m) long; *crown span*, 10 ft. (3 m); *trunk*, 30 ft. (9.1 m) tall and 8–12 in. (20–30 cm) thick

CULTURE *hardiness*, 15°F (–9°C); *exposure*, sun or part shade; *soil*, adaptable; *climate*, cool tropical, subtropical, warm temperate, Mediterranean

TOLERANCE *drought*, moderate; *salt*, high

HEAT REQUIREMENT moderate

USES AND EFFECTS foliage accent, groves and clusters, armed sentinels, floral design (leaves, leafbases, inflorescences, infructescences); *effects*, menacing, elegant, sculptural; *special use*, security; *avoid* planting where spines might pose a risk

ALTERNATE SPECIES *Copernicia* spp., *Trachycarpus* spp.

AVAILABILITY rare

Trithrinax campestris

CARANDAY PALM

One of the most fiercely armed of palms, the caranday palm's exquisite pewter-color leaves are as rigid as an agave's, each segment tip sharpened to a spine. Additional natural defense comes from leafbases composed of stiff spines, like its cousin the Brazilian needle palm. As a young plant it forms a mound of steely leaves. Older plants slowly become upright clusters, among the most memorable of palms when viewed in their savanna habitat. The metallic beauty of an established plant marries particularly well with succulents and grasses. In addition to being drought-tolerant, this slow-growing palm is adapted to summer rain inundations.

APPEARANCE *leaves*, 3 ft. (0.9 m) long; *crown span*, 6 ft. (1.8 m); *clump span*, to 15 ft. (4.6 m); *trunk*, 15 ft. (4.6 m) tall and 8 in. (20 cm) thick

CULTURE *hardiness*, 15°F (−9°C); *exposure*, sun or part shade; *soil*, adaptable; *climate*, subtropical, Mediterranean, desert, warm temperate

TOLERANCE *drought*, moderate; *salt*, presumed moderate

HEAT REQUIREMENT high

USES AND EFFECTS foliage, focal point, armed sentinel, security hedge, floral design, with care (leaves, leafbases, inflorescences, infructescences); *effects*, menacing, elegant, sculptural; *special use*, security; *avoid* planting where spines might pose a risk

ALTERNATE SPECIES *Chamaerops humilis* var. *argentea*

AVAILABILITY rare

Veitchia

A group of graceful, fast-growing, clean-looking, tall feather palms from the tropical southwest Pacific with conspicuous crownshafts and large, bright-red fruits, *Veitchia* species are commonly used in tropical and subtropical landscapes such as South Florida. Heat and moisture loving, a few can be coaxed to grow in very mild Mediterranean climates such as coastal Southern California, and a *Wodyetia* × *Veitchia* hybrid that grows with extra vigor has been successful there. Incidental hybrids within the genus are common, too.

above: *Veitchia arecina* at Punta Roquena, Florida Keys

left: *Trithrinax campestris* at the Ruth Bancroft Garden, Walnut Creek, California

Veitchia arecina

MONTGOMERY PALM

Native to Vanuatu in the southwest Pacific, this tall, charismatic palm bears leaves in a hemispherical crown above a pale, silvery green crownshaft marked with dark scales at the apex. Dying leaves barely turn yellow before peeling off the trunk, making for a tidy, vibrant plant. The semipendant leaflets, jagged and blunt at their tips, dynamic in breezes, appear to levitate. Branched inflorescences below the crownshaft are greenish white with large flowers that produce attractive bright red fruits nearly the size of a quail's egg; both flowers and fruits often decorate the ground below the tree. Beneath the crownshaft, dark rings separate silvery green internodes; both quickly fade to pale gray below. The proportion of the thin, sometimes gently leaning trunk to the broad, open crown is especially pleasing, even thrilling, when a group of these fast-growing palms arise from a flat lawn—a regular sight in South Florida. *Veitchia joannis* is a similar, slightly taller species with more languidly pendant leaflets and thus a more relaxed appearance.

APPEARANCE *leaves*, 6–12 ft. (1.8–3.7 m) long; *crown span*, 10–16 ft. (3.0–4.9 m); *trunk*, 60 ft. (18.3 m) tall and 12 in. (31 cm) thick, flared at the base

CULTURE *hardiness*, 32°F (0°C); *exposure*, sun or part shade; *soil*, adaptable; *climate*, tropical, warm subtropical, mildest Mediterranean

TOLERANCE *drought*, moderate; *salt*, moderate

HEAT REQUIREMENT high

USES AND EFFECTS groves and clusters, avenue planting, focal point, street tree, silhouette, floral design (leaves, leafbases, inflorescences, infructescences); *effects*, elegant, tropical, South Seas; *special use*, lawn planting; *avoid* frost, sustained cool weather

ALTERNATE SPECIES *Archontophoenix cunninghamiana, Ptychosperma elegans*

AVAILABILITY common

Verschaffeltia splendida

SEYCHELLES STILT PALM

The Seychelles Islands, near the equator in the western Indian Ocean, are home to an extraordinary handful of monotypic palm genera (including *Lodoicea mal-divica*, the coco de mer, a species that bears the largest seed in the plant kingdom). The monotypic, single-trunk genus *Verschaffeltia* is the only commonly grown palm from this fabled granite archipelago, partly thanks to its fast growth and ease of propagation, but especially because of its splendid appearance. Its pinnate leaves remain undivided in youth except at the apex, splitting into varied groupings of leaflets in the crown and resembling a loose feather duster. Spines arm the petiole and rachis of the leaf, especially on younger plants. Open inflorescences emerge among the leaves but often remain attached below the crown as the glossy round fruit develops. Neat leafbases do not form a crownshaft but nearly encircle the trunk; leaves sometimes briefly hang dead before fully detaching from the crown, revealing a trunk with spined rings. Most notable is the cone of thick, phallic stilt roots that seem to elevate the trunk and give the palm the effect of a dancer en pointe. The ensemble of sail-like leaves, thin trunk, and elevated base epitomizes the gravity-defying impression at which palm trees can excel. Best in moist tropical climates, this moderate-size tree looks beautiful in trios and small groves and beneath high canopy as well as in full sun.

Verschaffeltia splendida at Hale Mohalu, Big Island, Hawai'i

APPEARANCE *leaves*, 10 ft. (3 m) long; *crown span*, 8–12 ft. (2.4–3.7 m); *trunk*, 60 ft. (18.3 m) tall and 12 in. (31 cm) thick, with stilt roots at base

CULTURE *hardiness*, 35°F (2°C); *exposure*, shade or sun; *soil*, well-drained, moist, acid; *climate*, tropical, warmest subtropical

TOLERANCE *drought*, low; *salt*, low

HEAT REQUIREMENT high

USES AND EFFECTS groves and clusters, focal point, subcanopy vertical element, silhouette, floral design, with care (leaves, leafbases, inflorescences, infructescences); *effects*, Jurassic, tropical; *special use*, trios; *avoid* drought, cold

ALTERNATE SPECIES *Phoenicophorium borsigianum* (tropical)

AVAILABILITY uncommon

Washingtonia

A genus comprising a pair of fast-growing, large, single-trunk, fan-leaf species from Baja California, Sonora, Mexico, and the southwesternmost United States, *Washingtonia* is grown as commonly for ornament as almost any other genus in the family. Dead leaves with fiercely thorny petioles cling to the trunk, layering themselves into a straw-colored skirt or beard unless pruned. The leaves can be used to thatch roofs.

Washingtonia filifera

CALIFORNIA FAN PALM, DESERT FAN PALM

The majestic palm native to the creeks and springs of the low-altitude deserts of California, northern Baja California, and western Arizona has been expanding its range with human and animal help to Death Valley National Park and even the San Joaquin Valley, where feral seedlings have been making new groves and new generations. It's now the northernmost spontaneously growing palm in North America, and accordingly hardy, especially in drier climates. Giving Palm Springs its name, the grand palm oasis—a ten-minute drive away in the Indian Canyons in the Agua Caliente Band of Cahuilla Indians' ancestral land—is a must-see for visitors to the desert cities. Also near Palm Springs, the pool and marshes of Thousand Palms Oasis at the Coachella Valley Preserve offer a different, equally breathtaking, experience of this gregarious palm's ecology and beauty.

It's an excellent, speedy, hardy, very large palm for warm to hot, dry areas such as southern Nevada, Arizona, Central Texas, and California's Inland Empire and Central Valley. Even favored spots of southern Utah and New Mexico grow a nice *W. filifera*. Heavy, untapered columns and jade-colored crowns of these palms frame the California State Capitol building grounds in Sacramento and mark grand houses in farm country. Closely planted or sun-seeking individuals will develop leaning trunks, but this phenomenon is rarely seen outside of habitat. Long, branched inflorescences with whitish flowers push out of the crown in spring and summer and hang down, especially once the currant-size black fruits have formed. A pleasingly fine-textured skirt of dead leaves persists through most of the palm's life unless burned or pruned off. Leafbases can remain attached after cutting petioles at the base, or trunks can be "skinned" with a carpet knife to expose the trunk surface.

Rather drought-tolerant, but not xeric, it thrives with regular moisture and crowds the watercourses to which it's limited in its desert home. Although native

to the state of California, the palm has a desert-dweller's preference for warm, dry weather that limits its long-term viability in the densely populated coastal regions of the state. There, the nightly moisture of marine air in the dry season and cool rains in winter nurture fungal diseases in the palms' crowns that conspire to kill the trees over the long run. Even in hot-summer areas with long winter-wet seasons, such as the Napa Valley, crowns deteriorate through the rainy season, regaining a fresh, green look through summer's dry heat. The same problems can occur in warm, summer-wet subtropical and tropical climates. (The best desert fan palms in Hawai'i grow on the dry, leeward sides of the islands.) It's a worthy plant for the desert and semiarid tropics, in addition to colder realms.

APPEARANCE *leaves*, 11–13 ft. (3.4–4.0 m) long; *crown span*, 15 ft. (4.6 m); *trunk*, 66 ft. (20.1 m) tall and 20–36 in. (51–91 cm) thick, subtly flared at the base

CULTURE *hardiness*, 14°F (–10°C); *exposure*, sun or part shade; *soil*, adaptable, tolerates calcareous soils; *climate*, desert, Mediterranean, dry subtropical, dry tropical

TOLERANCE *drought*, high; *salt*, high

HEAT REQUIREMENT moderate

USES AND EFFECTS avenue planting, focal point, street tree, groves, silhouette, floral design (leaves, leafbases); *effects*, oasis, Hollywood, Palm Springs; *special use*, skyline tree; *avoid* saturated soils

ALTERNATE SPECIES *Brahea armata, B. clara, B. edulis, Livistona nitida*

AVAILABILITY common

left: *Washingtonia filifera* in habitat, Palm Springs, California

below: *Washingtonia robusta* at Tongva Park, Santa Monica, California, designed by James Corner Field Operations and John Greenlee

Washingtonia robusta

MEXICAN FAN PALM

The Mexican fan palm is an easy, low-cost palm tree for many people . . . well, at first. It's the tall, skinny fan palm that grows all over lowland California (as an ornamental or a weed), but native to desert oases around the Gulf of California, where it acquired a tolerance for humid air and ferocious heat. It will tolerate the chilly fog belt (but not look very nice) and the salty air of the West Coast, growing 5 to 8 feet (1.5 to 2.4 m) per decade with plentiful water. Away from the coast, it will thrive and become a 40-foot (12.2-m) skyline tree in twenty to forty years. The problem with this speed demon is that it needs regular pruning to keep it looking neat. Those who admire the natural, if messy, shag of dead leaves hanging below the crown will save money on pruning until it begins to peel off spontaneously in middle age, often leaving a neck beard below the clean upper trunk to drop dribs and drabs indefinitely. In the coldest valleys of California and extreme winters of the Southeast and Gulf Coast, it will suffer occasional winter foliar damage. It can be the wrong selection because it gets too tall for home gardens and can become a literal lightning rod in thunderstorms.

For steady growth, plant it in sunshine. In cooler areas, shade slows it way down. Its salty beach tolerance ranks it with *Sabal palmetto* and just below *Cocos nucifera.*

APPEARANCE *leaves*, 6–8 ft. (1.8–2.4 m) long; *crown span*, 10–12 ft. (3.0–3.7 m); *trunk*, 100 ft. (30.5 m) tall and 12 in. (31 cm) thick, flared at the base

CULTURE *hardiness*, 22°F (–6°C); *exposure*, sun or part shade; *soil*, adaptable, tolerates calcareous soils; *climate*, desert, Mediterranean, subtropical, warm temperate, tropical

TOLERANCE *drought*, high; *salt*, high

HEAT REQUIREMENT moderate

USES AND EFFECTS avenue planting, focal point, street tree, clusters and groves, silhouette, floral design (leaves, leafbases); *effects*, oasis, Hollywood; *special uses*, skyline tree, seaside; *avoid* saturated soils

ALTERNATE SPECIES *Brahea edulis*, *Livistona australis*, *Saribus rotundifolius* (tropical, warm subtropical)

AVAILABILITY common

Washingtonia ×*filibusta*

This fast-growing hybrid of *W. filifera* and *W. robusta* falls between the two species in characteristics. It's favored in humid regions for a huskiness and stateliness conferred by the *W. filifera* parentage and the partial resistance to fungal diseases in moister areas that is the heritage of *W. robusta.*

Many of these spontaneous hybrids in the landscape confuse the eye—some of them first-generation descendants of the two species, others the product of several generations of mingling, and thus not perfect intermediates. Compared to the more common *W. robusta*, *W. filifera* has a thicker, shorter, untapered trunk; a broader crown with stiffer leaves of a more muted green; and longer petioles and persistent threads. *Washingtonia robusta* has rich green, shiny leaves with a distinct patch of white tomentum visible when looking up at center of the undersides of adult fans, and its thin trunk often flares at the base. The skirts of *W. filifera* tend to be even-textured, while those of *W. robusta* can seem irregular and messy. Mexico's *W. robusta* also goes through distinct phases in its lifespan—from dense-crowned and stiff in youth to graceful and dynamic in full maturity—a phasing that is subtle if it occurs in its California cousin.

Washingtonia ×filibusta in
a garden designed by Steve
Martino, Palm Springs, California

APPEARANCE *leaves*, 8–10 ft. (2.4–3.0 m) long;
crown span, 13 ft. (4 m); *trunk*, 100 ft. (30.5 m)
tall and 12–20 in. (31–51 cm) thick, subtly flared
at the base

CULTURE *hardiness*, 17°F (–8°C); *exposure*, sun
or part shade; *soil*, adaptable, tolerates
calcareous soils; *climate*, desert, Mediterranean,
subtropical, warm temperate, dry tropical

TOLERANCE *drought*, high; *salt*, high

HEAT REQUIREMENT moderate

USES AND EFFECTS avenue planting, focal point,
street tree, silhouette, floral design (leaves,
leafbases); *effects*, oasis, Hollywood; *special
uses*, skyline tree, seaside; *avoid* saturated soils

ALTERNATE SPECIES *Brahea edulis, Livistona
australis, L. nitida, Saribus rotundifolius*
(tropical, warm subtropical)

AVAILABILITY uncommon

Wodyetia bifurcata

FOXTAIL PALM, WODYETI'S PALM

A narrow endemic from northern Queensland, Australia, this popular, fast-growing, moderate-size to large crownshaft palm tree bears an open crown of densely plumose, arching leaves resembling a fox's tail. Its ringed, cylindrical white-gray trunk shows a subtle spindle shape in maturity, accentuated by the narrow, slightly glaucous crownshaft. Branched inflorescences packaged at first in bracts are displayed below the crownshaft, expanding laterally to bear large flowers and then

hanging with the weight of attractive orange-scarlet fruit. It prefers tropical and subtropical climates. Although these palms look reasonably healthy in milder parts of Southern California, they ride on hopes more than proof of success there. Presumably, they are coaxed to grow in irrigated landscapes of similarly mild Mediterranean climates. They prefer regular moisture, good drainage, and slightly acid soils, appearing yellow and chlorotic in Miami's alkaline substrates, and they grow best in full to partial sun. They also appear to survive monsoonal drought in habitat by tapping deep sources of moisture; plants in cultivation can tolerate drought but stall and lose color.

Its effect in the landscape is of a two-thirds–scale royal palm (*Roystonea* spp.)—tidy and proud. *Wodyetia bifurcata* is useful as a street tree, a single focal point, a small grove tree, a tree for allée planting, for its colorful fruit, and, like so many palms, for its attractiveness to honeybees and other pollinators.

A delightful hybrid of *Veitchia arecina* and *W. bifurcata*, ×*Wodveitchia* (the Foxy Lady palm) is more slender and less plumose than *Wodyetia*. It has proven more successful in California gardens than either parent, and one selection has a pleasing variegation. It also thrives in tropical and subtropical climates.

APPEARANCE *leaves*, 8 ft. (2.4 m) long; *crown span*, 14 ft. (4.3 m); *trunk*, 45 ft. (13.8 m) tall and 8–10 in. (20–25 cm) thick, subtly fusiform

CULTURE *hardiness*, 28°F (−2°C); *exposure*, sun or part shade; *soil*, adaptable; *climate*, tropical, warm subtropical, desert, mild Mediterranean

TOLERANCE *drought*, moderate; *salt*, low

HEAT REQUIREMENT high

USES AND EFFECTS street tree, avenue planting, groves, allées, focal point, floral design (fruit, inflorescence, leafbases, leaves); *effects*, tropical, uniform, formal; *special use*, color (fruit); *avoid* nutrient-poor or alkaline soils, cold and wet soils

ALTERNATE SPECIES *Roystonea regia, Syagrus romanzoffiana*

AVAILABILITY common

Wodyetia bifurcata at Hale Mohalu, Big Island, Hawai'i

RESOURCES

The International Palm Society

Palms.org

With local affiliates in the United States and worldwide, this organization of enthusiasts and researchers dedicated to the study of palms publishes the quarterly journal, *Palms*; hosts the palmtalk.org community; convenes an international biennial; funds research, conservation, and publication; and sells palm-related books and other publications. Local affiliates host regular meetings and garden tours, and many produce their own newsletters.

The Merwin Conservancy

merwinconservancy.org

Award-winning poet W. S. Merwin, the seventeenth Poet Laureate of the United States, has created an exceptional palm collection in his private botanical garden on Maui, Hawai'i. Under the auspices of a conservancy, this location is also becoming a center for poetry and palm knowledge, with a wealth of resources on its website: "The Merwin Conservancy's mission is to preserve the living legacy of W. S. Merwin, his home and palm forest, for future retreat and study for botanists and writers, for environmental advocacy and community education."

DESIGNERS

The work of several designers and landscape architects appears in this book (*). Others included here also design artfully with palms.

ARIZONA

* Steve Martino Landscape Architect, Phoenix: facebook.com/SteveMartino.LandscapeArchitect

CALIFORNIA

* Christopher Reynolds, San Francisco: reynolds-sebastiani.com

* Elysian Landscapes, Judy Kameon, Los Angeles: elysianlandscapes.com

* Eric Nagelmann, Carpinteria: (805) 689-5525, nagelmann@cox.net

* Exteriors Landscape Architecture, Hélène Morneau and Kris Sunderlage, Santa Rosa: exteriorslandscapearchitecture.com

* Flora Grubb Gardens, including Flora Grubb, Patrick Lannan, and Daniel Nolan, San Francisco: floragrubb.com

   GardenArt Group, Chris Jacobson, Saratoga: gardenartgroup.com

* Hood Design Studio, Walter Hood, Oakland: wjhooddesign.com

   Lisa Gimmy Landscape Architecture, Los Angeles: lglalandscape.com

* Living Green Design, Davis Dalbok, San Francisco: livinggreen.com

* Planet Horticulture, Roger Raiche and David McGrory, Sonoma County: Planethorticulture.com

* PWP Landscape Architecture, Berkeley: pwpla.com

* Sherry Merciari Designs, Oakland: (510) 638-4405

* Surfacedesign, San Francisco: sdisf.com

* Terremoto Landscape, San Francisco and Los Angeles: terremoto.la

FLORIDA

BURLE YATES DESIGN, Key West:
debrayates.com

Chip Jones, Fort Lauderdale: cycadflorida.com

Craig Reynolds Landscape Architecture:
craigreynolds.net

* D'Asign Source, Marathon:
dasignsource.com/landscapes

DDM Horticulture Services, Debra DeMarco,
Miami: ddmhort.com

Dre Joris, Key West: andrejoris.com

* Patrick Tierney Tropical Landscapes, Key West:
ptpalms@gmail.com

* Raymond Jungles, Miami: raymondjungles.com

HAWAI'I

* Brian Lievens, Big Island:
greenwizard@hawaii.rr.com

* Kaloli Landscape, Tom Piergrossi, Big Island:
tompiergrossi.com

OREGON

Sean Hogan, Portland: cistus.com

SOUTH CAROLINA

Glen R. Gardner, Landscape Architect,
Charleston: gardnerla.blogspot.com

* Jenks Farmer, Columbia: jenksfarmer.com

* Robert Chesnut ASLA, Charleston:
(843) 577-3673

Wertimer + Cline Landscape Architects,
Charleston: wertimer.com

OTHER LOCATIONS

Scott Ogden and Lauren Springer Ogden, Texas
and Colorado: plantdrivendesign.com

* SWA, various locations: swagroup.com

PUBLIC GARDENS TO VISIT

ARIZONA

Arizona-Sonora Desert Museum, Tucson:
desertmuseum.org

Desert Botanical Garden, Phoenix: dbg.org

CALIFORNIA

Capitol Park, Sacramento:
capitolmuseum.ca.gov/the-museum/capitol-park

City Park at Transbay, San Francisco:
transbaycenter.org/media-gallery/image-gallery/
city-park

Fullerton Arboretum, Fullerton:
fullertonarboretum.org

Ganna Walska Lotusland, Montecito:
lotusland.org

The Gardens at Lake Merritt, Lakeside
Palmetum, Oakland:
gardensatlakemerritt.org/palm-garden

The Huntington Botanical Gardens, San Marino:
huntington.org/gardens

Los Angeles County Arboretum & Botanic
Garden, Arcadia: arboretum.org

Los Angeles County Museum of Art, Primal
Palm Garden (by Robert Irwin): lacma.org

Mildred Mathias Botanical Garden, UCLA,
Los Angeles: botgard.ucla.edu

Palm Canyon, Balboa Park, San Diego:
balboapark.org/gardens/palm-canyon

Project Artaud, San Francisco:
www.projectartaud.org

The Ruth Bancroft Garden, Walnut Creek:
ruthbancroftgarden.org

San Diego Botanic Garden, Encinitas:
sdbgarden.org

San Diego Zoo botanical gardens:
animals.sandiegozoo.org/plants

San Francisco Botanical Garden: sfbotanicalgarden.org

Santa Barbara County Courthouse: sbcourts.org/gi/loc/sbcourthouse.shtm

Sherman Library and Gardens, Corona Del Mar: slgardens.org

South Coast Plaza luxury shopping, Costa Mesa: www.southcoastplaza.com

University of California Botanical Garden, Berkeley: botanicalgarden.berkeley.edu

Virginia Robinson Gardens, Beverly Hills: robinsongardens.org

FLORIDA

Alfred B. Maclay Gardens State Park, Tallahassee: floridastateparks.org/park/Maclay-Gardens

Fairchild Tropical Botanic Garden, Miami: fairchildgarden.org

Gizella Kopsick Arboretum, St. Petersburg: www.stpeteparksrec.org/gizella-kopsick-arboretum.html

Kanapaha Botanical Gardens, Gainesville: kanapaha.org

Leu Gardens, Orlando: leugardens.org

Marie Selby Botanical Gardens, Sarasota: selby.org

Miami Beach Botanical Garden, Miami Beach: mbgarden.org

Naples Botanical Garden, Naples: naplesgarden.org

National Tropical Botanical Garden: The Kampong, Miami: ntbg.org/gardens/kampong-plantcol.php

GEORGIA

Atlanta Botanical Garden, Atlanta: atlantabg.org

Coastal Georgia Botanical Gardens, Savannah: coastalgeorgiabg.org

HAWAI'I

Big Island

Hawai'i Tropical Botanical Garden, Papaikou: htbg.com

Pana'ewa Rainforest Zoo, Hilo: hilozoo.com

University of Hawai'i at Hilo Botanical Gardens, Hilo: (808) 932-7446

Kaua'i

National Tropical Botanical Garden (Allerton, Limahuli, and McBryde): ntbg.org

Maui

National Tropical Botanical Garden (Kahanu): ntbg.org

O'ahu

Honolulu Botanical Gardens (Foster, Ho'omaluhia, Koko Crater, and Wahiawa): honolulu.gov/parks/hbg.html

Lyon Arboretum, University of Hawai'i at Mānoa, Honolulu: manoa.hawaii.edu/lyonarboretum

Waimea Valley Botanical Collection, Hale'iwa: waimeavalley.net/botanical-collection

NORTH CAROLINA

J. C. Raulston Arboretum, Raleigh: jcra.ncsu.edu

OREGON

Cistus Nursery, Sauvie Island, Portland: cistus.com

Hoyt Arboretum, Portland: hoytarboretum.org

Lan Su Chinese Garden, Portland: lansugarden.org

SOUTH CAROLINA

Riverbanks Zoo and Garden, Columbia: riverbanks.org

TEXAS

Beaumont Botanical Gardens, Beaumont: beaumontbotanicalgardens.org

Moody Gardens, Galveston: moodygardens.com

Peckerwood Garden, Hempstead: peckerwoodgarden.org

Zilker Botanical Garden, Austin: zilkergarden.org

WASHINGTON

Carl S. English Botanical Gardens, Seattle: nws.usace.army.mil/Missions/Civil-Works/Locks-and-Dams/Chittenden-Locks/Botanical-Garden/

Washington Park Arboretum, Seattle: botanicgardens.uw.edu/Washington-park-arboretum

HABITATS TO VISIT

ALABAMA

Choctawhatchee River bottomlands

AMERICAN SAMOA

National Park of American Samoa: NPS.gov/npsa/index.htm

ARIZONA

Palm Canyon Trail, Kofa Mountains National Wildlife Refuge: fws.gov/uploadedFiles/PalmCanyonFactSheet2014_508.pdf

CALIFORNIA

Anza-Borrego Desert State Park: parks.ca.gov/?page_id=638

Indian Canyons Palm Canyon, Palm Springs: indian-canyons.com/palm.html

Joshua Tree National Park: nps.gov/jotr/index.htm

Thousand Palms Oasis Preserve, Palm Springs: coachellavalleypreserve.org

FLORIDA

Bahia Honda State Park, Florida Keys: bahiahondapark.com

Big Cypress National Preserve: nps.gov/bicy/index.htm

Crane Point Hammock Museum and Nature Center, Marathon: cranepoint.net

Curry Hammock State Park, Marathon: floridastateparks.org/park/Curry-Hammock

Everglades National Park: nps.gov/ever/index.htm

Florida Caverns State Park, Marianna: floridastateparks.org/park/Florida-Caverns

Juniper Springs Recreation Area, Silver Springs: juniper-springs.com

Key Deer Reserve, Big Pine Key: fws.gov/refuge/National_Key_Deer_Refuge/

Larry and Penny Thompson Park, Miami: miamidade.gov/parks/larry-penny.asp

Maritime Hammock Sanctuary, Brevard County: brevardfl.gov/EELProgram/Sanctuaries/MaritimeHammockSanctuary

Torreya State Park, Bristol: floridastateparks.org/park/Torreya

GEORGIA

4-H Tidelands Nature Center, Jekyll Island: caes2.caes.uga.edu/georgia4h/tidelands

GUAM

San Carlos Falls: theguamguide.com/trek-to-san-carlos-falls-and-swimming-hole

HAWAI'I

Hawai'i Volcanoes National Park, 'Ōla'a Tract, Volcano: nps.gov/havo/index.htm

Ko'olau ridge trails, O'ahu

Koke'e State Park, Kaua'i: hawaiistateparks.org/parks/kauai/koke%CA%BBe-state-park

Punalu'u Beach, Big Island: hawaiicounty.ehawaii.gov/camping/all,details,57790.html

LOUISIANA

Barataria Preserve, Jean Lafitte National Historical Park and Preserve, Marrero: nps.gov/jela/barataria-preserve.htm

NORTH CAROLINA

Bald Head Woods, North Carolina Coastal Reserve, Bald Head: nccoastalreserve.net/web/crp/bald-head-woods

OKLAHOMA

Red Slough Wildlife Management Area, Idabel: fs.usda.gov/detail/ouachita/landmanagement/?cid=STELPRDB5090471

PUERTO RICO

El Yunque National Forest, Rio Grande: fs.usda.gov/elyunque

SOUTH CAROLINA

Hunting Island State Park: southcarolinaparks.com/huntingisland/introduction.aspx

TEXAS

Palmetto State Park, Luling: tpwd.state.tx.us/spdest/findadest/parks/palmetto

Sabal Palm Sanctuary, Brownsville: sabalpalmsanctuary.org

Westcave Preserve, Round Mountain: westcave.org

VIRGIN ISLANDS

Virgin Islands National Park, St. John: nps.gov/viis

NURSERIES AND CONSULTANTS

Several nurseries and consultants in the United States—with a concentration on the West Coast—sell palms or advise on the use of palms. These are retail establishments unless otherwise specified.

ARIZONA

Moon Valley Nurseries: moonvalleynurseries.com

CALIFORNIA

All Tropical Palms Nursery, Gilroy: alltropicalpalms.com

Cycads-n-Palms, Fallbrook, mail order: cycads-n-palms.com

Discovery Island Palms, San Marcos, by appointment: discoveryislandpalms.com

The Dry Garden, Oakland: thedrygardennursery.com

Flora Grubb Gardens, San Francisco: floragrubb.com

Golden Gate Palms, Gary Gragg, Richmond: goldengatepalms.com

The Good Earth Nursery, Fallbrook: palms4u.com

Jungle Music Palms & Cycads, Encinitas: junglemusic.net

KW Palms & Cycads, Lake Elsinore, by appointment: palms4U2.com

Las Palmas Ranch, Oceanside, by appointment: (760) 726-7488

Moon Valley Nurseries, Escondido: moonvalleynurseries.com

Palm Island Nursery, Dale Motiska, Vacaville: palmislandnursery.com

Rancho Soledad Nurseries, Rancho Santa Fe: ranchosoledad.com

Sea Crest Nursery, Santa Barbara: seacrestnursery.com

SLO Palms, Grover Beach: slopalms.com

XOTX-Tropico, West Hollywood: (323) 654-9999

FLORIDA

Caribbean Palms Nursery, Loxahatchee: (561) 792-0333

D'Asign Source Botanicals, Loxahatchee: dasignsourcebotanicals.com

Holton Nursery, Loxahatchee: (561) 965-6792

Jesse Durko's Nursery, Davie: jessedurko.com

Jones Landscaping Nursery, Fort Lauderdale: cycadflorida.com

Redland Nursery, Homestead: redlandnursery.com

Searle Brothers Nursery, Southwest Ranches, by appointment: rainforestcollection.com

Signature Trees & Palms, Miami: (305) 233-3139

West Coast Tropicals Botanical Garden and Nursery, St. Petersburg: wctropicals.com

HAWAI'I

Floribunda Palms and Exotics, Mountain View, mail order: floribundapalms.com

MISSISSIPPI

Mule Palms of Mississippi, Ocean Springs: mulepalmsofmississippi.com

NEVADA

Moon Valley Nurseries, Las Vegas: moonvalleynurseries.com

NORTH CAROLINA

Gary's Nursery, New Bern, by appointment: garysnursery.com

Plant Delights, mail order: plantdelights.com

OREGON

Cistus Nursery, Portland, retail and mail order: cistus.com

Hooked on Palms, Medford, by appointment: hookedonpalms.com

Oregon Palm Nursery: oregonpalms.com

Portland Nursery: portlandnursery.com

SOUTH CAROLINA

Palm Trees Limited, Ollie Olivier, Johns Island: Palmtreesltd.com

Penny's Palms, Leesville, by appointment: pennyspalms.com/index.html

TEXAS

Eastside Discount Nursery, El Paso: (915) 591-3333

Horticultural Consultants, Inc., Grant Stephenson, Spicewood: hciglobal.com

North Texas Cold Hardy Palms, McKinney: northtexaspalms.com

WASHINGTON

Palms Northwest, Auburn, by appointment: palmsnorthwest.com

BIBLIOGRAPHY

Balslev, Henrik, Finn Borchsenius, and Henrik Borgtoft Pedersen. *Manual to the Palms of Ecuador.* AAU Reports 37. Aarhus, Denmark: U. Aarhus Dept. Systemic Botany, and Quito: Pontificia Universidad Católica del Ecuador, 1998.

Bernal, Rodrigo, and Gloria Galeano. *Palmas del Departamento de Antioquia: Región Occidental.* Bogotá, Columbia: Universidad Nacional de Colombia – Centro Editorial, 1987.

Bornstein, Carol, David Fross, and Bart O'Brien. *Reimagining the California Lawn: Water-conserving Plants, Practices, and Designs.* Los Olivos, California: Cachuma Press, 2011.

Boyer, Keith. *Palms and Cycads Beyond the Tropics.* Milton, Queensland, Australia: The Publication Fund, Palm and Cycad Societies of Australia, 1992.

Braun, August. *Las Palmas Cultivadas en Ciudades Elevadas de la Parte Andina de America del Sur.* N.p, n.d.

Broschat, Timothy K., and Alan W. Meerow. *Ornamental Palm Horticulture.* Gainesville, Florida: University Press of Florida, 2000.

Burton, Pamela, and Marie Botnick. *Private Landscapes: Modernist Gardens in Southern California.* New York: Princeton Architectural Press, 2002.

Church, Thomas, Grace Hall, and Michael Laurie. *Gardens Are for People*, 3rd ed. Berkeley, California: University of California Press, 1993.

Clifton, Joan. *Courtyard and Terrace Gardens.* London: Aquamarine, 2002.

Cornett, James W. *Desert Palm Oasis: A Comprehensive Guide.* Palm Springs, California: Nature Trails Press, 2010.

Crandell, Gina. *Tree Gardens: Architecture and the Forest.* New York: Princeton Architectural Press, 2013.

Dallman, Peter. *Plant Life in the World's Mediterranean Climates: California, Chile, South Africa, Australia, and the Mediterranean Basin.* Berkeley, California: University of California Press, 1998.

Dransfield, John, and Henk Beentje. *The Palms of Madagascar.* Richmond, Surrey, United Kingdom: Royal Botanic Gardens, Kew, and The International Palm Society, 1995.

———. *Lexicon Palmarum: A compendium of botanical terms in five languages.* Marly-le-Roi, France: Editions Champflour, 1996.

Dransfield, John, Natalie W. Uhl, Connie B. Asmussen, William J. Baker, Madeline M. Harley, and Carl L. Lewis. *Genera Palmarum: The Evolution and Classification of Palms.* Richmond, Surrey, United Kingdom: Royal Botanic Gardens, Kew, 2008.

Eckbo, Garrett. *Landscape for Living.* New York: F. W. Dodge, 1950.

Eliovson, Sima. *The Gardens of Roberto Burle Marx.* New York: Harry N. Abrams, 1991.

Farmer, Jared. *Trees in Paradise: A California History.* New York: W. W. Norton & Company, 2013.

Francko, David A. *Palms Won't Grow Here and Other Myths.* Portland, Oregon: Timber Press, 2003.

Grau, Juan. *Palms of Chile.* Santiago, Chile: Ediciones Oikos, 2006.

Harrison, Robert Pogue. *Gardens: An Essay on the Human Condition.* Chicago: University of Chicago Press, 2008.

Henderson, Andrew. *Palms of Southern Asia.* Princeton, New Jersey: Princeton University Press, 2009.

Henderson, Andrew, Gloria Galeano, and Rodrigo Bernal. *Field Guide to the Palms of the Americas.* Princeton, New Jersey: Princeton University Press, 1995.

Hodel, Donald R. *Chamaedorea Palms: The Species and Their Cultivation.* Lawrence, Kansas: Allen Press, 1992.

———. *The Palms and Cycads of Thailand.* Lawrence, Kansas: Allen Press, 1998.

———. *The Biology and Management of Landscape Palms.* Porterville, California: Britton Fund, Western Chapter International Society of Arboriculture, 2012.

———. *Loulu: The Hawaiian Palm*. Honolulu: University of Hawai'i Press, 2012.

Jones, David L. *Palms in Australia*. Frenchs Forest, Australia, 1984.

———. *Palms Throughout the World*. Washington, D.C.: Smithsonian Institution Press, 1993.

Jones, Louisa. *Gardens of the French Riviera*. Paris: Flammarion, 1994.

———. *Mediterranean Landscape Design: Vernacular Contemporary*. London: Thames & Hudson, 2012.

Joyce, David. *Garden Style: An Illustrated History of Design and Tradition*. London: Pyramid Books, 1989.

Jungles, Raymond. *The Colors of Nature*. New York: The Monacelli Press, 2008.

———. *The Cultivated Wild*. New York: The Monacelli Press, 2015.

Kameon, Judy. *Gardens Are for Living*. New York: Rizzoli International Publications, 2014.

Kingsbury, Noël. *Dramatic Effects with Architectural Plants*. Woodstock, New York: The Overlook Press, 1997.

Lorenzi, Harri, Larry Noblick, Francis Kahn, and Evandro Ferreira. *Brazilian Flora: Areceaceae (Palms)*. Nova Odessa, Brazil, 2010.

Maurières, Arnaud, and Eric Ossart. *Paradise Gardens*. Vanves, France: Editions du Chêne, Hachette Livre, 2000.

McCurrach, James C. *Palms of the World*. New York: Harper Brothers, 1960.

Meerow, Alan. *Betrock's Guide to Landscape Palms*. Hollywood, Florida: Betrock Information Systems, 2000.

———. *Betrock's Cold Hardy Palms*. Hollywood, Florida: Betrock Information Systems, 2005.

Meninger, Edwin A. *Seaside Plants of the World*. New York: Hearthside Press, 1964.

Moran, Reid. *The Flora of Guadalupe Island*. San Francisco: California Academy of Sciences, 1996.

Muirhead, Desmond. *Palms*. Globe, Arizona: Dale Stuart King, 1961.

Ogden, Scott, and Lauren Springer Ogden. *Plant-Driven Design: Creating Gardens that Honor Plants, Place, and Spirit*. Portland, Oregon: Timber Press, 2008.

Okita, Yoshihiro, and J. Leland Hollenberg. *The Miniature Palms of Japan: Cultivating Kannonchiku and Shurochiku*. New York and Tokyo: Weatherhill, 1981.

Racine, Michel, Ernest J.-P. Boursier-Mougenot, and Françoise Binet. *The Gardens of Provence and the French Riviera*. Cambridge, Massachusetts: The MIT Press, 1987.

Rainer, Thomas, and Claudia West. *Planting in a Post-Wild World: Designing Plant Communities for Resilient Landscapes*. Portland, Oregon: Timber Press, 2015.

Riffle, Robert Lee, Paul Craft, and Scott Zona. *The Encyclopedia of Cultivated Palms*, 2nd ed. Portland, Oregon: Timber Press, 2012.

Ritter, Matt. *A Californian's Guide to the Trees Among Us*. Berkeley, California: Heyday, 2011.

Smith, W. Gary. *From Art to Landscape: Unleashing Creativity in Garden Design*. Portland, Oregon: Timber Press, 2010.

Stilgoe, John R. *What Is Landscape?* Cambridge, Massachusetts: The MIT Press, 2015.

Streatfield, David C. *California Gardens: Creating a New Eden*. New York: Abbeville Press, 1994.

Titley, Norah, and Frances Wood. *Oriental Gardens: An Illustrated History*. San Francisco: Chronicle Books, 1991.

Travis, Richard. *Palms for South Texas*. Raleigh, North Carolina: Lulu Press, 2005.

Walker, Jacqueline. *The Subtropical Garden*. Portland, Oregon: Timber Press, 1996.

Wijaya, Made. *Tropical Garden Design*. Singapore: Archipelago Press, 1999.

———. *Modern Tropical Garden Design*. Singapore: Periplus Editions, 2007.

ACKNOWLEDGMENTS

I am grateful to you who read this book and to everyone who helped me prepare for, research, illustrate, and write this book. As it is the culmination of the abiding intellectual interest of my adult life, the number of names recognized here spills beyond the scope of the project itself.

Its germ came from my cousin, Maggie Rudy, who encouraged me to submit a proposal about palms to Timber Press; it took twenty years for me to do it. Flora Grubb's ideas and inspiration launched that proposal and permeate this book. Jared Braiterman and Shu Kuge shared my palm love and helped turn my interest toward a vocation, one that Saul Nadler and Flora have nurtured.

That I had the luck to collaborate with Caitlin Atkinson, whom I esteem as an artist, thinker, professional, and friend, amazes me.

My step-grandmother, June Harbett, gave me my first palm book, answered all my questions, and shared the love.

Tom Fischer and Hazel White were wise, helpful, patient, and encouraging, as editor and writing counsel, respectively. I thank Lisa Theobald for her assiduous, thoughtful, and patient copyediting. Brandy Kuhl made the Helen Crocker Russell Library of Horticulture a fruitful place to work.

Davis Dalbok and the late Michael Postl instilled in me the importance of design with palms, and Darold Petty and Garrin Fullington brought me into the Palm Society and its attendant exhilarations. The late Dick Douglas was a welcoming host to his extraordinary palm garden and shared his decades of growing experience and observations freely.

Accompanying and instructing me in writing and design have been my friends and colleagues Lisa Lee Benjamin, Hank Jenkins, Zenaida Sengo, Daniel Nolan, Johanna Silver, Patrick Lannan, and Beth Mullins. At Flora Grubb Gardens and East West Trees, Clarke de Mornay, Zann Cannon Goff, Gregg Opgenorth, Court Blackburn, Peter Doljanin, and Jim Kumiega and his display team have guided me with their designs and plant knowledge.

Scott Zona was generous and kind. He and Paul Craft were of crucial help. Don Hodel, Matt Ritter, Jenn Yost, Don Mahoney, David Kruse-Pickler, Ted Kipping, Kathy Musial, Brian Kemble, Doug Wildman, Mike Sullivan, Jacob Uluwehi Knecht, Ken Greby, Dick Turner, Virginia Hayes, John Dransfield, Eric Hupperts, Chuck Swanson, Christy Dewees, Warren Roberts, Benjy Young, James DeVinny, Dale Motiska, Gary Gragg, Marc Jeanson, Matt Bradford, Jeff Marcus, Bill Stowe, Jeff Wright, and Kyle Wicomb each taught me something about horticulture, biology, and botany. For years Adam Greenspan and I have carried on a discussion about plants we love and, refracting it through his eyes, we put something of that to paper here. Conversations with Sean Hogan, Gustavo Vazquez, Brandon Tyson, Bonnie Fisher, Scott Ogden, David Godshall, Frank Eddy, Michael Collins, Marion Brenner, Ron Lutsko, Lia Lund, Carole Bowen, and Barbara Van and Howard Wollner fortified my design thinking.

Many designers, gardeners, and landscape architects gave their time to help Caitlin and me see and document their work: Patricia Bullis, Andy Cabe, Franco and Nicholas D'Ascanio, Richard Gervais,

Alejandro Gonzales and Jim Smeal, Mike Harris, Paul Humann, Judy Kameon, Chris Jacobson, Brian Lievens, Sherry Merciari, Helene Morneau and Kris Sunderlage, Eric Nagelmann, Dat Pham, John Pierce, Jeff Seyfried, Michael Stancliff, Andrew Street, Pat Tierney, Michael Turcotte, Mary Alice and Bear Woodrum, Roderick Wyllie, and Steve Martino. I'm thankful for the chance that Jenny Andrews, Megan Padilla, and Sarah Kinbar at *Garden Design* and Lorene Edwards Forkner at *Pacific Horticulture* gave me to write; this book draws upon articles for both publications. Wise informants and generous fixers like Cristi Walden, Jenks Farmer, Joe Le Vert, Betsy Flack, Sandy Shapiro, Matt Power, Ben Noyes, Chip Jones, John Cressy, Greg Haines, Cousin Park Dougherty, Nancy Hart, Ollie Olivier, Jean Marie Seely-Hing, Wendy Proud, Debra DeMarco, Phyllis Nolan, and the late George Nolan shaped my writing and got Caitlin and me through the garden gate.

To the many friends and family members who gave me moral support over the years I worked on (and toward) this project I am grateful, especially to my father, Michael F. Dewees, and my brother, Nathanael "Gnat" DeWees. My aunt, Helen Harbett, cheered me on. Among those who gave me encouragement to write and safe harbor are Kate Aurthur and Rebecca DuMoulin, Richard Alden and Maggie Rudy, James DeVinny and Mark Schaefer, Dan Worden and Emmanuel Donval, X-topher Budz, Roquin-Jon Siongco, Elaine Katzenberger, Julie Chai, Jane Scurich, Tina Andropoulos, Karen Ahn, Kim Wong Keltner, Carolyn Miller, Eleanor Burke, Eleanor McBride, Liz Greenberg, Midge Donalds, Marsha Irwin, Christina Crosby, Nancy Armstrong, the late Lois Wallace, Todd Malensek, Kirsten Menger-Anderson, Susy Rudy, Alexander Chee, Daniel Mendelsohn, and especially Henry Abelove.

INDEX

ABOUT THE AUTHOR AND PHOTOGRAPHER

JASON DEWEES is a writer and horticulturist born and living in San Francisco. He is currently staff horticulturist at Flora Grubb Gardens and East West Trees in San Francisco. Responsible for the Tree Canopy Succession Plan for the San Francisco Botanical Garden, he serves on the San Francisco Conservatory of Flowers Advisory Council. He advises landscape architects, designers, public agencies, and gardeners on planting design and plant selection, especially involving palms and trees.

CAITLIN ATKINSON wrote and photographed *Plant Craft* and has also provided exquisite photos for other Timber Press books. She has worked in floral design and at Flora Grubb Gardens as an interior merchandiser. An accomplished freelance photographer, she captures gardens, interiors, and still life. See more of her work at www.caitlinatkinson.net.